TEN WAYS TO WEAVE THE WORLD: MATTER, MIND, AND GOD

—Volume 1—

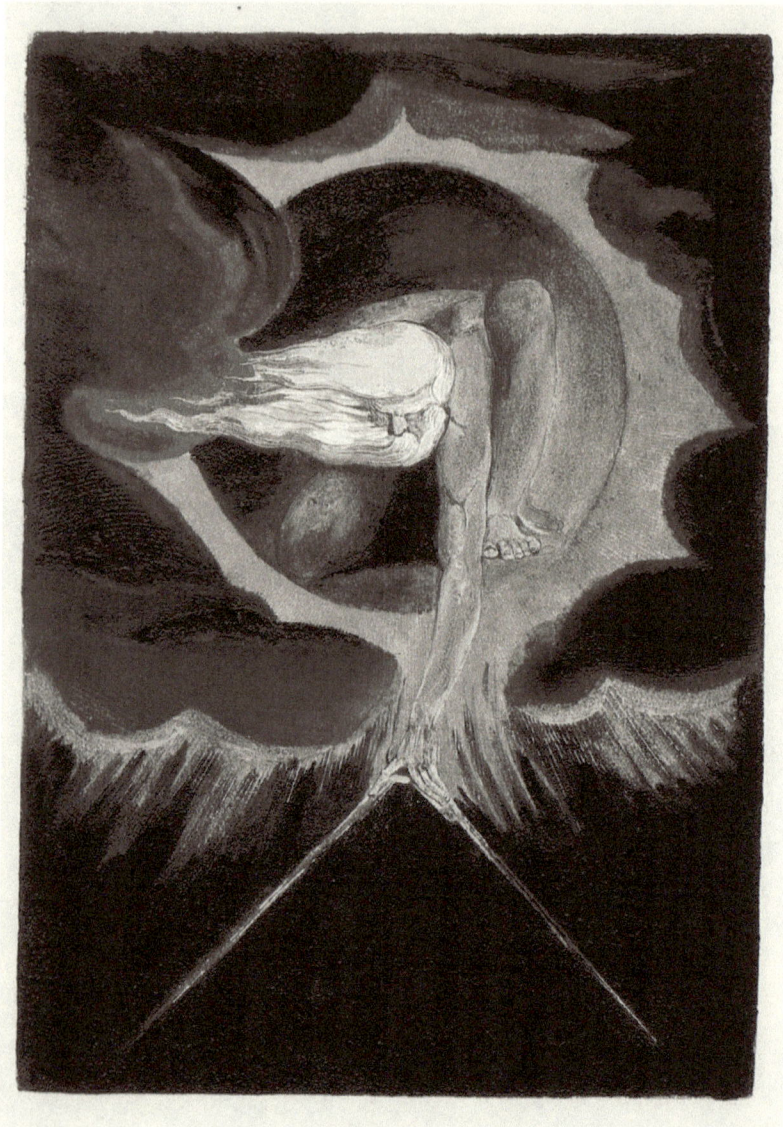

Blake: The Ancient of Days

TEN WAYS TO WEAVE THE WORLD: MATTER, MIND, AND GOD

—Volume 1—

Outgrowing Materialism

Ross Thompson

CASCADE *Books* • Eugene, Oregon

TEN WAYS TO WEAVE THE WORLD: MATTER, MIND, AND GOD
—VOLUME 1—
Outgrowing Materialism

Copyright © 2022 Ross Thompson. All rights reserved. Except for brief quotations in critical publications or reviews, no part of this book may be reproduced in any manner without prior written permission from the publisher. Write: Permissions, Wipf and Stock Publishers, 199 W. 8th Ave., Suite 3, Eugene, OR 97401.

Cascade Books
An Imprint of Wipf and Stock Publishers
199 W. 8th Ave., Suite 3
Eugene, OR 97401

www.wipfandstock.com

PAPERBACK ISBN: 978-1-7252-7682-6
HARDCOVER ISBN: 978-1-7252-7683-3
EBOOK ISBN: 978-1-7252-7684-0

Cataloguing-in-Publication data:

Names: Thompson, Ross, 1953– [author]

Title: Ten ways to weave the world: matter, mind, and God, volume 1 : outgrowing materialism / Ross Thompson.

Description: Eugene, OR: Cascade Books, 2022 | Includes bibliographical references and index.

Identifiers: ISBN 978-1-7252-7682-6 (paperback) | ISBN 978-1-7252-7683-3 (hardcover) | ISBN 978-1-7252-7684-0 (ebook)

Subjects: LCSH: Philosophy and religion | Metaphysics | Philosophy of mind | Materialism | Realism | Reality | Dualism

Classification: BD418.3 T46 2022 (paperback) | BD418.3 (ebook)

VERSION NUMBER 120522

To Dennis

CONTENTS

Acknowledgements | ix

Introduction to *Ten Ways to Weave the World* | 1

Introduction to *Outgrowing Materialism* | 17

{1} Is Naivety Original? Naïve Realism | 21

{2} The Haunted Machine: Dualism | 35

{3} Bits and Pieces: Materialism | 73

{4} Music of the Universe: Structural Realism | 132

{5} Everything That Can Happen Must: The Multiverse | 168

Conclusion to *Outgrowing Materialism* | 195

Bibliography for *Outgrowing Materialism* | 197

Index | 203

ACKNOWLEDGEMENTS

No one travels alone, and there are several people I need to thank for helping me on the journey that is this book. The first is my father, Dennis, who was ever interested in the scientific and philosophical issues discussed in these two volumes, though as a longstanding agnostic, his conclusions were very different from mine. He died half-way through the writing—as it were, in the space between the two volumes. He would not have believed he now has a viewpoint from which to assess the book, though I am not so sure. I dedicate this first volume to him, and the second to my brother-in-law Mark, who also died during the writing, and whose indomitable cheerfulness and energy in work and life helped provide the context in which I wrote at Grove Cottage, Mere in Wiltshire, UK.

Two others have been especially important in generating my interest in philosophy. One is Tony Williams, who taught me Greek at Godalming Grammar School, and instilled in me a great love of Plato and philosophy in general. Readers will note how central Plato and Aristotle are to my central thesis. The other is Denys Turner, who supervised my PhD thesis, "Objectivity and Religious Symbol," and imparted to me a commitment to combining theological imagination with philosophical rigor (or is it the other way round?), which I hope I have gone a little way to fulfilling.

Then there is my beloved wife and companion, Judith, who bore with me in the times when the writing of this book filled my horizon, and not least, carefully proof-read and commented on the text. And I must also acknowledge Wipf and Stock, my publisher, who through my editor, Robin Parry, allowed me the freedom and flexibility to create what must be quite a risky book (indeed, allowing it to become two books).

Finally, there is life itself, grounded in goodness, the contemplation of the enigmatic beauty of which has nourished the whole undertaking.

Ross Thompson, May 2022.

INTRODUCTION TO *TEN WAYS TO WEAVE THE WORLD*

MUCH INK HAS BEEN spilled of late on a purported debate between science and religion. But the idea of a debate here seems to me to rest on a kind of category mistake. Religion and science are quite obviously different categories of enterprise, rather like cooking and football, or gardening and music. Between cooking and football, or gardening and music, there can be no debate. It would be pointless to debate which is more beautiful, Stourhead Garden or Beethoven's 9th Symphony, or to argue from the proliferation of books and TV programs about cooking that football is in inevitable decline. It is true that beauty is a concept that applies to gardens and music, and probably cooking and football and science and religion too. All of these activities can be more or less beautiful—or creative, or innovative, and there are a host of other adjectives you might think of as applying to all of these. But these concepts apply in different ways; what makes a symphony beautiful is not what makes a garden beautiful, and what makes an act of worship beautiful is not what makes a scientific theory beautiful. There are (this book will argue) common factors in beauty, but these factors will apply differently depending on whether we are looking for beauty in notes and harmonies, trees and flowers, liturgy, songs and symbols, or models and formulae.

Without attempting a precise definition, we would probably agree that science, or the sciences, denote a range of methods designed to create theories to help us observe, explain, correlate, and predict phenomena in the world, and to test these theories through experiment. The methods vary from once science to another, but have in common processes that eliminate the particular values and standpoint of the one doing the experiment, mainly by enabling the experiments to be repeated by other observers. That is why science tends to progress, coming up with theories that eventually get accepted by most scientists, and that then form the basis for further observations. Of course, there are many issues on which scientists have yet to reach consensus: the origins and destiny of the universe, the processes at work in evolution, the relation of the brain to conscious phenomena, the ultimate constituents of nature, and even what matter is—its intrinsic qualities as opposed to the structure and relationships of these ultimate constituents—to name but five. But there remains the hope that these questions will one day be resolved, and consensus achieved, not by the decree of some supreme scientific magisterium, but by examination of appropriate experimental evidence.[1] Finally, the sciences enable technology: the theories that have the best experimental results also tend to have practical results in terms of extending our powers over the world, enabling us, for example, to fly, compute, communicate more widely, cure diseases, and create new ways of destroying each other. Science here is ethically neutral: science is what enables us to burn fuels and create global warming, and also it is what tells us about global warming and its causes, so as to be able to slow it down if we (collectively) want to.

Religion is harder to define, but we could probably loosely agree that a religion denotes a collection of teachings and practices designed to help us live better lives, and to achieve transformation into a better state, usually in some kind of community with others and often in relationship to higher beings. The better state and the higher beings are variously defined, but all religions set forth a goal, such as heaven, or nirvana, or satori. Immediately we note the differences from science. There are differences in method: religious do not have tests that decisively prove one belief true over against another. Hence through history religions have increased rather than decreased in number; consensus is never reached. There are differences in approach: while science tries to screen out the subjective bias of the scientist, religions work by drawing on, motivating, and intensifying the subjective experience and values of participants. And while science aims at a true description of the world that enables people to change and control it (for better or worse), when religions describe the world, it has an ethical intent. Religions typically argue that the world is such and such; therefore, this is the appropriate attitude to take to it; by taking this approach and doing these things you will know the truth and become better people. The Buddhists describe the world as full of suffering in order to invoke in us an attitude of detachment and ego-lessness leading to nirvana; the Christians describe the world as full of sin and injustice in order to invoke a repentance and a thirst for justice that will lead us to the kingdom of God. It is in and through the subjective self that religions work, in terms of what is invoked, and what is sought.

---

1. In the course of the book, however, we will come to doubt whether all of these issues can be resolved by science alone.

Now of course, the promoters of science and religion often confuse the boundaries. We all witness how religious people are often in denial about the root subjectivity of their position, seeing weakness in what could be a strength. They then (to the embarrassment of most of their co-believers) make absolute and universal claims for their particular faith or sect, as if it told the only true story of how the world is; claims that only a science has a right to make, within its limited sphere. This tendency has of late been especially evident in the claims of certain believers to find in their texts accounts of how the world began, and how species came to be; claims that it is appropriate for a science rather than a religion to adjudicate. But equally, we have witnessed some advocates of "science" (to the embarrassment of most of their fellow scientists), notably the "New Atheists,"[2] sounding off like high priests of a new cult, in which "science" takes on the role of molding our subjectivity and telling us how we should behave. They speak as if the absence of subjective value from the world were a discovery of science, rather than its methodological presupposition. And yet they also argue that science itself can somehow fill the gap in value it has opened up, with new values that sound strangely like toned down versions of the old religious values of love, justice, and peace.

In terms of the future, then, it seems to me that science is likely to continue to progress; unless, that is, the politics of the future are such that the scientifically discovered methods of destruction prevail over those that give life, or the remedies for climate change advocated by science fail to prevail over human greed; in which case science will vanish from the earth along with religion and life itself. But in no way need the continued advance of science be seen as entailing the decline of religion. If what I have argued is true, the reverse may be true. The advance in science leaves us more aware of the gap: the value-neutrality of science, its dogged agnosticism regarding the subjective and everything we call "mind" or "soul," leaves us wanting and needing something that will appeal to our hunger for personal transformation, as well as the transformation of society into something that can harness its scientific powers over the earth and use them for good.

Some will no doubt find what they need in eclectic new-age amalgams drawn from several spiritual traditions; others will go to the other extreme, and adopt a faith as if it replaced, rather than complemented, the cautious rationality of scientific method. But in between there are those who will value the discipline of a particular religious faith, without needing to build this discipline into an absolute truth-defining taskmaster. It is probably mainly

---

2. The core of the New Atheists are the so-called "four horsemen of the non-apocalypse": the biologist Richard Dawkins, the neuroscientist Sam Harris, the journalist Christopher Hitchens, and the philosopher Daniel Dennett.

to this last group of disciplined yet reasonable believers, and perhaps to some of the first group of multi-faith explorers, that this book is addressed.

The Debate behind the Debate

The two-sided "science v. religion" debate, then, is founded on a category mistake. But this mistake does not mean that there is nothing at stake in the debate, or that all the argument, rhetoric, and sheer emotion vented on both sides is but "a tale told by an idiot, full of sound and fury, signifying nothing."[3] As I hope this book will clarify, behind the ill-conceived conflict, and perhaps motivating it, lie a tangle of issues—for the most part philosophical issues—concerning the nature and relations of mind, consciousness, experience, subjectivity, quality, value, and the like. As physiologist and writer Denis Noble has written with regard to the New Atheists,

> Whether the authors know it or not, they are in fact speaking not on behalf of science but rather on behalf of an alternative metaphysical viewpoint, and often enough they do not appreciate the need for humility in the face of deep uncertainties.[4]

Needless to say, the same could be said of many of those who purport to speak on behalf of religious faith. In this book I hope to dig out some of the deep metaphysical issues before which we should be humble.

What is at stake in and motivates the popular debate is not whether "science" or "religion" should "win" the debate or prevail in the future. Rather, it is the question of how the world of supposedly "objective" and quantitative description relates to the world of supposedly subjective experience and qualitative value. The dilemma can be presented as the relation of matter to mind, or quantity to quality, or fact to value; and the relation of "God" to each of these. All of these converge on the philosophy of mind. The metaphysics the New Atheists advocate is materialism, or scientific naturalism, which eliminates mind, consciousness, and value, and consequently God, from the discussion. The metaphysics they mainly abominate, as we shall see, is substance dualism, which views mind and matter as separate substances. Materialism has proved to be a respectable and productive metaphysics, but it and dualism are not the only metaphysical fish in the sea, and there are several ways of thinking about mind and matter equally worthy of consideration, which pre-date and may well survive the dominion of these two. Looking at those different views can open up and liberate the

---

3. *Macbeth* 5.5.26–28.
4. Noble, *Dance*, 254.

debate, making it less polarized and more creative, even for those who in the end return to their original viewpoint. Limiting the discussion to views of mind and matter, and by implication views of God, may mean we lose out on a few subtleties. But it will make the discussion just about manageable within the scope of a book, which would not be the case if we had to cover the whole of metaphysics!

Philosophers have debated the nature of mind a great deal recently, possibly more than any other metaphysical issue. But these debates are largely unknown to the wide popular audience that avidly digests the "science v. religion" debate. Among the New Atheists, only Daniel Dennett has any real grasp of philosophy, and he (see World {3}) more clearly than the others proposes we simply ignore, disregard, or eliminate from consideration anything to do with the subjective mind or consciousness. He believes, as we shall see, that we should build morality, instead, on science and sociobiology. He is not alone here, but follows a trend. For while philosophically materialism has proven to be deeply flawed—more flawed than most of its rivals, as we shall see—a methodological reductionism has come to pervade what were once "the humanities," such that materialistic accounts of everything from art to altruism carry a certain academic "street cred." Arguably the science v. religion debate is a kind of cover for ideological warfare concerning this development.

On my understanding, what is involved is more complex than a case of "hard objective fact" versus "soft subjective story." On the contrary, each perspective can be viewed both as a philosophical system and as a world narrative (or what the postmoderns call a metanarrative). It is rather, as with an Estate Agency, you can see the house for sale as a plan or as a set of photographic pictures. The plan has all the objective dimensions on it, but it leaves out a lot of what it would be like to live in the house. The pictures contain more of the latter (the beautiful view from the living room, the wonderful fitted kitchen) but there is greater possibility of distortion (no picture of the motorway at the bottom of the garden; no measurements to show how cramped the kitchen must actually be; no indication of what lies in that unlabeled space that is so obvious when you look at the plan). So each philosophical alternative is related to a story, a way of construing the world, which evokes a spiritual response.

In a way, each worldview, even the most austerely atheistic and materialistic, is religious in the sense of being related to a narrative that calls for a subjective response of belief and commitment to action. So far, so "postmodern." But then again, I argue that some of the stories have flaws, or other reasons for not believing them. So my postmodernism does not entail a total relativism. Rather, I follow philosopher Nelson Goodman in believing that though there are many "ways of worldmaking," there are reasons for preferring some to others.[5] Though, by definition, we can only view the world through a particular view, some views offer a wider view than others, some a clearer and more precise view, some a less conflicted view, some a more beautiful or inspiring view. Or to change to the story analogy, some stories "outnarrate"[6] others in the sense of telling us clearly and simply about things that in others are confused or ignored, or in the sense of not including things that in others are "tall stories." So there are reasonable and unreasonable (though not necessarily "hard" or decisive) and attractive and unattractive (though not necessarily "soft" or subjective) ways of constructing belief and value.

Beyond that I do not wish to say much about the criteria for choosing between "worlds," since any worked out set of criteria is bound to have been worked out from within one of the worlds, and will inevitably judge favorably with respect to that world *vis à vis* the others. That is the essential point postmodern relativism is making. On the other hand, the writing of this book has forced me to return to my first love, philosophy, in order to find a kind of language in which science and religion can speak to each other. It is not that (as some believe) philosophy is the supreme adjudicator of scientific and religious claims: the grounds of both kinds of claim lie largely outside of philosophy. Nevertheless, when I returned to the philosophical debate, what I found was no longer the largely inconclusive battles between idealism, dualism, and materialism, and between realism and relativism, that my earlier studies had presented. What I found was a limited kind of progress and development. No worldview had simply won the day, but certain battles were trending in a definite direction. Some arguments, while they had not been decisively won or lost for all time, were proving more probable than others, and certain "hard problems" for particular views were still proving unresolved. It was not that one could no longer be, say, a materialist or a dualist. But dualism was proving, in the face of philosophical argument, too hard to defend for most (as well as, for many, proving less desirable to defend). Meanwhile the moving of materialism towards views that could be regarded as in some sense idealist (structural realism on the one hand and panpsychism on the other), while not philosophically inevitable, carried the momentum of many arguments.

---

5. Goodman, *Ways of Worldmaking*.

6. The term is used by Radical Orthodox theologian John Milbank, but probably in a more "postmodern" way than I intend by my use. Sometimes for him the term seems to mean to outwit or overpower with superior rhetoric. What I mean is indicated by the following sentence.

In other words, the battle of worlds needs to know more about these philosophical arguments; not because they have decided the battle, but because those arguments tell of the detailed cost you have to pay if you wish to maintain a given worldview. It is then for you decide whether the cost is worth paying. The difficulty here is that most of the philosophical argument is very detailed, very complex, and versed in a pithy mode that only other philosophers will easily understand. (This is not a particular fault of philosophers; most science, and much theology, is highly jargonized, for partly good reasons.) So it is that I have felt a need to relate philosophical arguments, some of them at the limits of my own understanding, in order to tell the broader story of their possible impact regarding the Worlds. Philosophers, please forgive me if I have at certain points misunderstood the detail. I hope I am right in terms of the broader sweep of philosophy, which tells a story that needs telling, and has not yet been told, in order for us properly to assess the Worlds.

Two groups of readers will not like this book's emphasis on philosophical and metaphysical viewpoints. On the one hand, neo-orthodox and post-liberal theologians in the lineage of Karl Barth, who still form a significant number of academic theologians in our universities, will protest that theology should not take its cue from philosophy of any kind, for to do so is to commit the "sin" of ontotheology.[7] Rather they would have the argument start from the truth of biblical revelation and/or church tradition, and work out the metaphysics of mind and matter from that. On the other hand, the New Atheists in the lineage of Dawkins et al. would take a view that is almost a mirror image of this, arguing that science should not start with philosophy, but work out its philosophy on the basis that the method and content of science has got it all right. Such approaches are fine for those who are prepared to put all their faith in Barth's kind of Christianity, or in Dawkins's take on science. In the fourteen volumes of his *Church Dogmatics*, Karl Barth does not give science a mention except in connection with his claim that theology itself is a science; while mentions of specific theologians and religious teachings are exceedingly rare in the writings of the New Atheists.

If, however, you regard both science and religious faith as sources of wisdom, then you face the problem of the *prima facie* incompatibility between of the worldviews presented. The Bible refers to angels and demons, a "good" creation, and an apocalyptic end of the world; science refers to a very different timescale, an indifferent universe, and forces and particles

---

7. My *Interfaith Imperative*, chapter 8, considers ontotheology and why it is not necessarily a sin, though some cruder versions of it may be.

never mentioned in Scripture. Those wishing to honor both traditions cannot avoid doing some metaphysical thinking, either to reconcile them or to clarify the choices between them. Reflecting philosophically, as this book encourages, opens up alternative worldviews and practices of living that may be both biblical and scientific.

Now it is not part of my aim to deprive the ardent theologians and atheists of their convictions. Rather these are my broad aims:

1. To draw the interested reader's attention to the philosophical debates about mind and matter that lie behind what is often simplistically presented as a two-sided debate between science and religion.
2. Debates in the philosophy of mind have all too often been conducted only among philosophers using abstruse examples. I aim to set the philosophical debates in the wider context, as offering ten distinct "Worlds" with different implications for God, ethics, and spirituality.
3. Without offering definitive conclusions in debates that have continued unresolved for centuries, or on the other hand arguing that my ten Worlds are self-contained and incommensurable, to offer my own evaluation of the strengths and weaknesses of each, in order, if possible, to discover and commend a view of my own.

It remains my task in this introduction first to offer an outline of the ten Worlds that form the main chapters of this book; and then to say a bit about my personal reasons for writing it.

Pattern of the Parts and the Chapters

The project of this book is a large one and falls into two roughly equal volumes. The theme of each is depicted on the cover. This first volume, *Outgrowing Materialism*, shows Blake's picture of *The Ancient of Days*. It is commonly understood as a picture of God, but in Blake's mythology it depicts the demiurge, Urizen, a patriarchal parody of the God of deism. He sets his compass on the deep, but measures only the abyss, while he himself seems trapped in the circle or globe he should be measuring, his beard swept sideways by a mighty wind. I see him as a figure for the God whom materialists and atheists wipe out of the dualistic picture, making the measurable world all that is, only to find that the mathematical compass finds nothing substantial, only abstract relation. *Outgrowing Materialism* tells the philosophical story of how that came about. The second volume, *Embodying Mind*, offers another Blake picture: *The Reunion of the Soul and the Body*. That volume will describe ways in which meaning and "soul" may return to the material cosmos

Outgrowing Materialism has something of a historical structure, and tells the way dualism has given way to materialism, but by its own logic, materialism has unraveled into two opposing ways beyond it. Counting through the ten Worlds, I begin with the a-historical {1},[8] the World of those who look with non-philosophical eyes, and take it just as it seems to be. I do this in order to get to grips with {2}, where this seeming identity begins to be doubted, and how things are, according to science, begins to diverge from how things seem to be. In {2} a distinct world or reality is posited on either side of the divide, creating a substantial dualism between matter and mind, and equally, between God and world: the deist God of Blake's picture first clearly emerges. {3} arises from precisely this World, by disregarding mind as recalcitrant to scientific study, and leaving only the world of matter. It is here that we find most clearly the world advocated by the New Atheists. {4} then arises as the process of disregarding becomes more and more strict, so that most of the qualities associated with matter are themselves discarded, leaving only the quantities and relations in our mathematical equations. However, a realist understanding of these may give rise to a Platonic realism regarding the Good. Finally in {5}, mathematical criteria for reality begin to overtake the empirical ones, and we allow for the existence of a multiverse because it makes the mathematics simpler, and because it is the easiest way to reconcile the remarkableness of our universe with the elimination of metaphysical factors, as materialism requires.[9]

The trajectory described in this volume is not logically necessary. There is nothing illogical or incoherent about stopping the story at any given point, and remaining in one of the Worlds without moving to the next. I am enough of a materialist myself to acknowledge that the steps in the story just told arise not only for conceptual reasons, but also for material historical ones. The story of modernity does seem to move on with the need for society to produce ideas and technology in line with changes in its own means of production, as Marxists would have been quick to tell us, were many of them still around. However, it is not part of my purpose in this book to enter intractable controversies around the material or social contexts and causes of the Worlds I discuss; my purpose is to present and evaluate them, and finding the causes of an idea is no part of evaluating its truth.

The second volume presents worldviews that have prevailed before the rise of modern dualism and its main modern rival, materialism. In our own

---

8. For {1} read World 1. See next section on abbreviations.
9. The introduction to the first volume, below, offers a fuller outline.

time these Worlds may be beginning to overtake dualism and materialism, and perhaps the modern science-led secularizing project as such. Constituting the "before and after" of the story told in Volume 1, it is inevitably less historical in order, beginning with pre-modern views such as panpsychism, idealism, and Aristotelianism, before moving on to more recent views, in a dialogical building toward my own understanding.

Broadly speaking, the Worlds discussed in Volume 1 relegate mind to a partial or non-existent role in the universe, while those in Volume 2 embrace the role of mind, albeit in very varied ways. So {6} holds on to reductionism and naturalism but regards mind as an aspect of nature all the way down to its ultimate constituents. In terms of the God debate, such a view would tend to give rise to a kind of pantheism or even polytheism. {7}, on the other hand, abandons reductionism of any kind, and dispenses altogether with the idea of matter, regarding all reality as fundamentally mental. Of all the alternatives to materialism, it is probably the least fashionable worldview among philosophers today, though it has in the past prevailed from India through the Neoplatonists in Greece to modern German Romanticism, giving rise to a God who is a primordial Mind from which all minds emanate. {8} is the ancient and mediaeval view of Aristotle and Aquinas: the hylomorphism that bases its model of reality neither on the machine nor on the mind, but on the living organism as a unity of matter and form. Aristotelianism gives rise to the classic "proofs" of the existence of God as necessary existence, grounding all beings: the proofs we find in mediaeval Judaism, Islam, and Christianity alike. The study of living and other self-organizing complex structures, pioneered by Aristotle, has brought into view {9}, which focuses on various ideas whereby life, mind, and consciousness are understood as emerging as a higher level of what, at the lowest levels, consists of physical particles. Finally, {10} arises when we combine the idea from {9} that mind emerges from matter, with the notion from {4} that matter is grounded in the multiverse of conceptual possibilities via a kind of selection by consciousness; or as {7} would have it, matter is experienceable structure. This combination results what has been called a "strange loop"; however, the whole universal loop may be seen as grounded in goodness, existing just because it is good. But good is active and profligate, justifying panentheism and process theology, which speak of good as a self-surpassing process in which God becomes God through the universe, just as the universe becomes itself through grounding in God.

Each World's chapter has a similar order, though not always the same balance, of elements. To set the scene, there is an initial sequence of quotations relating to the World in question, which will be referred to in the chapter. This is followed by a summary of the basic ideas at work in the

World, and an indication of how the World may answer questions raised regarding other Worlds. There follows a short historical outline of how the World developed, leading into a more detailed and critical appraisal of the philosophical presuppositions of the World, with reference to contemporary exponents; and then an exploration of how the World sits with ideas of God—or not. I move from there to a sketch of the aesthetic, ethical and spiritual aspects of the story or stories at work in the World. Underlying each World, I discern a distinctive "plot" in the sense described by Christopher Booker.[10] I have been deeply influenced by his description of seven basic plots in world literature. Though the ten Worlds do not each correspond with one of his plots, and I would not limit the plots to Booker's seven, I believe each philosophical approach represents a distinct way of telling the world's story, and that we are often drawn to a certain philosophy because we find a certain kind of plot attractive.

At the end of my examination of each World, I raise a series of questions that lead us on to consider other Worlds. These question sections, which in some cases are almost as long as the rest of the chapter, delve more into the thickets of current philosophical argument, and in that way give more solid grounding to the broader-brush treatment elsewhere. It is because Worlds raise questions that other Worlds may answer better than they do, and vice versa, that, though no World has the right to stand in judgment on all the others, the Worlds are not entirely self-justifying and incommensurable. There may be trans-World pathways that it makes sense to take, and the pathways may converge somewhat, while leaving considerable room for subjective choice.

It is possible to imagine your way through the two volumes as a trans-World journey, in which you linger in the well-developed plains of each World, meeting and conversing with interesting philosophers that come your way. Then you climb the sparser mountains, taking a look back at the general view in the sections on story and spirituality. After that, in the questions, you explore the precipitous trans-World pathways before descending into the next World. On the other hand, if you are unacquainted with contemporary philosophy, on a first reading you may wish to skip the questions, or those of less immediate interest to you, so as to get a clearer sense of the argument as a whole. It is your journey, to undertake as feels best.

---

10. Booker, *Seven Basic Plots*.

Terms and Abbreviations

Each of the philosophies-cum-metanarratives is called, for the sake of simplicity and elegance, a "World" and identified by a numeral in curly brackets. The term "World" is meant to refer to something more robust than a mere "worldview" or opinion about the world. A World is a cluster of understandings of which we expect both philosophical coherence and material rootedness in a culture or spirituality. But I am not suggesting totally independent and incommensurable "conceptual worlds"; for the questions open genuine reasons for moving between Worlds, albeit not in a deterministic direction.

The curly brackets seemed appropriate for three reasons. The first is simply that this kind of bracket is the least often used, so that the simple presence of the brackets is enough to make it clear that the number is referring to a particular "World." Most often I dispense with the word "World" and refer simply to {1}, {2}, and so forth; the latter should be read as "World 2," etc.

The second is that these brackets are used in set theory to refer to a set or collection. Ultimately a "World" is a collection of everything that exists: Worlds differ according to what entities are believed to be in them. However, listing a denumerable or perhaps non-denumerable infinity of entities is likely to be impossible. But it may prove possible to define Worlds in terms of what is *not* believed to exist in them, or by *kinds* of thing so believed to exist, or ways of conceptually *constructing* things from other, more fundamental things. So one World may allow material objects but not thoughts and ideas, others the reverse; yet others may construct material things out of thoughts, or the reverse, and so on. A World is then a way of specifying or constructing everything believed to exist, while ruling out non-existents, and perhaps deconstructing apparent existents.

But if this sounds too precise, the final reason for the brackets is that they curl round the number in a broken and wiggly circle. At one stage I considered identifying Worlds by numbers in circles, but the wiggly broken circle suggests something less logically tight and defined, more capable of spilling over into other Worlds.

The questions are listed "?{1}a," "?{1}b," "?{2}a," and so forth, where "?" denotes "Question," the bracketed numeral denotes the number of the World, and a, b, c, etc., differentiate the specific questions relating to that World. This may seem artificial, but will make it easy to identify the questions being referred back to later; for as we shall see, there will be quite a tangle of interrelated questions. For each World resolves questions raised by the previous World or Worlds, but also raises questions that require still further Worlds, or lead us back to Worlds discussed earlier. Only by the end will it emerge whether the chain of questions and Worlds leads us anywhere, or (as anyone versed in the philosophical debates will probably expect) whether it spins unresolvable circles or tangles of question without ultimate answer.

The World Stories and My Story

In this complex web of discussion, the first person I have to convince is myself. The next to convince would be those like me, those who share my perverse combination of openness to different perspectives and need to find one that makes sense to me. This being the case, I need to say a bit about where the writing of this book sits in my personal journey. After all, I argued that the reasons for choosing a view are at once subjective and objective, and some of the subjective reasons can be tough and demanding, while some of the objective reasons are fuzzy and ambivalent. Having outlined the abstract plan of the book, I need to say some more on the personal aspect.

I have had to write this book because of changes in cosmology and changes in my own spirituality, and especially and more urgently as time has gone on, in order to find a place in this wonderful, ever-shifting, and vulnerable twenty-first-century world where I might take a stand, before I move on to . . . . Well, what I believe I am moving on to depends on my worldview, which is precisely what this book is trying resolve

My spiritual journey has included many of the Worlds. When I was eight years old I, like Dawkins, "outgrew" the God of my childhood and became a hardline atheist. Unlike Dawkins, I went on in my mid-teens to outgrow my rejection of religion, being drawn to Buddhism, and later converted to the Christian faith.[11] The title of this first volume reflects this autobiographical element, which makes me view not only naïve religious faith but also naïve atheism as dogmas to be outgrown. Obviously, my title is intentionally provocative, designed to echo the provocation of Dawkins's *Outgrowing God*. Whether, in the process of outgrowing, you become a considered believer, or a considered atheist, what matters is that you have considered seriously the rich variety of alternative ways of understanding the world and our place in it, which is what I hope this book will present.

Now at the time of my conversion to atheism, and for several years thereafter, I was an avid reader of *Knowledge*, a wonderful magazine whose weekly editions could be bound together to form an encyclopedia. It was

---

11. I remain deeply influenced by both Buddhism and my earlier atheism. In *Buddhist Christianity* I argued that it is possible to be both Buddhist and Christian, but I have since come to doubt that this strictly applies in my own case.

there I first began to learn, among other things, about cosmology. I learnt that there were two equal contenders for an understanding of the universe. There was the steady state theory, advocated by Fred Hoyle, according to which matter was constantly being created and destroyed in the universe, leading to a balance that enabled it to last, essentially unchanged, forever. And there was the big bang theory, advocated by Edwin Hubble, which saw the universe as expanding from a massive initial explosion. In general, people who believed in God tended to prefer the big bang with its suggestion of an initial creation and a universe that changed and evolved, even if its end, as the universe expanded into a dreary infinity of cold space, was not likely to be happy. But at that time, I was a dogmatic atheist, and preferred the steady state universe, because it sustained itself without resort to a creator, and justified more optimism about the (very) long-term future. Despite its infinity and eternity, Hoyle's universe had a metaphysical coziness about it, whereas Hubble's poised us alarmingly between a one-off past catastrophe and a slow but inevitable future death.

By the time I published *Holy Ground* in 1990, the big bang had decisively won the day, for a variety of reasons. A wide range of thinkers—some, like John Polkinghorne, committed Christians; others, like Paul Davies, John Barrow, and Frank Tipler, sympathizers—noted the extraordinary coincidences in the laws and conditions that enabled such a chaotic "bang" to give rise to complex living creatures, including ourselves. They developed the anthropic cosmological principle, which made it a rule of the initial conditions in the big bang and the laws of nature that they should be capable of giving rise to sentient life. Though subject to strong and weak interpretations, which {5} will explore, the principle did have the effect of reversing the tendency of science to see us sentient human beings as a meaningless slime on the surface of an insignificant planet. Humanity, *anthropos*, was once again center stage.

I was then in the middle of my ministry as parish priest in the suburbs of East Bristol, and a committed Anglo-Catholic more than ready to leap upon this cosmological bandwagon. In my book I contended for a theistic view that saw the universe as sacramentally brimming with the glory of God. While parts of the book were moving towards seeing the sacred in a more "Buddhist" way, in the interdependence of things and the unity of spirit and matter, the book ended by justifying belief in God on "anthropic" grounds: only God could have tweaked the laws so finely as to produce us from an initial bang.

Since then, three things have happened that have made it necessary not so much as to rewrite *Holy Ground* as to write a different book on the same themes. The first is that not many of my friends said they understood that book, and the book in general did not have quite the wide effect I had hoped it would. Even though it was written for a broad audience, I needed to redouble my efforts to write as simply and clearly as I could. The second is that since then cosmology has become more complex and confusing. The third is: so have I, and so have my beliefs. In view of all this, there is a need for a book that is both clearer and more complex and nuanced—difficult aims to combine—even if something of the old apologetic aim remains.

The changes in cosmology can be left to the book, especially {5}. Suffice it to say that what we may now call the "classical" big bang is no longer the sole contender. Meanwhile—as is less widely known or acknowledged, but as {6} and {9} will explore—the notion that was becoming widespread in the 1990s, that mind or consciousness might seamlessly "emerge" from matter, has also been challenged from both idealist and materialist sides. My conviction in *Holy Ground* that mind and matter flow from each other in seamless sacramental unity cannot so easily now be established; there could be more of mysterious rupture in the universe than I had liked to acknowledge. It may seem now that the best we can do is set different stories of the world alongside each other, each with their strengths and lacunae. Such an approach might accord best with the "postmodern" ethos that has more and more prevailed; though in the end I would argue this is a temptation to be resisted.

As for me, I have changed from being a definite if liberal Anglo-Catholic through a rapprochement with the Buddhist faith of my teens. After publishing a series of books (*The Sacraments, Christian Spirituality, Spirituality in Season*) designed to help students and others study and understand the Christian faith, I wrote *Buddhist Christianity* and *Wounded Wisdom*, in which I wholeheartedly grasped the nettle of dual Buddhist and Christian belonging. Then came *The Interfaith Imperative,* which developed an apologetic for this approach without resorting to a free-for-all relativism.[12] However, it might be argued that the basis of this apologetic was my old liberal Catholicism. In many ways this book continues these trajectories. It could be seen as applying the understanding I have developed over the years to the issues that have long concerned me, about which I wrote my first book. Its approach is irenic, looking to affirm a great deal in each worldview; but also apologetic, since in the end not everything in every view is compatible, and amid them all, I have to find and argue for a stance of my own.

And this is the crucial point: this book is part of the process of finding. Only part: I do other things too, like pray, and meditate, and read novels, and poems, and books on science and philosophy. But it is in the writing

---

12. Full details in the Bibliography.

that these different approaches come together. So writing this book is for me a genuine adventure. I do not know as I write these particular words in October 2019, what conclusion I will come to;[13] whether I will be able to chart a pathway that for me at least makes sense, or whether I will be left with a preponderance of unknowns. I am sure that I will not abandon all that I have received from Christianity and Buddhism, and that I will also remain committed to a critical, rational approach that holds science in high regard. But I do not at this stage know whether I will end up as an idealist holding—after the Buddhist Yogacara school, the Jewish Spinoza, and the Anglican Bishop Berkeley[14]—that mind alone is real, or whether the bodily and material will have much more of a place. I do not yet know whether I will be convinced by the idea that mind "emerges" from matter, or the other way around, or paradoxically both. I do not know whether my final position will be such that Buddhists or Christians, or both or neither, will regard me as an orthodox co-believer; or whether the more liberal-minded scientists and philosophers will regard my work as wise in their terms, or as purveying what Brian Cox has described on TV as "mystic twaddle"!

---

13. The book was completed in May 2022.
14. I am not assuming, of course, that the views of these three are identical.

INTRODUCTION TO *OUTGROWING MATERIALISM*

THE FIRST PART OF this book tells a story that is often told, though in different versions. One version is the "Whig interpretation of history," which describes how a dark, superstitious period called the "Middle Ages" was succeeded by the triumph of modern, secular rationality. The Renaissance opened us to the wisdom, art, and democratic politics of classical Greece and Rome, always presented in a benign, rose-tinted way so as to contrast with the darkness of Gothic cloisters and cathedrals, and the witch-hunts and persecutions of an intolerant "age of faith." The Reformation is presented similarly, as the triumph of individual freedom of conscience over religious dogma, as if Luther, Zwingli, and Calvin were libertarian freethinkers with no interest in dogma themselves. Then Descartes "fathered" (a significantly patriarchal term) modern philosophy, setting it on a course of systematic doubt in which one by one the old certitudes were called into question; the role of God as Savior from doubt, in Descartes's system, was quietly occluded. And though in reality Christians did much to pioneer the rise of science, the latter is portrayed in a way that makes the most of relatively minor incidents surrounding Galileo and the Darwin debate, to wrongly suggest that the church was a violent persecutor of science. Finally, the French Revolution came along to erase the last tracers of "unfree" pre-scientific thinking; it being forgotten, in this account, that the means of establishing freedom, equality, and brotherhood included the guillotine, and the movement was pioneered not by ardent secularists but by deists who desired to replace Catholicism with a rational religion of their own devising. From then on secularism has advanced unchecked, with science enabling us to eradicate diseases and other causes of suffering. We progress towards the "end of history" in our own time, as the need for war and conflict gives way to a rational, disenchanted, democratic mutual respect.[1]

---

1. Cf. for example, Fukuyama *End of History*; Pinker, *Better Angels* and *Enlightenment Now*.

This story probably sounds familiar to you, even though in many circles it has been replaced by another story, which is like its mirror image, and perhaps equally far-fetched. According to this, a patriarchal Greece and Rome—which were only ever democratic for brief periods and among an elite of free men, and largely ran on the basis of tight-knit family groups—gave way, however gradually and imperfectly, to a society based on ideas of justice and the common good, the medieval guilds containing the seeds that would eventually flourish as liberal democracy.[2] The emphasis on divine law, prevalent in Christianity and the other monotheistic faiths, enabled a development of science not seen in the context of any other religion. However, the golden Middle Ages, with its sacramental cosmos full of meaning, suffered a "dissociation of sensibility,"[3] ceding the physical world to more mechanistic ideologies, associated first with a dualistic, deistic variant of Christianity, and later with an atheistic materialism that opposed dualism but took many cues from it. Divested of its spiritual dimension, the material world was opened up to capitalist exploitation and colonization. So Christian faith began to be swallowed up by the science to which it had given birth, and by an empty secularism, ruled by a hollow technology, and threatened by the development of the methods of mass destruction and genocide (of which the twentieth century saw more than any of those preceding it)[4] and the earth-destroying hypertrophy of globalized industry. In this context many began to look to the old faiths for a sense of rootedness and the re-establishment of harmony within society and with the earth. The modern began to give way to a postmodernism in which the modern secular monoculture is replaced by a respect for all cultures and religions in their diversity.[5]

"Science" and "religion" are standard-bearers in the ideological and political struggle between these two stories. The truth might lie in an uneasy reconciliation of the two. But it is not the purpose of this book to take on the immense challenge of that reconciliation. Rather it will try to trace two more logically tractable but all-important threads of the greater story: those that relate to the philosophy of mind, and to religion and spirituality. And the tracing will not be a strict historical tracing, showing the development of ideas from one another, but a logical one, focusing on implications and

---

2. Cf., for example, Siedentop, *Inventing the Individual,* and Holland, *Dominion.*

3. The phrase was first used by T. S. Eliot in his essay titled "The Metaphysical Poets."

4. Though in previous centuries, deaths from the Mongol invasions and several Chinese conflicts come close: see https://en.wikipedia.org/wiki/List_of_wars_by_death_toll.

5. Cf. Taylor, *Secular Age.*

arguments. The aim will not be to understand world history better, but to locate and develop our own beliefs better.

Thus my "story" does not begin in an account of the historical positions that preceded Descartes. The "world" that modernism finally demolished (though it was already being eroded) will be touched on much later, mainly in World {8}. My beginning is the logical beginning, and in probably more cases than mine, the biographical beginning. {1} describes the naïve realism (much less sophisticated than the Aristotelian-cum-mediaeval realism) with which most of us start. This the Cartesian doubt shatters, dividing a kind of wholeness (albeit a complex wholeness, not necessarily monistic) into the mind-body duality of {2}. We shall see how this shattering sucked meaning and purpose into the mental world, leaving the physical with a purely mechanistic description. It only remained for the materialism[6] of {3} to exorcise the ghost of the mind, and the corresponding ghost of the deist God, in a move that the New Atheists seem compelled to repeat. For the God they attack—among the rich and varied understandings of God that have evolved in human culture—is so often the designer, the watchmaker God of William Paley, who is so to say a mere ghost of God's former medieval self. Such a move does indeed leave us with matter, but once again it is only one among many possible accounts of matter, namely dualistic matter with dualistic mind subtracted: precisely, mindless matter.

{4} and {5} represent the unravelling of mindless or mechanical matter, showing that if we wish to preserve the reductionism of dualism and materialism, we have to forgo the idea of matter, as normally understood, as the ultimate stuff or substance of the world. {4} shows how the advance of physics and cosmology has rendered matter less and less fundamental, more questionable and curious, as we move into a World where mathematics reigns. That is to say, the fundamental concepts at work become mentally real, in the sense in which Plato's world of forms and Popper's third realm are mentally real. The search for mathematical necessity in our explanations of why the world is the way it so remarkably is leads us to World {5}: the multiverse. But the alternatives to the multiverse turn out to seem to the innocent eye in many respects more reasonable. And whether we prefer the mental-seeming austerity of World {4} or the superabundance of {5}, in one way or another we have lost sight of matter as the mindless stuff of dualists and materialists. Whisper it not among the New Atheists, but by its own internal logic materialism leads us beyond itself to reconsider understandings that preceded it, and have never seriously been out-argued,

---

6. {3} gives reasons for preferring "materialism" to "naturalism" as a description of this world. Naturalism is a much broader and, to me, more plausible concept, not limited to {3}.

though they have often been ignored or confused with the dualism, which is the only account that atheism has arguably slain, the dualism that is in fact the conceptual brother of materialism.

This then will be my telling of the story of the modern insofar as it relates to issues of mind, body, and religion. It is a story that leads us logically to retell the alternative pre-modern stories that preceded it, which may yet come together in a story we do not quite have yet. The second volume of the book will be groping towards that.

{1}

IS NAIVETY ORIGINAL?

Naïve Realism

We all start from "naive realism," i.e., the doctrine that things are what they seem. We think that grass is green, that stones are hard, and that snow is cold. But physics assures us that the greenness of grass, the hardness of stones, and the coldness of snow are not the greenness of grass, the hardness of stones, and the coldness of snow that we know in our own experience, but something very different.[1]

If other things and other people are to be manifest to me then they must have the natural capacity to appear as they are. That is to say that the manifest properties of things can be themselves the ways in which things appear. There is no need for a mental intermediary or representative, for a quale or a concept, to stand in for manifest properties. No, the idea that some of the properties of things are manifest is on its face the idea that they, and not their mental surrogates, figure in the relation of appearing.[2]

'We are here,' he said. "We really are here."
Some people laughed, some yelled out that if he wasn't going to talk sense, he should shut up his bloody gob.
"He means this isn't a dream," Gerry tried to explain. "He means that this isn't just some kind of story."[3]

---

1. Russell, accessed at www.goodreads.com/quotes/8047059-we-all-start-from-naive-realism-i-e-the-doctrine-that on March 4, 2020.
2. Johnson, *The Manifest*, opening of chapter 5.
3. Beckett, *Dark Eden*, ch. 16, Loc. 2979.

I HAVE A STRANGE memory from my childhood, when I was about nine or ten years old. I vaguely remember it happening in my back garden, but it is all very unspecific, and I do not recall what occasioned the thought. But I remember thinking that the world had somehow lost its immediacy, its vividness. I was no longer immersed in the world. It was as if the veil of thought had intervened. Whereas before it had never occurred to me that the world was not as it seemed—full of real objects like cats and trees and people, and full of real qualities like the green of the grass and the black of the blackbird—now a little philosopher had grown up in me, telling me a quite different scientific story of a world that consists of atoms and space and light rays, none of them colored. And though I had no doubt that there were people in the world other than myself, I felt, now, that I could not tell at all how other people saw what I saw as green or black. Their "worlds" were closed to me, and mine to them.

However, as I describe this now, I use the philosophical questions and categories I have since grown used to. What I experienced then was much more direct, much more like a bereavement of the childhood perception I had once had. But had I ever really had such a perception? The curious thing is that most of my memories begin around the age when I think I had this sense of loss. I cannot remember much of my life before the age of eight, and what I can remember is the opposite of vivid perceptions, more like verbal reconstructions put together from what people have told me, or I had told myself, I had done.

A World of Real Things and Qualities

I write this preamble to introduce {1}, the pre-philosophical World of what is often called "naïve realism," though as we shall see, this is as problematic a notion in general as it is in our own experience. Essentially naïve realism (sometimes called, less pejoratively, direct or commonsense realism) denotes the belief that the world contains objects with qualities, that these exist independently of our perception of them (hence "realism"), and when we perceive these objects, we perceive them approximately as they really are (hence "direct," "common sense," or—more critically—"naïve"). "We really are here," and so are the things we perceive. Experience is taken at face value. The red squirrel outside my window really is red, its nut really brown, and the lawn it is sitting on really green. And if I shut my eyes, or cover my face in the curtain so that I cannot see them, these things go on being as they are (contrary to the even more naïve early childhood idea that when I do this, people disappear, or at any rate, can no longer see me).

For naïve realism there is no need for what is called the correspondence theory of truth. According to that theory, what we perceive are various representations of the world: ideas or statements or images of how things are in the world. These representations in turn are true if they correspond with how things are in the world. Thus I see an image of a red squirrel or the lawn, or I think the thought, "there is a red squirrel on the lawn." Correspondence theory presupposes an "indirect" realism, according to which what I perceive are things (verbal or mental things) that may or may not correspond with things in the material world.

Indirect realism and the correspondence theory work well in {2}, the dualist World, which posits a mental world alongside the physical, so that comparisons between the mental and the material can (somehow) be made. We can then ask whether my mental squirrel is like the squirrel on the lawn; though as we shall see there are tremendous problems concerning what might constitute likeness between an idea or thought or statement, on the one hand, and physical realty, on the other. Philosophers have also tried to square correspondence theory with {3}, materialism, though this involves even more mental contortions, since for this World there are no mental entities, and the comparison has to be between the material brain state that somehow corresponds with my thought about the squirrel, and the material squirrel itself. The correspondence is between, on the one hand, the neurological material thing in the brain that corresponds with my thought, and the physical material thing on the other. ?{2}d and ?{3}f will return to these problems regarding the correspondence theory.

The beauty of naïve realism is that it dispenses with the intervening layer involved in indirect forms of realism. For naïve realism, it is not that I see or say or think some object that may or may not correspond with the physical object. I do not see a seeming-squirrel, or think a thought-squirrel, or utter a squirrel-statement, which may or may not be "like" the real squirrel. What I see, or think about, or describe is *the squirrel itself*. As Bertrand Russell suggests in the opening quote, for naïve realism (albeit not the scientific view he himself supports), things don't just happen to correspond (or fail to correspond) to what they seem to be; things *are* what they seem. Or as Mark Johnson argues in the second quote, what appear to us are the properties of things themselves, not mental surrogates such as sense-data or qualia (of which more soon).

Philosopher and AI scholar Ricardo Manzotti has recently argued that instead of looking for a naturalistic explanation of consciousness in terms of an identity between mental events and events in the physical brain (as in reductionist materialism—see {3}), it is much simpler to seek an identity between experiences and their objects. "One's experience of an object is the object one experiences."[4] Though Manzotti does not use the term, he is effectively arguing a direct or naïve realist position. His position is vulnerable to the same critiques as naïve realism generally, namely the question of how different experiences of different people, or the same person at different times, can be identical with one and the same object. He responds by arguing that the same object may have different aspects, depending on the conditions in which it is experienced (moonlit or sunlit, for example) and on the person who is experiencing it. A physical object is then not a single thing but a complex of interactions with different persons, who are themselves physical bodies. Mark Johnston likewise rejects the need for a layer of representation intervening between the observer and the object, arguing that we experience aspects of objects as the object gives itself to a variety of experiences. ?{2}d will return to these arguments, but at this stage note that the idea of an "aspect" is an important qualification on the directness of direct realism: for precisely how an does an "aspect" differ from a "representation"?

In naïve realism, rather than merely pointing to thoughts or ideas that might "correspond" with reality, all parts of speech disclose something real "out there." For example, the statement "A red ball is rolling slowly down the road into the muddy gutter" draws our attention to the real ball named by the first noun and the real place named by the second noun; the adjectives direct us to real qualities of redness and muddiness qualifying their respective nouns; the verb indicates a real movement of rolling; a quality of slowness really qualifies that verb; and the prepositions "down" and "into" point out for us real spatial relations. These realities do not "correspond" with aspects of the knowledge in my mind; they are directly disclosed in the act of speaking or thinking. In naïve realism, what you see and know is what you describe in language, and what you get in reality.

In this book we will encounter Worlds that place trust in only some parts of speech: only nouns denoting things, only adjectives denoting qualities, plus spatial relations in both cases, for example. Naïve realism denotes a democratic trust in all of the parts of speech. Volume 2 will argue that Aristotelian direct realism {8} represents a more sophisticated trust, a metaphysics that arises from giving due weight to all parts of speech. In both naive and Aristotelian realism, to use the analogy from Plato's *Phaedrus*, language carves reality at the joints, while other Worlds arise from carving reality in some more sophisticated or artful way. In {1} and {8}, language is trusted to describe the world, more or less, as it really is; but equally, the world is trusted to be as language describes it, and our minds and thoughts

---

4. Manzotti, *Mind-Object Identity*.

are trusted to be right about the broad structure of the world. This does not mean that our realism is naïve enough to believe that our language or our thought *always* gets the world right—we can be mistaken about the facts—but the structure of thought and language cannot be so systematically misleading that we can *never* get it right.

Why should we not believe this commonsense view? The reasons will emerge in the questions below, and in the discussion of the dualist and materialist views that replaced naïve realism, at least in the minds of the philosophers. But at this stage it is worth noting that up till the advent of those views in the modern period—broadly speaking following Descartes—this kind of realism was the consensus view. For Aristotle, and the medieval scholastics who developed his views, there was no reason to doubt that grass was really green, or that we could really see green grass. There were views that threw into doubt the greenness along with the grass, and departed from realism in an idealist direction. Many schools of Mahayana Buddhism, for example, adopted the view that objects, qualities, and the self that seemed to perceive them were systematically illusory. The Advaita Vedanta school of Hinduism saw the world as the dream of Ultimate Reality or Brahman. Meanwhile Greek thought called into question fundamental aspects of what we like to call reality. Parmenides argued that change was an illusion, while Heraclitus argued against the reality of anything other than change. For Plato, the reality of material objects was shadowy to say the least, and the Neoplatonists took this trajectory of thought further, affirming one true Reality from which all else has fallen.

These philosophies we only mention here, leaving them to be explored in more depth in later Worlds. The point that matters at this stage is that all these views challenged naïve realism, not in the interests of a non-naïve realism, but in the interests of a non-realism that often had something of a religious motive. It was not the qualities of objects that was questioned, but the objects themselves, leaving the qualities as it were to float free in a transformed understanding of what made for their reality.

This was reversed in the modern attack on naïve realism, which sacrificed the naïve understanding of the reality of the qualities in favor of a "harder" understanding of objective reality. That is the story to be told in {2} and {3}. At this point we just need to be clear about these two alternative ways of departing from naïve or direct realism: one affirms directness at the expense of "reality," while the other affirms reality at the expense of naïve directness. In the former case, we affirm what we can see and hear as real in itself, rather than inhering in supposed real objects: this is the approach of {7}, idealism. In the latter case, we affirm the reality of objects independent of our experience of them, even when this calls aspects of our experience into question: the approach of {2}–{4}.

Meanwhile it needs to be emphasized that in the medieval West, despite the temporary success of Gnosticism in the early centuries, and the Cathars in the twelfth, the idealist challenge eventually failed. Christian philosophy in the Western church had drawn from Aristotle an understanding of how there could be real knowledge of real qualities inhering in real objects, in a sacramental cosmos that was thoroughly material and yet thoroughly spiritual. In a sense this represented the most materialist understanding the world has ever seen, without ceasing to be full of spirit, full of value. The art and culture of the period reflected this understanding—in its eye for detail and intensity of quality, and gradually in the development, in the Christian West, of perspective and other techniques that give to paint, paradoxically, the appearance of reality. {8} will explore the philosophical underpinnings that enabled what would otherwise be naïve or "merely commonsense" realism to generate a sophisticated direct realism.

Just as, biographically, the Cartesian doubt broke the vividness and confidence of my naïve childhood world (in a process certainly not unique to me!), so historically it would break asunder the sacramental unity of quality and thing, or meaning and matter, that characterized the medieval view.

Naïve Faith

Medieval theology, following Aristotle, developed a very sophisticated (and some would say, a somewhat obscure and remote) understanding of God. But this sophisticated God would surely have no force in the minds of ordinary believers if it did not resonate with some very simple, primitive, and naïve approaches to God. It is often argued that children, and animist peoples, have an intuitive belief in gods or spirits, and find it easy to talk to God, until dispossessed of those intuitions by sophisticated-sounding rational argument. This is affirmed by many on both sides of the "science versus religion" debate, the difference between the two sides being that where some would see insight and intuition, others would see superstition; and where some would see mature reason, others would see mere sophistry and sophistication.

The Bible contains many levels of reflection on God. In the earliest strands God walks and talks with human beings, as in the Garden of Eden (Gen 3:8), wrestles with Jacob (Gen 32:22–32), and later converses with Moses face to face as with a friend (Exod 33:11). Such passages are amenable to a naïve interpretation in which God seems as anthropomorphic as any Greek god. However, such texts are nearly always juxtaposed with others that challenge such a literal reading: for example, only nine verses after the "face to face" passage we read (Exod 33:20) that no one can see God's face and live. By such editing, and later writing, it became clear not only that the Hebrews ought to serve only one God but that there *is* only one almighty God, who created heaven and earth, and will eventually bring these to an end (e.g., Isa 40:25–6; 42:5–8; 43:10–13); whose glory fills all the earth (Isa 6:3), but whose nature transcends anything in the universe and can never be fully grasped. Less and less, in the Bible, does this God converse with ordinary individuals. Rather, God addresses humans through the mediation of angels, prophets, and priests.[5] God becomes more like the God of medieval theology, the uncreated creator of all; yet paradoxically this God always retains, in the eyes of faith, something of the original, naïve intimacy, such that the God of the philosophers will always be in creative tension with the personal God of naïve faith.

Of course, the God of naïve faith is a very easy target for the New Atheists. The apparent anthropomorphism lends itself to the notion that God is a purely fictional character along the lines of the tooth fairy so maligned by Richard Dawkins. It is not surprising, therefore, that believers of a philosophical bent (Origen, Spinoza, Kant) have often tried to rid God of the naïve elements, while others (Tertullian, Luther, Pascal, Barth) have striven to eliminate the metaphysics and rely on faith alone, despite, or even because of, its apparent absurdity. (Tertullian is often misquoted as saying, "*credo quia absurdum*," I believe because it is absurd.) However, this book will argue that many of the Bible stories are subtler than they appear, while metaphysics (including materialist metaphysics) never finally transcends narrative. So, to parallel the Gospel saying in Matthew 10:16, authentic belief needs to be metaphysically sophisticated as a serpent, and naïve as a dove. I hope this book will show several ways of achieving this.

Arguably a similar tension arises in so-called primitive art, which is generally not at all naïve. The earliest works of art we know—the rotund "venuses," some of them dating from around 500,000 years ago, through the cave paintings of El Castillo (approximately 39,000 BCE), to the Lion Man of the Hohlenstein Stadel (38,000 BCE)—look far from "realistic"; many of these seem deliberately to transform their object into something stylized and geometric. There is a cartoon-like naivety about the Christian icon, and yet also a sophistication that embeds in stiff egg tempera paint the theological mysteries of Trinity and incarnation. Meanwhile modern art often tries

---

5. In *God: A Biography*, Jack Miles argues that in the Hebrew Bible, God is never again quoted after his long speech at the end of Job. God, he believes, fell silent.

to return to a dreamlike, icon-like naivety that is likewise subtler than it seems: as in the expressionism of Chagall, the modern icons of Rouault, the strangely convincing life forms of Klee, the uncanny fable-laden realism of Rousseau and Spencer. And yet it was in the age of faith that artists turned to perspective painting and the precise rendering of surfaces: painters like Van Eyck (notably in his Arnolfini portrait, which seems partly to be a painting about representation) open up uncanny depth in the bright and precise surfaces of things, convincing the onlooker that these painted qualities must be real, just as they are.

Questions Regarding {1}

Modern philosophy, as noted, is often seen as beginning with Descartes's radical break with the realism that went before it in both the logical and historical senses. It is possible to trace three interwoven strands of question. The first reflects Descartes's method of doubt in relation to uncritical realism. The second reflects the progress of science, which Descartes himself helped pioneer, which had the effect of constructing a "real world" that is quite unlike the world of naïve perception. The third introduces a suspicion as to whether the naïve world can be as innocent and as pure of metaphysical reflection as it seems. This "postmodern" suspicion could spell the end of more than just naïve realism, proving fatal to all "modern" or post-Cartesian approaches to truth.

The main discussion of these questions will appear in {2}, {3}, and {7} respectively; at this point the questions are simply outlined and set in relation to one another.

?{1}a: The Possibility of Illusion

Descartes—of whom more in the next World—pioneered the method of systematically doubting everything that can be doubted, in order to affirm what remains standing as an indubitable foundation for knowledge. To return to our example, I may doubt whether the squirrel, or the lawn, really exist. After all, as Descartes points out, when we dream, we believe the objects in our dream are real; only when we awaken do we realize they are not. Could this waking world not just be a dream on another level? (And as Buddhist and Hindu thought often suggest, may there be a further awakening, such that we wake up and realize all the things we chased after or feared in this life are as nothing?) Is there anything at all that it is impossible or unreasonable to doubt?

Descartes invokes a deceiving demon to drive home the idea that the contents of our minds may be deceptive, relating to nothing real. Twentieth-century philosophers created other more sophisticated devices to the same effect. Perhaps we are just brains in vats wired up to electrical currents that give our brains the illusion of walking around in a real world and communicating with real people, when all that really exists in the universe is a brain, a vat, and sundry demonic scientists operating these items in a laboratory. Or perhaps—as the film *The Matrix* explored—I am a software program running on a computer, designed to create the experience of life in a real world, when the only thing in the universe is the computer and the malevolent beings who run it. Australian philosopher David Chalmers discusses many such possibilities in his recent book, *Reality+*, but as he there points out, despite their sophistication, these variants add little to Descartes's demon analogy. In fact, they detract from its simplicity, by introducing elements of real hardware like brains and vats and computers, which confuse the basic issue.

There are actually three ways in which simple identity between word, idea, and thing can unravel. As well as delusion, on which Descartes's critique focused, which consists in a mismatch between world and both language and mind, there is the possibility of the lie (a mismatch between language and both world and mind) and the possibility of misunderstanding (a mismatch between mind and both world and language). All three possibilities prize open the simple identifications presupposed by naïve realism, and invite us to consider notions of correspondence (or mismatch) between word, idea, and thing.

In practice, it takes some reflection to break our naïve realism. If everything is delusory, the words delusion and reality lose their meaning, which is gained only by their contrast with one another. If there is no way of telling reality and illusion apart, the proper conclusion to draw is not that "all is illusion" but that we cannot decide as to things' illusion or reality. However, regarding some things as more real than others does have considerable practical advantages, like not stepping aside to get around the "illusory" cat only to bump into the "real" table. It helps us for practical purposes to describe some real-unreal things as "unreal" and others as "real." But then why not remove the quotation marks and make do with real and unreal? So *in practice* some kind of realism, even a naive realism, is logically bound to return. So Chalmers argues that in a "virtual" world our responses remain "real"—we can act ethically in a simulated world as in a real world, and enjoy and appreciate its contents just as much. He argues this justifies the idea of "real virtual reality."[6] Or as C. S. Lewis put it,

> Although the whole of life were said to be nothing but a dream and the physical world nothing but a phantasm, I should call this dream or phantasm real enough if, using reason well, we were never deceived by it.[7]

?{1}b: Does Science Render Naivety Impossible?

A more modest, less draconian doubt is possible. We may concede that the squirrel is really there but doubt whether he is really red. After all, when I look out at night on my moonlit lawn, my squirrel becomes a grey squirrel. Has he really changed species? Surely it is more reasonable to suppose that what has changed is not the squirrel himself, but the qualities I can perceive in him.

And this is the hypothesis most of us would adopt. By night the squirrel is the same squirrel, but appears grey, because our eyes cannot register color at low levels of light. If I were a cat or an owl with better night vision, he might still look red. And if I were a bat "seeing" the squirrel mainly by echolocation, I cannot imagine what I would see, since my imagination is based on human, not chiropteran experience. I am tempted at this point to say that the squirrel *appears* grey at night, but *really* he is red, as he appears by day. But why privilege the daytime version? Is not red merely how the squirrel appears to a human being by day. An eagle, with much more refined eyesight, might see the squirrel more perfectly than I ever could. On the other hand, we could say with the philosophers that day has better conditions for seeing, or enables us to see more of the things that there are. The real squirrel is then the squirrel we observe "in optimal conditions."

Following Galileo, Descartes, and others, the empiricist John Locke took a more radical approach. He distinguished the primary qualities a squirrel really has—things that can be measured, like mass, size, shape, and motion—from the secondary qualities like redness, which are dependent on our perceptions and vary with lighting conditions and suchlike. Basically, the primary qualities are the ones that science applies to objects, while the secondary qualities are the ones that science explains away by reference to the primary. For example, the red of the squirrel is explained in terms of the chemical construction of squirrel fur and the way it responds to light. The

---

6. Title of Chalmers, *Reality+*, Part 4.
7. Cited in Davies, *God and the New Physics*, 205.

atoms of the fur and the light waves have only primary qualities like length, amplitude, and mass. And this avoids the circularity of explaining the redness of the squirrel by redness in its fur.

On this basis modern science discovers a world full of real things, but unlike the world of naïve realism, it contains no colorful squirrels. What *appears to us* as a red squirrel *is in fact* a bundle of atoms in a web of rebounding light rays, a bundle of atoms organized as a nut-processing machine. Though more modest than the total doubt of Descartes, the progress of science casts a wider and more pervasive doubt on the world of common-sense realism. It retains a kind of realism: realism regarding objects and their primary, scientifically measurable qualities, and perhaps what is called indirect realism, the idea that the events in our brain are caused by external realities and result in brain-events that are partially accurate representations of those realities. But the bright innocence of naïve realism darkens, as we enter {2} and {3}, though there would be many a rear-guard defence of that original light.

?{1}c: Is Realism Ever Naïve?

The third question is not so much about the reality of objects described by nouns, or qualities described by adjectives, as about whether the way we construct sentences and use language as a whole reflects reality. My belief that there is a squirrel on the lawn may reflect the way language, or thought, works, rather than the way the world is. It may be that language does not carve reality at the joints, but imposes its own structure. Most languages have a structure that consists of subjects, verbs, and objects, with appended adjectives, adverbs, and prepositions. But does this structure work because it reflects the structure of the real world: because it actually consists of things with qualities, causing changes in quality, substance, and relation to happen in other things? Or do we see the world in this naïve way because language is structured the way it is?

So is naïve realism as naïve and innocent of metaphysics as we think? Or when we see the world as we do, have we already interpreted it by means of language and cultural systems? A young child or a tribal hunter will probably "naively" see the world as full of spirits, many of them hostile. When a child describes the things she fears, a parent in an animist society will probably tell her to make an offering to the gods responsible and the evil spirits will go away, thus affirming the validity of her naïve belief. I remember that as a child I was quite often troubled by fears of nightmarish figures, and later, intruders under the bed, and tornadoes (though these were rare indeed in Surrey!). But my parents did not tell me to placate these evil forces with offerings. Instead, they told me that they were not really there, or not likely to happen, and I didn't need to fear them. Was that not because they were twentieth-century Western parents, so that even when I was naïve and had no metaphysics of my own, I was imbued with theirs, while in other cultures different "naïve" beliefs would be encouraged?

With postmodernism we are all familiar with the idea that the way we see the world is never innocent, but always shaped by our basic stories and beliefs. But this idea is by no means new. Mahayana Buddhism distinguishes between "conventional reality," which is the world of naïve experience, corresponding with the conventions of our language, and "ultimate reality," in which subject and object are undifferentiated and there is no self and no objects we can lay hold of and name. Immanuel Kant argued, in a parallel way, that things as they are in themselves, are unknowable, but that in order to be able to speak of and deal with the world, our minds structure things with the categories of space, time, causality, and so forth.

Note that it is not just that, to describe the real red squirrel eating his nut on the lawn, I have to employ categories like "squirrel" and "eat" and "on." It is equally true that, to identify the patch of red as a squirrel shaped patch, I have to import from my idea of the external world the category of "squirrel." I use my mental experience to structure my experience of the world, but also, conversely, I need beliefs about the external world, as containing things like squirrels and nuts, to organize my mental experiences into something I can describe. This is something postmodernism often misses, so creating its lopsided relativism, for which the world is mind-structured (or language-structured) but the mind and language are not world-structured.

Ask yourself the question of whether you see people as getting smaller as they move away from you. Some will say, "of course," and others "of course not, they are still the same size." Look at a picture by a child or an early mediaeval artist: the people depicted are all the same size (except, perhaps, "important" ones). Now look at one by a Renaissance or post-Renaissance artist; or a photograph. In these, people get smaller as they approach the "vanishing point." This is because these artists have learnt to paint in perspective; and the camera depicts the world in perspective because of the way light impacts on a flat screen. They have applied a theory, a technique, or a machine that embodies a technique.

So how you see the people depends on your theory, or technique of seeing. Probably in the street we do not immediately experience people as inflating as they come along the road toward us. But we all know about paintings and cameras and films, and we understand immediately what is meant when it is said that people further away look smaller, even though actually, they aren't. We seldom actually confuse people at the bottom of our garden with little fairies! So which is the reality I "naively" experience: the one in which people get smaller as they move away, or the one in which they stay the same size?

Again, consider our inability, above, to identify any one style of "naïve" art. Are we to understand "reality" in terms of cave paintings, or icons, or Van Eyck, or the modern styles of art, many of which indeed capture something naïve from "primitive" antecedents, but in a manner that is really quite sophisticated? There seems to be not one naivety, capturing reality as it is, but many, each of them stylizing reality in a different way.

Experience, it would seem, is always already laden with interpretation, and our minds are subtle enough to grasp different ways of describing the world in language. A world experienced without interpretation would be a nightmare, as we will see in the case of Funes the Memorious in {7}. As with our other two questions, we merely raise this question now, to receive more of an answer in later Worlds, especially {2}, {3}, {6}, and {7}.

Résumé: Inescapable Naïvety?

Like our childhood innocence, naïve realism is a kind of reference point about which there is little to say; which is why this chapter has been so short. For as soon as we start to philosophize, we move away into other worlds in which there is much more to doubt and argue about. The Worlds arise through questioning naïve realism, but each World retains something of the naïve.

- {2} I doubt, therefore there is a doubter and a doubtable, a self and a material world.
- {3} I never experience the doubter, so there is only the material world.
- {4} But the material world is dubious too; there is no matter, only mathematics.
- {5} ... and no way of knowing which mathematical world is "true," so they all must be.
- {6} But surely there are fundamental realities; but to be fundamental to my reality, they must be both matter and mind.
- {7} The only matter I know is what I experience, so experience is all.
- {8} Not so! Ordinary language carves reality at the joints; things are what they seem.

{9} Yes, reality is many and varied, but all emerges out of one process.

{10} And that process is grounded in goodness, through which naive trust returns.

{2}

THE HAUNTED MACHINE
Dualism

In the old cosmology the universe was . . . like a very rich literary text, full of hidden symbolism. Values, purposes, omens, portents, occult meanings and forces abounded in everything. A human being's fulfilment lay in harmoniously fitting himself into this vast given order. . . . By contrast, we have experienced the disenchantment of the world. For us the world is what the sciences of nature have shown it to be—morally and religiously neutral and without magic. It is bureaucratic, in the sense that all particular events are processed in accord with general rules. . . . In order to learn to see what nature is really like, we have been obliged quite consciously to forgo all the old rich "meaningfulness."[1]

I have, on the one hand, a clear and distinct idea of myself taken simply as a conscious, not an extended, being; and on the other hand, a distinct idea of a body, taken simply as an extended, not a conscious, being; so it is certain that I am really distinct from my body, and could exist without it.[2]

Still unwittingly adhering to the grammar of mechanics, [Descartes] tried to avert disaster by describing minds in what was merely an obverse vocabulary. The workings of minds had to be described by the mere negatives of the specific descriptions given to bodies; they are not in space, they are not motions,

---

1. Cupitt, *Taking Leave of God*, 17–18.
2. Descartes, Sixth Meditation, in *Philosophical Writings*, 114–15.

they are not modifications of matter, they are not accessible to public observation. Minds are not bits of clockwork, they are just bits of not-clockwork. . . . As thus represented, minds are not merely ghosts harnessed to machines, they are themselves just spectral machines. Though the human body is an engine, it is not quite an ordinary engine, since some of its workings are governed by another engine inside it—this interior governor-engine being one of a very special sort. It is invisible, inaudible and it has no size or weight. It cannot be taken to bits and the laws it obeys are not those known to ordinary engineers.[3]

DUALISM IN THE BROADEST sense has a long history. People of all cultures love the story of the world as a battle between two opposing forces. A force of good, light, law, spirit, and often maleness is often depicted as being locked in eternal combat with a force of evil, darkness, chaos, materiality, and often femaleness. In the Babylonian creation myth, the warrior god Marduk creates the world by slaying and dismembering the serpentine body of the sea goddess Tiamat. This story crept into the edge of the Bible (though not its main creation myths) in God's slaying of the sea-monster Rahab, and the slaying of the dragon by the Archangel Michael (or alternatively in later Christian fable, St.. George). Meanwhile the Zoroastrianism born in ancient Persia depicted an eternal struggle of good versus evil. Such ideas continued in the Manicheanism, with which early Christianity itself struggled. The Islamic idea of jihad—which primarily denotes a person's spiritual struggle, and derivatively the holy war—uses the same language. Though, of course, in all the monotheistic faiths, God can never be seen as engaged in a struggle with an *equal* power, the notion is common to Islam and Christianity, and has often brought them into political conflict. Of course, in any cosmic battle, it is always the believer and those like her who are on the side of the good . . . .

In other mythologies, to which Volume 2 returns in {7}, the world itself is created by a catastrophic fall, or the work of a demonic creator. Many have argued, perhaps unfairly, for such dualistic tendencies in Plato, with his world of eternal forms set against the inferior (though not for him evil) world of transient matter. In Gnosticism this picture darkens: the good and the spiritual are seen as locked in an intrinsically evil bodily and material realm, having to struggle to break free to re-join the true God beyond the created order. Christianity has often had to struggle with such ideas, and has sometimes expressed itself in terms that are either Manichean or gnostic.

3. Ryle, *Concept of Mind*, 21.

The dualism of {2} is neither Manichean nor gnostic, nor is it based on the Babylonian or any other creation myth. Nor is it simply a dualism in the sense that the above myths continue to haunt many more sophisticated worldviews, such as the Platonic, the Aristotelian, and the Catholic Christian. These worldviews all hold to the comforting immortality of the soul, and all inevitably therefore see the soul as in some way "other" than the mortal body; but such views find their home in other Worlds equally well, if not better than in {2}.

The dualism of {2} represents a contrasting struggle: the struggle to overcome the mythologies of struggle, in favor of a scientific worldview. Yet a struggle against struggle cannot be without paradox. The early modern struggle against myth and superstition has often been depicted in terms that are themselves mythological. In place of the old sea-monster, modern dualism slays the monsters of religious dogmatism and priestcraft so as to establish the new order of reason and light. As is often the case with struggles, the victorious new dualism takes on many of the features of the conquered: the division of the world into two kinds of substance; one the spiritual and mental locus of everything that gives life meaning; the other material and bodily, and essentially without value or meaning, fit to be divided up, investigated, and exploited. Some of the power of this substance dualism may reside in the way it evokes earlier myths. It would be ironic indeed if the rise of modern science, so often seen as a triumph of reason over superstition, and of the world-affirming over the world-denying, was in fact facilitated by a return to dark mythologies that Christian faith and Aristotelian metaphysics had temporarily dispelled.

Modern Western philosophy has often swallowed this kind of myth of its origins in terms of the (much exaggerated) struggles of scientists like Copernicus and Galileo against a monstrously persecutory mother church. And as with the ancient religions, modern philosophy looks to a founding patriarch. Authentic philosophy is often seen as being "fathered" by René Descartes. A few minor predecessors apart (mainly Plato and Aristotle), Descartes is seen as initiating the core problematic for philosophy, which is understood to be the question of epistemological method, or how we can work out a way of getting to know truths. Though by no means all modern philosophers are dualists in the strong sense in which Descartes was (i.e., an ontological dualist who posited mind and matter as distinct substances), arguably a kind of dualism is implicit in the epistemological problematic of modern philosophy, which is understood in terms of the question of how mental contents can correspond with material contents, or how our minds can correctly "mirror" the world.

So when materialism comes to reject the need for "mind" in favor of a metaphysics of matter alone, the "mind" that is rejected is mind conceived by dualism, and the matter that is left is likewise the matter first conceived by the mechanist philosophies in the context of which Descartes's dualism was born. The monism of materialism {3} is arrived at by way of subtraction of one part of the older dualism {2}. Materialism is dualism minus mind; its matter is still the soulless matter of substance dualism (not for example the "soulful" matter to be found in {6}). And dualism had made that subtraction easier, by rendering mind itself soulless and in a sense (witness the opening quote from Gilbert Ryle) mechanical.

Or so I shall argue in this chapter. Which is why, to tell the story of the Cartesian kind of dualism, substance dualism,[4] we need to begin before Descartes, in the late Renaissance period in which Aristotelian realism came to be supplanted by a different kind of account of reality, one that both arose from, and contributed to, the rise of scientific method. There has been a tendency in the history of ideas to delve ever earlier for the origins of "modernity," in previous medieval departures from the Aristotelian/Thomist account. Candidates include Duns Scotus's notion of the univocity of being, that is to say, his belief that "exists" means the same thing when applied to God and to created realities. (Aquinas believed in the analogy of being: for him, existence in the case of God is eminent existence, surpassing existence as we know it, which stands as a pale analogy for divine existence.)

The other major candidate for the origin of modernity is the nominalism pioneered by William of Ockham (famous for his "razor"), which rejects the notion (common to Plato, Aristotle, and Aquinas) that universals like "green" and "triangle" refer to realities (more on this in {4}). According to Ockham, only singular things—particular green blades of grass and particular triangle-shaped things—are real. This view has been argued to be a step towards science and its (arguable) attention to particular details rather than abstract relations. However, we shall see next that the great pioneers of modern scientific method—Copernicus, Kepler, Galileo, and Descartes himself—were the opposite of nominalists, being revivers of Platonic realism. Nominalism in fact does not sit well with substance dualism since the latter is committed to the substantial reality of mental contents. However, nominalism, particularly via the influence of Thomas Hobbes, did help ease the route from dualism to thoroughgoing materialism. Reductionism

---

4. It has been argued that Descartes is not a substance dualist. In "Panpsychism?," for example, Galen Strawson argues that Descartes rejected the idea of a substance as something separable from its attributes, so when he speaks of mind and body as substances, he is in fact espousing a kind of quality dualism. However, I will follow the scholarly consensus that Descartes epitomizes substance dualism.

arguably follows from nominalism, and we shall see reductionism prevail in {3}, though receding from view again in {4}.

So nominalism was not an influence on Descartes and his form of dualism, and we do not need to consider it at this stage. Much more important to consider is the revived Platonism and faith in mathematics that lie at the metaphysical root of the mechanical worldview of early modern science, which is the real context of Descartes's dualism. This chapter will examine the metaphysical foundations of modern science, arguing that Descartes's dualism arose as their negative corollary: the withdrawal of meaning to a ghostly realm, leaving the material world disenchanted and modelled on the machine. We shall see how this mechanization prepared the way for the banishing of the ghost by the kind of materialism that is now, rightly or wrongly, associated with science. This chapter considers the variety of forms whereby dualism has adapted to the severe critique it has received in modern philosophy especially after this move to materialism. It examines the God and the kinds of spirituality and root story associated with dualism, and finally, summarizes several kinds of question faced by dualism.

Eight Principles of Scientific Method

A popular view—expounded by the New Atheists—would regard the heroic pioneers of modern, sun-centered astronomy, such as Copernicus, Kepler, and Galileo, as contending for empirical evidence against the dogmatic pronouncements of mother church. In fact, it was only Galileo who was (mildly) persecuted, and his main opposition lay not in the church as such so much as the academics who were committed to an Aristotelian view. And far from drawing on new evidence, these pioneers were actually contending *against* the evidence. For we all certainly experience the world as solid and static, and the sun as moving in the sky; try as we may, we cannot for long experience what Copernicus and the others tell us is true, that at sunrise the sun does not move, rather the horizon tilts downward as the earth revolves. The earth-centered Ptolemaic system that was then in favor accounted for the evidence completely, albeit cumbersomely, in its cycles and epicycles; the evidence that would favor the Copernican (and later, the Einsteinian) understanding was unavailable to the measuring instruments of the day.

What made Copernicus and the others contend for the sun-centered view was not evidence but a new theoretical framework, and a new set of priorities. What was involved was what Thomas Kuhn has taught us to call a "paradigm shift," in which theory does not change in the light of new evidence; on the contrary, the evidence itself is reinterpreted in the light of the new theory. The latter is favored not because it "corresponds" better with the evidence, but for reasons that include "appeal to the individual's sense of the appropriate or the aesthetic—the new theory is said to be 'neater,' 'more suitable,' or 'simpler' than the old."[5]

We do not have to follow Kuhn all the way regarding the incommensurability of paradigms, and the much-debated relativism that follows, to appreciate that the rise of modern science was accompanied by a profound paradigm shift. Kuhn is well-known, and drew heavily on less celebrated earlier thinkers such as Alexander Koyré[6] and Michael Polanyi.[7] Both argued that though science presents a mathematical world divorced from lived experience, it does of course rely on lived human intersubjectivity and traditions of practice. Koyré in turn was influenced by an underrated maverick, A. E. Burtt, whose classic, *The Metaphysical Foundations of Modern Physical Science*, argued that a turn from Aristotelian to Neoplatonic, mathematically based metaphysics ousted humanity from its previously central place in the cosmos, so facilitating the rise of modern science. For the purposes of this book, it is not necessary to get involved in disputes about causal order: whether it was a change in metaphysics that enabled the rise of scientific method, or vice versa; doubtless things worked both ways. Nor need we share Burtt's tendency to lament the loss of the anthropocentric cosmos. But the clarity of Burtt's categories and analysis is very helpful, and establishes the basis of the scientific worldview in what I summarize as eight basic tenets. Each represents both an aspect of scientific methodology and a metaphysical view that both supports and depends upon the methodological tenet. Let us consider the first two tenets together.

1) Nature Is Governed by Laws

. . . and . . .

2) These Laws Are Discoverable by Human Beings

The idea that nature is law-governed is widespread, indeed perhaps universal to all civilizations complex enough to need laws to govern behavior. Witness the Hindu and Buddhist concept of *dharma*, the Hebrew concept of *torah*, and the Greek notion of the *logos* or rational order. In most cases

---

5. Kuhn, *Scientific Revolutions*, 155.
6. Koyré, *From the Closed World*.
7. Polanyi, *Personal Knowledge*.

the primary reference is to a moral law, but there is often an extension to the notion that nature obeys laws and that its order may be compared with the moral ordering of society. The Greek philosopher Heraclitus regarded the sun's obedience to law as being enforced by the same beings as human justice, declaring, "The sun will not overstep his measures; otherwise the Erinyes, ministers of justice, will find him out."[8] And the Hebrew Psalm 19 moves smoothly from contemplation of the sun's orderly procession in the heavens to considerations of the sacred law of the Lord:

> In the heavens he has set a tent for the sun, which comes out like a bridegroom from his wedding canopy, and like a strong man runs its course with joy. Its rising is from the end of the heavens, and its circuit to the end of them; and nothing is hid from its heat. The law of the LORD is perfect, reviving the soul; the decrees of the LORD are sure, making wise the simple.
> (Ps 19:4b–7)

But though the idea that law governs nature is widespread, science has not proven to be a widespread activity among human cultures. For science to develop, more has to be believed about the nature of the laws. There has to be hope that human beings can discover the laws ordained by God or the gods; and this hope has often been absent. The Bible often emphasizes the inscrutability of those laws. In the prophet Isaiah we hear, in relation to God's forgiveness:

> My thoughts are not your thoughts, nor are your ways my ways, says the LORD. For as the heavens are higher than the earth, so are my ways higher than your ways and my thoughts than your thoughts.
> (Isa 54:8–9)

In context, admittedly, this passage is making a specific point about God's willingness to forgive and bless his people, contrasting this with human judgmentalism. However, God's words from the whirlwind at the end of Job raise bigger questions about human ability to discern the purposes of God.

> Where were you when I laid the foundation of the earth? Tell me, if you have understanding. Who determined its measurements—surely you know! Or who stretched the line upon it? On what were its bases sunk, or who laid its cornerstone when the morning stars sang together and all the heavenly beings shouted for joy?
> (Job 38:4–7)

8. Cited in Kirk, *Presocratic Philosophers*, 201.

God proceeds with a catalogue of wonders in creation to which human wisdom cannot hope to penetrate (though arguably, science has in fact now put most of them within the range of human understanding). On the other hand, we find contrary passages concerning the law.

> Surely, this commandment that I am commanding you today is not too hard for you, nor is it too far away. It is not in heaven, that you should say, "Who will go up to heaven for us, and get it for us so that we may hear it and observe it?" Neither is it beyond the sea, that you should say, "Who will cross to the other side of the sea for us, and get it for us so that we may hear it and observe it?" No, the word is very near to you; it is in your mouth and in your heart for you to observe.
> (Deut 30:11–14)

The wisdom writings in the Bible (including Job, many psalms, Song of Songs, Ecclesiastes, and many apocryphal writings) describe wisdom—the order and beauty that accompanied God's making of the world—as a practical quality which humans can learn through the practice of virtue. And theologically, the universe was created good and orderly by divine intent and command (Gen 1:1—2:3); human beings bear the image of God, so a hope pervades the Jewish tradition (and the other monotheisms, Christian and Muslim, that sprang from it) that human beings may come to learn the divine laws that govern the cosmos.

We find then in these traditions a sense of mystery—an otherness to the divine laws that transcends ultimate understanding—combining with a sense of accessibility to the intellect shaped by virtue. Such hope is broadly absent from the polytheistic traditions in which the gods are often arbitrary or threatening (at least until Greek philosophy penetrated beyond Greek polytheism) and from those Eastern religions for which the physical world is the emanation of an unknowable divine. It is absent, too, from modern materialism, following its rejection of the God to whom Descartes delegated the task of rendering the world trustworthy; see ?{3}b.

So the belief that the universe is governed by laws, and the belief that the laws are discoverable by human beings, are far from universal. But they are not new to the rise of science in the modern period. As Stanley Jaki's monumental study[9] has shown, science *only* continued to grow in cultures that acknowledged a single, orderly creator and a law-governed creation. But it did not grow in *all* of those that made this acknowledgement. Though scientific observation, especially of the heavens, as well as the practice of mathematics (see next), were widespread in many of these cultures, scientific

---

9. Jaki, *Science and Creation*.

method and actual discovery were rare. Through the Middle Ages, Chinese civilization was in advance of the monotheistic cultures in these and many other respects. For these two beliefs are necessary for the rise of science, but they are not sufficient to ensure it happens. For science to develop, the hope for the possibility of knowing the universe's laws needs to be supplemented by practical means of realizing this possibility. It is this supplement that is supplied in the remaining six tenets, which serve to translate the theoretical notion of discoverable law into a method of discovering laws in practice.

3) The Laws Are Mathematically Formulable

Perhaps the most decisive move in this respect is the idea that the laws of nature can and should be expressed in mathematical form. We shall consider in {4} how this idea dates back to Pythagoras's notion that nature was governed by number and harmonic ratio. This concept had a profound influence on Plato, for whom geometrical figures were paradigmatic among the eternal forms. Aristotle largely spurned the notion, but Burtt argues that the Platonic revival at the time of the Renaissance was one factor that facilitated a return to the idea that observations of the heavenly bodies ought to be correlated by geometries that were as simple as possible. This principle guided the likes of Kepler, Copernicus, and Galileo to prefer a sun-centered system to the old Ptolemaic geocentric one, in the face of what seemed obvious facts. As Burtt (followed here by Kuhn) notes, "as far as astronomy is mathematics, both [systems] are true, because both represent the facts, but one is simpler and more harmonious than the other."[10] It was not that mathematics revealed new facts, but rather that it provided a way of correlating a complex set of facts under simple laws. For Johannes Kepler, according to Burtt, "of a number of variant hypotheses about the same facts, that one is true which shows why facts, which in the other hypotheses remain unrelated, are as they are, i.e., which demonstrates their orderly and rational mathematical connection."[11] He regarded himself as "having shown the necessary and rational ground of the new structure of the world, as having penetrated to the mathematical connection of facts formerly held distinct."[12]

Kepler's ardent Platonism, which was one factor in his (correct) insistence on the sun as a worthy center of the solar system, also led him astray in his attempt to correlate the orbits of the then known planets with the five Platonic solids. But in time scientists developed a more discerning use of

10. Burtt, *Metaphysical Foundations*, 49.
11. Burtt, *Metaphysical Foundations*, 65.
12. Burtt, *Metaphysical Foundations*, 63.

mathematics, aided by the development, in the fifteenth and sixteenth centuries, of algebraic notation, which enabled scientists to detach themselves from their dependence on geometry and draw on algebraic formulations, which were often easier to manage.[13]

To be sure, mathematics works well in the formulation of celestial motions, and in the formulation of earthly movements such as the trajectories of cannonballs and the fall of stones: the very areas in which science progressed so dramatically in this period. Mathematics continues to be fundamental and successful in physics and cosmology. It seems less applicable in the other sciences, which is perhaps one motive for the later materialist attempt to reduce all scientific fact to physical elements and laws. We shall see that the mathematical tenet remains fundamental, and even capable of carrying science through materialism and beyond, to {4}.

In any event, to work as an explanation the mathematical laws have to be translated into descriptions and predictions that can be tested empirically (see next section). Though sometimes it is argued that the mathematics alone is sufficient to express relations between data observed, most would argue that to be fully explanatory, the mathematics has to correlate with physical models (such as the Bohr model of the atom) that map the formulae onto observed events, so explaining how and why the mathematics works. {4} and especially ?{4}a will return to this issue.

4) The Mathematical Laws Must be Measured and Tested by Experiment and Observation

The mathematization just mentioned pushes in an abstract direction, but of course, science has also a very concrete, empirical thrust in its reliance on testing theories by experiment and observation. If people know anything about science they know, first, that it is expressed in formulae, and second, that it involves experiment. Aristotle had placed great emphasis on observing and classifying the natural world, but the new emphasis on mathematics enabled observation and experiment to be precise, and to take the form—at least in the cases of physics and astronomy—of objective measurement rather than qualitative description.

The remaining four tenets effectively spell out the consequences and requirements if the first four tenets are to work. Summing up, if nature is governed by (2) knowable, (4) observable and testable, (3) mathematical (1) laws, it requires (5) spatiotemporal uniformity, (6) quantifiability, and (7) efficient causality, such that it (8) operates like a machine.

13. Burtt, *Metaphysical Foundations*, 43.

5) Space and Time Form the Uniform Background to the Operation of the Laws

Mathematical laws can only work in the study of remote facts like distant stars, and can only be thought to extend laws of the past to make predictions in the future, if they are uniform throughout space and time. This uniformity was lacking in the Aristotelian perspective, in which different laws and even different materials were believed to exist in the superlunary and sublunary worlds: the celestial world "above the moon" and the earthly realm below. Moreover, everything moved by virtue of its natural relation to different parts of space: some, like fire, strove to rise towards their natural home in the fiery heavens, while others, like stone, fell downward aiming for their earthly home. With the new science, all this changed. In the world picture that gained its masterly completion with Newton, the orbits of stars and the fall of apples were subsumed under the same mathematical laws. All things, wherever they are, were believed to move at uniform speed in a straight line, unless accelerated or decelerated in a certain direction by the forces of nature.

The uniformity of natural laws had four aspects:

1. *Space*. As just described, space is uniform in terms of the matter and forces operating in it. There are no specially privileged spaces, like the earth. Space itself, as Burtt points out, does not loom large in the Aristotelian framework, but assumes immense importance in the world of modern science. The seventeenth-century philosopher Henry More (of whom more in {6}) regarded space and time as God's infinite presence, while Newton saw it as God's sensorium, the organ through which God perceives all things.

2. *Time and Predictability*. Likewise, there are no privileged points in time, and the laws of nature remain the same. This is vital if laws relating events in the past are to hold in the future, enabling science to make predictions. Predictions are essential for two reasons: theories can be tested by testing the predictions they make, and they can lead to new technology. The success of the new scientific worldview was due in no small part to the fact that, on the one hand, its theories were testable, and could be established without resort to authority; and on the other hand, they powered a new technology leading to inventions that were of great benefit to humankind (as well as others, like weaponry, that were not, but served the interests of various elites).

3. *Repeatability.* The repeatability of experiments in different times and places, and by different individuals, ensured an objective truth that was lacking in other bodies of belief, such as the religious ones, which (as exploration was now making clear) varied immensely from place to place and people to people.

4. *Reversibility.* The laws of motion of the heavenly bodies are not only translatable throughout space and time, but reversible in both space and time. If the universe is turned on its head, or swapped left to right, or even run backwards in time, the same laws operate. This means, of course, that just as the past is fixed and determined, so must the future be; hence Laplace's declaration that given the position and momentum of bodies now, the entire past and future of the universe is knowable.[14]

6) Science Discovers "Primary" Quantities and Their Relations, and Ignores "Secondary" Qualities

If nature is to be measurable and describable in terms of laws that are mathematical, it, or what is objective and scientifically accessible in it, needs to be describable in terms of quantities rather than qualities. From Galileo through Descartes and on into the more explicit discussions of the English philosopher John Locke, the new science relied on a distinction between primary and secondary qualities. As noted in ?{1}b, the primary qualities are those that can be measured, like length, velocity, weight, and number, while the secondary are those that cannot be quantified, but only described, like color, smell, taste, and texture. In the preceding, Aristotelian framework, greenness was a real property of the "substantial form" of the grass on my lawn. In the new framework, by contrast, mere greenness is too subjective a matter to be considered integral to the grass, unless, for example, it is explained in terms of light that does have a certain measurable amplitude and wavelength.[15]

---

14. Reversibility has since collapsed. It turns out that the "weak" force is not reversible: a mirror-image of the universe—whether attained through a left-right swap or a reversal of time—would be slightly different. See Gardner, *Ambidextrous Universe*. And for different reasons the second law of thermodynamics, whereby order inevitably decreases through time, is evidently not time-reversible. The latter means that while the future may *in principle* be predictable from the present state of affairs, the past cannot be fully reconstructed from it; the loss of order means the universe "forgets" some of its past.

15. It is the quantifiability of the primary that sets them apart as amenable to scientific method, unlike the secondary; which is why I feel entitled to write throughout of "primary *quantities*" and "secondary *qualities*."

Galileo therefore urges the scientist to disregard those (secondary) qualities that depend on the sense organs of the particular observer.

> I judge that, if the ears, the tongue, and the nostrils were taken away, the figure, the numbers, and the motions would indeed remain, but not the odors nor the tastes nor the sounds, which, without the living animal, I do not believe are anything else than names.[16]

According to Galileo, then, it is the primary qualities that are in the world, independent of our sense organs. Galileo anticipates Descartes's dualism by consigning the secondary qualities to the soul.

Note that among the senses sight is not mentioned in this quote. One might ask, if the eyes were taken away, would figure, number, and motion then become secondary, being surely dependent on measurements only the eye can register? Does the primary/secondary distinction rely on a privileging of the experience of the eyes over that offered by the other senses?

For Plato and Aristotle, matter was a primal inchoate "something" that is nothing unless shaped by the forms. The new privileging of matter and its primary measurable quantities, as the main object of science, represents another profound reversal. All that we value in nature seems to lie in its secondary qualities. We cherish things because they are beautiful, comfortable, delicious, and suchlike—all secondary qualities, or arising from them, surely—rather than in primary quantities like weight or speed. So Burtt laments:

> In the course of translating this distinction of primary and secondary into terms suited to the new mathematical interpretation of nature, we have the first stage in the reading of man (sic.) quite out of the real and primary realm. Obviously, man was not a subject suited to mathematical study. His performances could not be treated by the quantitative method, except in the most meagre fashion. His was a life of colors and sounds, of pleasures, of griefs, of passionate loves, of ambitions, and strivings.[17]

A. N. Whitehead put it more ironically, paradoxically twisting the matter in a more humanist direction:

> The poets are entirely mistaken. They should address their lyrics to themselves, and should turn them into odes of self-congratulation on the excellency of the human mind. Nature is

---

16. Cited in Burtt, *Metaphysical Foundations*, 88.
17. Burtt, *Metaphysical Foundations*, 89.

a dull affair, soundless, scentless, colorless: merely the hurrying of material, endlessly, meaninglessly.[18]

7) Efficient Causes Are Necessary and Sufficient to Explain Events

Aristotle (see {8}) distinguished four kinds of cause: final, efficient, material, and formal. We may explain events in terms of *final* causes, that is, the reasons or aims or tendencies: things in the future that make things behave as they do now. So we may explain an acorn in terms of the oak it has the potential to grow into, or a person's actions in terms of what they want to achieve. Or we may explain them in terms of *efficient* causes, the things in the past that make present things behave so. We explain the acorn in terms of the oak it fell from, or a person's actions in terms of hidden complexes from childhood. Or we may explain in terms of *material* causes: the "stuff" or matter (we would say the DNA) that the acorn is made of that makes it grow into an oak. Finally, we may explain in terms of *formal* causes: the structures and patterns the matter of the acorn or person is shaped into.

The demand that we understand events in terms of mathematical, measurable laws rendered final and formal causes problematic. Both require a qualitative and subjective—we might even say empathic—assessment of inner tendencies (which Aristotle terms entelechy). We cannot quantify purpose or tendency or the formal pattern of the whole with any objectivity. One historian might judge a political figure as selflessly aiming for the good of her nation, another would discern a narcissistic thirst for power. If we abandon these kinds of cause, we are left with efficient, and to some extent material causes. Such causes are necessary to the explanation of events: we cannot explain anything without them. And they are sufficient: no other kind of cause is needed. It remains possible to measure the movement of an object, and assess what other objects in its vicinity "caused" (in the efficient sense) that movement to take place, according to the mathematical laws we have elsewhere discerned.

So we move from a world in which purpose is immanent, full of final and formal causes, to one that consists of material objects and their measurable qualities interacting according to mathematical laws. "From being a realm of substances in qualitative and teleological relations the world of

---

18. Whitehead, *Science and the Modern World*, ch. 3, cited in Thompson, *Holy Ground*, 27.

nature had definitely become a realm of bodies moving mechanically in space and time."[19]

8) Mechanization: The Cosmos and Its Contents Work like a Machine

In other words, we arrive at the concept of the world as a machine. The metaphor of the machine occurs repeatedly in the literature of science, from Galileo through to Dawkins and his "blind watchmaker."[20]

The prevalence of this image is significant, in that a machine obviously involves final causality. A machine could be defined as a group of objects brought together by some external agent in order to effect some purpose defined by that agent. So aeroplanes are assembled in order to carry people or freight through the air; watches are assembled in order to tell the time. But whereas in, for example, living organisms, the parts are brought together to further the purposes of the organism itself (hence the Aristotelian term "entelechy"—the telos *in* the organism), in a machine the parts are brought together to further a purpose external to the machine itself; typically the purposes of human beings and their desire to travel and to tell the time. We might call machines cases of *ectelechy*, since the purpose is *outside* the machine. So when the analogy of the machine is applied to the natural world, the implication ought not to be that nature is mindless or purposeless, but that it is assembled for a purpose or purposes outside itself. *Pace* Dawkins, watchmakers are seldom blind, and never aimless in their designing work. Within this mechanistic framework, the much-maligned William Paley has logic on his side.

On the other hand, on the machine analogy, the universe has only efficient and perhaps material causality within it. Purpose is reserved to the Mind of God, who causes the universe in only the efficient sense of making it happen in the first place, and providing out of nothing the matter it contains. The creation no longer denotes a total dependency throughout time on God as beginning and goal, but solely an initiating operation at the beginning. Thereafter, in the modified theistic perspective, God adds an occasional later causal nudge; in the deistic perspective, even these interventionist nudges are lacking. In either case, the universe normally runs by efficient causality, like clockwork. Formal and final causalities exist only in the mind of the Watchmaker, and in human minds, no longer immanently in the universe. We may, like Paley, try to discover the existence and nature

19. Burtt, *Metaphysical Foundations*, 161.
20. For a classic account see Dijksterhuis, *Mechanisation*.

of God by rational deduction from the patterns that suggest a transcendent designer, but not by way of any sense of immanent meaning in things. And this rational deduction will prove fragile, since as Hume was the first among many to point out, it rests on too ready an analogy with our own minds: the purpose of God in creating x is identified with what would have been in *our* minds had we created it ourselves.

Broadly speaking the scientists of this period would accept the designer God in either theist or deist form, even finding it a ground for their own search for laws and design. The theists (including, Copernicus, Galileo, Descartes, and Newton) believed God both created the world and also intervened in it from time to time to put it right, or to reveal further truths not discernible from the observation of nature alone. The deists dispensed with the intervention and argued that a perfect God would have made the world with perfect laws, with all events foreseen and needing no further intervention.

The highly paradoxical, and perhaps frightening idea of the world as a purposeless or random machine came later, as atheistic materialism edged out the rather emaciated[21] idea of God as designer. Meanwhile note for later consideration that the mechanistic view tends to rely on, and preserve, a naïve realism regarding the parts of the machine, whether they be Descartes's vortices or, later, atoms. Though we now see the fundamental constituents of the cosmic "machine" as being more mysterious than that, the image of the machine presupposed atoms that were exactly like our pictures of them. The subtle secondary qualities may have been relegated to a subjective quasi-reality, but the primary ones became by contrast literally real with a vengeance: the world came to consist of hard objects definable in terms of number, position, movement, and mass, all working infallibly together according to divine law in the divine sensorium to make up the cosmic machine.

Descartes's Doubt and His Dualism

It may seem that we have allowed ourselves a huge digression before arriving at the dualism that is the defining feature of {2}. But in reality, we are already there. Our eight tenets have already established a stark duality between the secondary world of human feeling, value, and experience, and the primary world of science governed by testable mechanical mathematical

---

21. I think here of the death of the Ancient of Days in Pullman's *Amber Spyglass*, 430. This figure is old and frail, and once taken from his crystal chariot, begins to dissolve in the wind. Perhaps the crystal chariot is the lawful machine of dualism.

laws. In the face of this duality, we have three choices: to deny the world of science and secure a Romantic idealist world of spiritual feeling; to deny the independence of mind and value so as to clear the path for science; or to embrace both worlds in an explicit dualism. The first two options will be discussed in {7} and {3} respectively. But most of the scientific thinkers we have been discussing did not take either of those options. They were dualists, still believing in God and the human soul, while giving most of their attention to the exciting new discoveries regarding the material world. Far from being a pioneer of a new philosophy with a new method starting from doubt, Descartes's doubt was already firmly embedded in the dualism of his time, and what he did was to articulate in explicit philosophy an understanding that was already pervasive.

It is not only that the new scientific methodology reveals a new world that operates mechanically and without purpose, by contrast with the world of mind. The methodology is in itself based on dualist metaphysics. Contrary to the way it is most often presented, modern dualism is epistemologically dualist because it is ontologically so, involving what philosopher Daniel Dennett has called the Cartesian theater.[22] The notion of observation involved posits an observer on the one hand, and an observed world on the other. "In here," behind my eyes and other senses, lurks a mind observing what is "out there" in the material world. The eyes and other senses are obviously parts of the material world, but at some point, they connect up with something that registers sensations and reasons them into the mathematical law-governed artifice that is then posited as being "out there." Even to describe things so suggests much more of a tangle than a duality: the mathematics is worked out "in here," in the mind, but then projected outwards as in a cinema onto the screen of matter. Matter impacts on material objects like eyes and ears, but these project what they receive from "out there" inward, into the mind.

The scientific tenets were designed to unravel the tangle into a duality, such that the mind would interfere as little as possible with the perceptions concerning matter. Things like values, secondary qualities, and reasoning needed a place where they could do their thing without interfering with the world of matter, and this place was called mind, seen as something tucked away and hidden from objective view behind my eyes. Observer and observed, mind and matter: a dualism between the two was presupposed. And yet, of course, there could be no observation without some interaction

---

22. Dennett, *Consciousness Explained*, ch. 5. Dennett argues that the Cartesian theater persists in many materialist accounts. For once, I agree with Dennett.

between the two; yet we shall see that this interaction, which dualism was meant to clarify, proved problematic within dualism.

At the beginning of his first Meditation, Descartes explains his method of doubt:

> Some years ago now I observed the multitude of errors that I had accepted as true in my earliest years, and the dubiousness of the whole superstructure I had since then reared on them; and the consequent need of making a clean sweep for once in my life, and beginning again from the very foundations, if I would secure some secure and lasting result in science.[23]

He goes on to state the need "to withhold assent no less carefully from what is not plainly certain and indubitable than from what is obviously false."[24] To this end, he writes, he does not need to doubt everything he believes, because if the fundamental beliefs are challenged, "the superstructure will collapse of itself."[25] The image here is clearly that of a logical building, erected on uncertain foundations. The building has to be demolished by destroying the shaky foundations, then new foundations need to be put in place, and a sound building erected on that. The foundations need to be "certain and indubitable," and joined to levels above by logical inference. This kind of "logical building" is modelled in turn on Euclidean geometry, with its self-evident axioms and logical deductions from them to the sure and certain theorems of geometry.

As is well-known, Descartes presents his dualism as emerging logically from his doubt. First there is the assurance of the cogito, the thinking self:

> I suppose, therefore, that whatever things I see are illusions; I believe that none of the things my lying memory represents to have happened really did so; I have no senses; body, shape, extension, motion, place are chimeras. . . . I have convinced myself that nothing in the world exists—no sky no earth, no minds, no bodies; so am not I likewise non-existent? But if I did convince myself of anything, I must have existed. "But there is some deceiver, supremely powerful, supremely intelligent, who purposely always deceives me." If he deceives me, then again I undoubtedly exist.[26]

---

23. Descartes, *Philosophical Writings*, 61.
24. Descartes, *Philosophical Writings*, 61.
25. Descartes, *Philosophical Writings*, 61.
26. Descartes, Second Meditation, in *Philosophical Writings*, 66–67.

Descartes's demon had reduced the possibility of delusion to the possibility of a systematic lie or deception. But if I wonder whether I am deceived, there must be something doing the wondering. If I am deceived by the demon, there must be a real "I" to be deceived. I can doubt the reality of the squirrel on the lawn, but I cannot doubt that I am doubting it. I doubt; therefore I exist; or in the more famous phrase, *Cogito ergo sum*: I think, therefore I am. From this certitude regarding the self, Descartes "proves" the existence of God. God then guarantees the existence of the material world over against the self; for unlike a demon, a perfect God would not deceive us. Everything is then constructed as in a geometrical proof based on foundational axioms, leading us from doubt through self and God to world.

But why would Descartes expect the real world to work on this kind of logical-cum-geometrical model? Clearly, like all the scientists of the early modern era, he is assuming geometrical and logical deduction will provide a surer clue to how the real world is, than mere experience can. It is hardly surprising that the reality that emerges from Descartes's method is a dualist world: a world of mind, which is what we know most clearly, applying the laws of logic; and a world of matter, relatively obscure, but discoverable if we apply those laws to it carefully. One part of reality does the rational thinking and deduction of the laws; the other responds to that logical thinking by way of operating mindlessly and mechanically in space according to those laws.

So in his way of arguing for epistemological doubt, Descartes is already a metaphysical dualist. Though dualism seems to follow from his reasoning, in reality his prior dualism conditions his thinking, which only serves to entrench it by seeming to be deduced from it. Descartes proves to be not the father of modern philosophy, but rather, perhaps, the midwife. His doubt is not primordial to philosophy, but something that can only seriously emerge when the scientific methodological background, and its associated metaphysics, is in place, and a world of scientifically measurable quantities, contrasting with our familiar quality-laden world, can be taken for granted.

The global kind of doubt that Descartes urges as the foundation of all rational thinking is actually irrational (see ?{2}f). It can only seem to be reasonable at all, let alone a ground for rationality, within certain thought-contexts, prominent among which is dualism. Significantly, Descartes expressed his doubt in terms of the real (efficient) causality of a real demon, and conversely, found the remedy for doubt in the (efficiently) causal activity of a trustworthy God. In view of our arguments so far, augmented below, Descartes is on the right track here. Our assurances about the external world and its lawfulness need some kind of metaphysical, if not theistic, underpinning. But possibly the resort to God could take him too far, or rather, right back to square 1, in that if God is trustworthy, why should God not validate *all* of our perceptions? We could be left without any possibility of delusion or hallucination, let alone the skepticism about secondary qualities on which Descartes himself draws. For would an all wise and benevolent God (such as Descartes believes he has proved) allow us to have any delusions, or any perceptions of secondary qualities that were not grounded in reality?

Once Descartes's doubt, and his perhaps excessive remedy, are in place, they entrench dualism. The doubt supposedly reveals an I "in here" whose doubting, and hence thinking, cannot be doubted, by contrast with the material world "out there" that can. Descartes is right that when doubts arise, thinking is going on. But why ascribe it to a thinking *subject*, an "I"—if there is possibly no world to contrast that subject with? If there is no real universe, can there be a real I? Granted, there is doubting going on, why ascribe it to a subject when all analogies of subjects in the world are in doubt? Once again, dualism between self and world is written into Descartes's *cogito*. It is not surprising, therefore, that what seems to emerge from Descartes's method of doubt is *substance* dualism, the kind of dualism that regards—as in the heading quote—the mind and the body are "really distinct": the former a *res cogitans*, a thinking substance, the latter a *res extensa*, an extended substance. Matter is one kind of substance with its own kind of qualities, viz the primary qualities of number, shape, motion, and extension in space. The mind is another, with none of those spatial qualities, but existing only in time, in the reception of impressions from the senses and (more important for Descartes) the formulation of ideas, thoughts, and arguments. As really—that is, substantially—distinct from our bodies, our minds do not depend on our bodies for their existence; hence the inference in the opening quote to the possibility of my soul existing without my body. Though obviously, without my body, I would not be able to perceive and do material things, Descartes argues that I could go on doing the things my mind does—reflecting, arguing, contemplating.

Before examining the difficulties of this dualism, we need to examine its implications. How far did World {2} "make" the modern world?

The Machine in the Machine

Gilbert Ryle famously parodied Descartes's account as "the Ghost in the Machine."[27] The Platonic and Aristotelian worlds had been dualistic in the sense of distinguishing matter from idea or form, but in such a way that matter was informed by, or participated in, idea and meaning. Descartes's

---

27. Ryle, *Concept of Mind*, 21.

substance dualism sucks the meaning out of matter, leaving it mechanical, and relocates meaning in a ghostly, unreachable, private realm of mind, which itself becomes in a sense, as Ryle shows, mechanized. Plato's realm of objective forms, geometries, and values is spirited away from the material world into the inner world of consciousness and mind. In the process, matter and also mind are mechanized, and God reduced to the designer and kick-starter of the cosmic machine. Let us explore these developments, just introduced: (a) mindless matter, (b) disembodied mind, and (c) the absent designer God.

a) Mindless (yet Strangely Autonomous) Matter

To render it susceptible to scientific measurement, the world for Descartes and dualism generally has become purely material and mechanical. All that makes us cherish the world—color and melody, touch and scent, value and purpose—are now attributed to an altogether different substance, the mind. As theologian Don Cupitt eloquently puts it in the header quote, the world has become "disenchanted," no longer being the place where values, good and ill, objectively reside. Cupitt, in line with many modern ethicists of an existentialist bent, celebrates the freedom this gives us humans to create our own values. No longer at home in a universe of value, we are now to be conquerors of the world in the interests of the good that resides (only) in a largely absentee God and the human mind.

More negatively, poet and critic T. S. Eliot described in a famous phrase how "in the seventeenth century a dissociation of sensibility set in, from which we have never recovered."[28] Before the dissociation, the Metaphysical poets expressed a seamless unity of thought and feeling; after that time, feeling and value tended to be at odds with science and rationality. Though Eliot does not explicitly link the dissociation of sensibility with the rise of science, the connection cries out to be made, and for the Romantic poets of the late eighteenth and nineteenth centuries, science, technology, and industry were certainly seen as being the opponents of poetry and art. William Blake saw Newton and his mechanical cycles as the arch enemy, along with the deist God, whom Blake parodied in his often misunderstood picture, *The Ancient of Days*, setting his measuring compass on the face of the deep.

But it was not only Romantic poets that set their faces against the loss of the old unity. Burtt argues that many of the major modern philosophers, "Berkeley, Hume, Kant, Fichte, Hegel, James, Bergson—all are united in one earnest attempt, the attempt to reinstate man (sic.) with his high spiritual

28. Eliot, "The Metaphysical Poets."

claims in a place of importance in the cosmic scheme."[29] But the situation is more paradoxical than Burtt and the Romantic poets would have us believe. On the one hand, the law-governed rational accessibility of the dualistic cosmos renders it susceptible to exploitation by "man." Having, according to Descartes, no soul or mind of their own, animals and other living forms were regarded as mere machines that could be experimented on and used to render the maximum human benefit in terms of the technological "progress," which had become the unseen god of the modern era. But because of this very same seamless rational order, there is an autonomy about the dualist cosmos, which runs on in complete indifference to the existence of humankind. We create things that are good on our terms, but there is no objective reference point that defines the goodness of our good. Without any concept of a global, ecological good, we each seek our own little good things, oblivious of anything wider than the national or tribal good. In the process, not only does it become easy to dismiss God from his role, but human meanings become obscure. A spirituality of discernment and contemplation of the values inherent in the world is replaced by a spirituality of conquest, which parcels out the world as my territory versus yours. In the "age of discovery," the dualistic duel of Marduk and Tiamat returns.

b) Disembodied (yet Strangely Mechanical) Mind

Many would follow Cupitt in celebrating the loss of the idea of an order of meaning to which the individual is called to submit; as if mind and meaning would stand out all the more clearly once liberated from this demand. But the mind of dualism is an obscure and lonely ghost, as Gilbert Ryle has documented. Many of us accept something like the Cartesian theater, or mind as a kind of cinema for one, in which each of us projects a world of sensation onto a *tabula rasa* or blank screen, and then reflects in solitude on what we see. In this context we are unable to know how far what we see on the screen represents a real world beyond. Each of us plays out our own narrative, while when we look at other people, we cannot know what story—if any—may be being played out in the cinema that is at work in the mind within the machine of their body.

Many of our Worlds (for example, versions of {6}) accept some type of property dualism, the idea that the mental and the physical refer to different

---

29. Burtt, *Metaphysical Foundations*, 25. It is Burtt the humanist speaking here, and it might be contested that the older view was primarily theocentric, and only through being God-centred does it support humanity's "high spiritual claims." The philosophers cited, Berkeley apart, could justly be termed anthropocentric.

kinds of property. Naturalistic or emergent forms of dualism (see {9})—which posit minds as emerging from matter by natural laws rather than imposing miraculously their own distinct causality—also have their advocates. Aristotle's hylomorphism, which regards form and matter as uniting to form substances rather than being themselves distinct kinds of substance, has been revived too.

Substance dualism however, is something else. In it the subject of experience—the "I" or person—has no physical properties, merely temporarily inhabiting a body that has them. In the commonsense view, as expressed in ordinary language, I have mental properties like thinking, but also physical ones like being so many inches tall, having brown eyes, and often walking to my allotment. This is how a property dualist would put it: persons do some mental activities, like reasoning, and some physical ones, like walking. Strictly a substance dualist has to say that "I" am a mind, a thinking thing, and that I, this mind, am (in some curiously non-spatial sense, since only bodies have spatial properties) "in" a body, which does the spatially extended physical things like walking.

This approach, besides seeming unnatural, raises a several questions: ?{2}b–d. As Ryle expresses in the header quote, it renders the mind itself mechanical: the mechanical projector of the world's sensations, and the mechanical calculator of its laws. Because its crucial role is to represent and operate within a mechanical world, it has itself to be mechanical, following the laws of reason and deduction as the world follows the corresponding physical laws. Though it may contain someone's values, the spiritual aspect of mind is now ghostly indeed, and the path is open for the exorcism of the ghost, leading to a materialistic interpretation of mind itself, as in {3}.

c) God the Ghostly Designer

In dualism, the relation whereby God relates to the cosmos parallels that by which mind relates to matter. That is not to say that dualism posits God as the mind of the cosmos; that would suggest the pantheism related to {6}, which is alien to dualism. For in dualism, our minds are not regarded as efficient causes of our bodies (though what kind of causal relation does exist between mind or body, or mental events and physical ones, is obscure, witness ?{2}c). Nevertheless, the evolution of these relations—between God and world, and mind and body—do seem to move historically in parallel, and there is perhaps a kind of imaginative rationale behind that parallelism. As the one relation becomes more tenuous and obscure, so does the other, until the materialistic banishment of mind leads, in the imagination if not strict logic, to the banishment of God.

In the old (medieval) cosmology, God was both transcendent and immanent: strongly connected to and present in the universe by the very kinds of causality whereby God transcended it. God was the efficient cause of creation in both its material and spiritual aspects, and the formal pattern and final cause or goal of all things. But with the abolition of the latter two or three kinds of cause, in the dualist framework God could only be understood as an *efficient* cause. As Burtt argues, in the old scholastic framework,

> God was the final cause of all things just as truly and more significantly than their original former. Ends in nature did not head up in the astronomical harmony; that harmony was itself a means to further ends, such as knowledge, enjoyment, and use on the part of living beings of a higher order, who in turn were made for a still nobler end which completed the divine circuit, to know God and enjoy him forever. God had no purpose; he was the ultimate object of purpose. In the Newtonian world, following Galileo's earlier suggestion, all this further teleology is unceremoniously dropped. The cosmic order of masses in motion according to law, is itself the final good. Man exists to know and applaud it; God exists to tend and preserve.[30]

God is now only the transcendent other, no more present in creation than a watchmaker is in the watch. We can too easily, perhaps, infer the watchmaker from the watch, but apart from a certain painstaking attention to detail and a desire to tell the time, we can know nothing of the watchmaker from the watch; we cannot work out from the watch (forgive the pun) what makes the watchmaker tick.

The dualist World shows, perhaps, the watchmaker-like cleverness of God, but the cosmos is no longer "full of God's glory" (Isa 6:3). Most of the early scientists were orthodox Christians, being theists who believed in a special revelation in Christ. They believed, too, that their discoveries laid bare the laws by which God had designed things. And many would believe, with Descartes, that God was needed, not only to frame and uphold the laws, but to guarantee the basic veracity of our perceptions and our science. But the logical tendency was toward deism. The more perfect and self-sufficient were the cosmic laws, the more they revealed the transcendent hand of God. But also, the more they did so, the less need was there for God to intervene and tinker, because that would only be necessary if the laws were not perfectly framed, but allowed for occasional error needing correction. So God,

---

30. Burtt, *Metaphysical Foundations*, 296.

within modernity, becomes steadily less immanent, more a transcendent designer and guarantor.

Such a God would prove remote from people's faith, and it is logical, within the dissociation of sensibility, that a tender, personal provider God also arose within modernity, in many pietistic and evangelical revivals. At the same time both the absentee designer and the personal provider proved easy to separate off and abolish from the natural world. Arguably, however, the resulting materialism never found a comparable guarantor for natural laws. Materialism, therefore, can be characterized as dualism minus the dualist mind and the dualist God. Atheists such as Dawkins never seriously consider any God other than the dualist God; the dualist God is, for them, what the term "God" means.

Questions regarding {2}

Dualism generally, not just in the Cartesian "substance" form, has become quite unfashionable in philosophical and in theological circles, and the term, when used, usually introduces a critique of some kind. However, philosopher Robert Koons, who produces a long list of recent philosophical arguers and arguments against materialism (listed in {3}), cites only three arguments against anti-materialism (by which at this point of the argument he seems to mean mainly substance dualism). These are the arguments based on complexity, the regularity of psychophysical occurrences, and the problem of mental causation.[31] These arguments are discussed below as ?{2}a–c, while the following question ?{2}d brings out a familiar epistemological issue that lies behind ?{2}b and c. The next two questions concern the Cartesian doubt: ?{2}e whether it necessitates dualism, and ?{2}f whether global Cartesian doubt makes sense at all. ?{2}g is posed from a completely different, religious angle, while ?{2}h asks if non-substantial forms of dualism fare better in the face of any of these questions.

?{2}a: Are Two Substances Too Many?

Materialists often argue that dualism defies Ockham's Razor, the medieval philosopher's aphorism that "entities should not be multiplied beyond necessity." In other words, dualism makes the universe over-complex, positing two kinds of substance when we need only one, matter, to explain things adequately. Materialism is simpler, being monistic, that is, ascribing all reality

---

31. Koons, *Waning of Materialism*, Loc. 20–23.

to one kind of substance. The dualist (and some of the other) alternatives to materialism are more complex, involving in the case of dualism two kinds of substance.[32]

Now there is something aesthetically unappealing to some (myself included) in the idea that the universe contains precisely two kinds of thing. Frankly I would be happier with a pluralistic universe that allowed for many kinds of substance, to allow for the many complex ways in which we do in fact describe the world. It is not clear that numbers, political ideals, imaginary characters, God, emotions, sensations, strings, waves, and middle-sized objects should all be reduced to just two kinds of thing, mental and material. I also have much more time for a threefold categorization, following Plato and Karl Popper—see {4}. Monism has its appeal, nevertheless, but as we shall see, materialism is not the only monism on offer; phenomenalism, panpsychism, and absolute idealism likewise ascribe just one kind of substance to the world.

But these are matters of aesthetic preference, and while aesthetic criteria are not irrelevant, they are inevitably partly subjective and so less than universally decisive. We may dislike dualism because it is too complex to be elegant, or perhaps, not complex enough to be rich as the real world is rich; but that is not a sufficient reason for rejecting dualism. Ockham's razor states that we shouldn't posit more kinds of thing in the universe *than are necessary*: if some complications are necessary in order to understand the universe, we should accept that. In other words, we should choose the simpler model only when all other reasons for choosing between them are equal. However, there are many other reasons for not choosing dualism, at least in its "substance," Cartesian form.

?{2}b: Why Do Mental Events Often (Perhaps Always?) Depend on Material Ones?

The next three questions concern whether, given the dualistic split, the world can be put together again. The first concerns the fact that physical events often cause mental events. The second questions how it can be that the mind can cause things to happen in the material world, given that the mental "substance" involves a different kind of causality from the material. The third asks the epistemological question of how, if mental and material

---

32. Later, {9} will distinguish *substance* monism—the idea that there is only one kind of thing—from *existence* monism—the idea (to which materialists are of course not committed) that there is only one thing—and *priority* monism—the idea that everything is grounded in one thing.

substances are really distinct, the former can correspond with and represent the latter.

The most often cited argument against substance dualism is the way changes to my body—in particular to my brain—seem to effect changes to my mind. On the other hand, my mind seems only to be able to make or experience physical changes via changes in my physical body. Without physical limbs, I cannot move things around. Without sense organs, I cannot experience material things. Very obviously my perceptions involve changes to my sense organs, nerves, and identifiable parts of the brain, which have been shown to correlate with different kinds of perception.

Moreover, operations on the brain, such as trepanation or craniotomy (drilling holes in the skull to release fluids), often result in loss of perceptions and/or motor abilities. Most significantly, people who recover from this loss do not report having continued as thinking beings frustrated by the loss of the perceptions, as if an intact mind were "locked inside" an incapacitated body and brain.[33] This is indeed what tends to happen in cases of bodily paralysis and the like, but when brain activity is suppressed, the result is a general loss of thought and memory, as in deep sleep. When the brain is affected, it is not like the loss or malfunction of a bodily part, as we would expect if the mind were simply located in a brain and body, and capable of continuing its thinking and imagining functions apart from them. If this were what was experienced, there would be grounds for considering the mind or soul as an independent entity capable of surviving after bodily death, as Catholic teaching (believed by Descartes and—differently—by the neo-Aristotelian Thomas Aquinas) holds. The soul after death, Thomas taught, experiences an impaired and unnatural state after death in the absence of the body, until reunited with its resurrection body. But the evidence is that brain and mind exhibit a stronger unity than that. Whether this should be conceived in terms of the substantial identity of brain and mind, a strong causal interconnection, the "supervenience" of mind states on brain states, or the Aristotelian understanding of the substantial unity of mind and body as a case of the broader unity of form and matter, or in some other way, will be discussed in {3}, {8}, and elsewhere. For now, it is sufficient to note that the philosophical consensus would surely be that Cartesian substance dualism does not do justice to the way mind and brain are experienced to be related.

---

33. For a clear, succinct discussion of these points, see Johnston, *Surviving Death*, 130.

?{2}c: How Can Mental Events Causally Interact with Material Ones?

As well as these problems in describing what happens in special cases of brain damage or surgical interventions in the brain, Cartesian dualism faces problems in clarifying what goes on in the normal case whenever our minds cause things to happen to the body—as when we intentionally do anything like walk or talk or kick an object—and what goes on whenever our minds register perceptions by way of our material sense organs, as when we see or hear or touch objects in the material world. As Ryle asks, "How can a mental process, such as willing, cause spatial movements like the movements of the tongue? How can a physical change in the optic nerve have among its effects a mind's perception of a flash of light?"[34]

The problem arises because of Descartes's substance dualism. According to Descartes, the material world consists of things extended in space, operating only in response to efficient causes, whereas mind is not spatial, and operates on final and formal causality, following purposes and plans. Thus the question, "Why did my foot move towards the ball" can be answered, "because I wanted to kick it" (mental, final cause) or "because muscles in my knee contracted, impelling my shin and foot forward" (physical, efficient cause). But if I am two substances, a mind and a body conjoined, then how are there not two things going on here, a disembodied mental striving to kick a ball (which is bound to be futile since disembodied minds cannot kick) and a mindless physical mechanism operating in my leg (itself unexplained because the material world contains no purposes)? And what does it even mean to say body and mind are "conjoined" if mind does not have spatial extension or shape? As Ryle noted in the heading quote, Descartes often yielded here to a pressure to compromise, giving the mind a spatial location in the pituitary gland, and a degree of mechanism in its operation; such moves may make mind-body interaction clearer, but at the expense of the purity of the dualism.

In the Aristotelian view,[35] there is no problem in discerning a single action here, and saying that I, because of my intention to score a goal, kicked the ball, in a process whereby nerves caused muscle contractions in my knee. For in this framework, which seems to accord with common sense, I am not two substances, a mind and a body, but a single subject, which is a unity of matter and form, or as we might prefer to say, material "stuff" shaped into a living and thinking organism. In my case, the matter is my

---

34. Ryle, *Concept of Mind*, 21.
35. Cf. Feser, *Aristotle's Revenge*, Loc. 3664.

body, and the form or pattern is my mind. When I do something, my mind causes me to do things following my intentions (final causality) and in the process my body causes a series of effects (efficient causality). But there is only one action, and only one agent or substance: me. Conversely when I experience things—say, seeing the ball go into the goal—there is a material chain of efficient causality whereby light rays rebound from the football and hit my eye, which transmits an impulse to the optical center in my brain, and there is the arising in my mind of the consciousness of having scored a goal, and probably feelings of elation a having achieved my goal (in another sense)—something I have only experienced once in my life! But again, there are not two things going on here, or many, but one perception by one substance, me, summed up as "I scored a goal."

This account, at this stage, raises as many questions as it answers (more answers, I hope, in {8}). And there are other, alternative ways of reducing what is going on to one thing. We can uphold one level of the account—the physical {3} or the mental {7}—as describing what is "really" going on, while the other is considered to be mere appearance. Or we can say there is one thing going on at two (or more) different "levels" {9}. But the implausible account by substance dualism is clearly inadequate.

And there are additional inadequacies. If bodies and consciousness are substantially separated, and lacking logical connection, how can we know which bodies have consciousness? How do we know when a body—a unified piece of matter—possesses mind? If the cries of animals do not persuade me that they are feeling pain, and if the use of tools by some animals to solve problems does not persuade me that they have the rudiments of reason, that may be convenient in that it will enable me to experiment on animals and vivisect them, knowing that their screams are merely a mechanical reaction; nothing more to worry about than the whistle of a locomotive. But then an even deeper problem opens up: why in that case should I even be persuaded that my fellow humans have minds like the one I find in myself? And then again, if I do, unlike Descartes, concede consciousness to some animals, where do I stop? If apes have minds, what about sharks, or woodlice, or amoebae, or fungi, or computers, or thermostats? This is a question that moves some philosophers towards the panpsychism of {6}.

?{2}d: Can (Mental) Thoughts "Correspond" with Physical Things?

{1} noted that naive or direct realism has no problem with the idea that what I see, in the above example, is the ball going into the goal; or that what I feel, consequently, is the elation of having achieved my goal. But as just noted, in dualism the goal (and all the apparatus of goalposts and balls and feet and kicking) inhabit a substantially different world, a world of spatial relations and efficient causes, from me in my mental world of intentions and perceptions. As noted, Descartes was able to doubt the existence of the material world only because he believed it operated differently from the mental, such that experiences and ideas in the mind might be no clue as to what was going on in the material world. Hence the need for a new theory of knowledge, or epistemology, based on the idea that structures in the mental world, might represent, or correspond with, structures in the material world.

According to this theory, our true statements about the world are true because they correspond with the things they describe in the world, and our true beliefs about the world are true because they correspond with how things are in the world. Sometimes correspondence theories emphasize the correspondence between language statements and the world, and sometimes that between mental contents and the contents of the world, and sometimes it is all three—language, mind, and world—that are said to coincide. In the strongest account, a threefold correspondence is looked for. The statement, "A red squirrel is eating a brown nut on my green lawn," is true, if it is true, because there is a red squirrel eating a brown nut on my green lawn; and in my mind there exists the experience of a red squirrel eating a brown nut on my green lawn.

Now to be sure, correspondence theory is not refuted by instances of non-correspondence. On the contrary, when we define lies, illusions, and misunderstandings in terms of a non-correspondence, we are in fact affirming that correspondence is the criterion we should use to judge these cases. But there may be a deeper difficulty involved here, in the very notion that ideas are the kind of thing that can correspond with reality, or either reality or ideas could correspond with language. What would it mean for a thought to correspond with a thing, or a sentence? On the face of it, things, thoughts, and sentences are unlike each other, the first consisting of things extended in 3-D space, the second taking place in time without any spatial dimension, and the third of a one-dimensional sequence of script or sounds. So how could a thought be like (or unlike) a thing? And there may be a sense in which a thought is like a sentence, but it is not naïvely obvious.

After all, in the case of the red squirrel, I can hardly compare the image of it in my mind with the actual squirrel out there, to see if it "corresponds." Nor can I measure up my verbal description of the squirrel with either the image of it in my mind, or the real one "out there." In a sense, the image and the language are all we have got. Are we to posit a noumenon of the squirrel, a real squirrel that nobody can see or describe? If we believe there is a real squirrel out there, it has somehow to be immanent in the coherence of my imagination, word-making, and action in the world.[36]

It is true that it is often obvious that a sentence expresses a thought that corresponds with how things are; but its correspondence does not consist in being *like* how things are. A famous example of correspondence theory is philosopher logician Alfred Tarski's saying that the sentence "snow is white" is true if and only if snow is white. But those words are nothing like or even unlike or in any way comparable with the whiteness of snow. And the fact that we can only refer to that state of affairs by repeating the words in our sentence, "snow is white," may give the game away: namely that it is the language that is determining both what thoughts we can have and what states of affairs in the world we can identify. The world may correspond with language and thought only because language has shaped thought and world and conformed them both to its own categories.

The correspondence theory has had many critics, from Ludwig Wittgenstein, who early on developed an intricate "logical atomism" based on it, and later criticized his own theory;[37] through Richard Rorty, who ridicules the "mirror mind";[38] to Mark Johnston, who argues that

> the resort to representations does no work; either we can say that thanks to the operation of our sensory systems items in the environment are made available, or we can say that thanks to the operation of our sensory systems there come to be representations that make items in the environment available. The first is a fact, and the second is a pseudoexplanation, for the idiom of representation does not in any way illuminate perceptual availability, the way in which objects of perception are THERE.[39]

Indeed, the only work "representations" and the idea of a mental mirror of nature do is enable us to preserve a mind-world dualism. It is only within dualism (and its derivative philosophies, such as materialism, which gets even more tangled in it; see ?{3}f) that a correspondence theory, and its idea of a mental structure that mimics the physical, is needed. Yet at the same time, within substance dualism, correspondence becomes truly impossible. Substance dualism both needs correspondence and undermines it.

---

36. A point argued at length in the phenomenological tradition that extends from Husserl through to Heidegger and Merleau-Ponty.

37. Cf. Wittgenstein, *Tractatus Logico-Philosophicus* and *Philosophical Investigations* respectively.

38. Cf. Rorty, *Philosophy and the Mirror of Nature*.

39. Johnston, *Saving God*, 143–44.

It is only once mind and matter are separate "worlds," that we need a structure that mediates between them and enables the former to know about the latter. But of course, the substantial separation of mind and matter only creates extra difficulties for the idea that the representations can be "like" their originals. The situation is rather like building a wall, instead of a bridge, to cross a river. If mind and matter are different substances, any correspondence between their contents has to cross an ontological rather than just an epistemological divide. Broadly speaking we could say that naïve realism was naïvely unaware of a gulf between thoughts and things. What naïve realism does is really to identify (or some would say confuse) the thought or experience of the thing with the thing itself. Because the relation between thought and thing is one of identity, the question of correspondence between them does not seriously arise. But in substance dualism there arises an ontological divide between mind and matter, such that the relation between contents of the mind and contents of the material world becomes much more problematic. When I look at the moon, what I see has to be mental, a content of my mind. So it is no longer that I seem to see the moon, as a naive realist might put it. What I see is a "seeming moon," or to employ the jargon that came to be used, "the phenomenal moon," or the "qualia" associated with the moon. And then the relation between this mental phenomenon and the actual moon—that lump of rock some 239,000 miles away from earth—becomes problematic, because the seeming-moon is an object in my non-spatial mind, while the real moon is a rock orbiting earth according to efficient causal laws. And that is not something just a bit different from the seeming moon; it is a wholly different category of thing, not just like the moon, not even quite different, but something that could not be compared at all.[40]

?{2}e: Can Doubt Be Resolved in Better Ways?

A big query (?{1}a) about the naïve realist approach, central as we have seen to Descartes's argument for dualism, concerned the genuine possibility of illusion. Naïve or direct realists claim that we do (sometimes) see the moon directly, without the mediation of a mental representation of the moon. But what distinguishes these cases from dreaming of the moon, or having some other kind of illusion that I am seeing the moon? Is there not a force in the Cartesian doubt, and the corresponding call for grounds of certainty, that is not so readily dismissed? This and the next questions respond to that query and ask, first: even if it is sometimes reasonable to doubt, is Cartesian

---

40. Cf. Thompson, *Holy Ground*, 35.

dualism the best answer to such doubt? And secondly: is global doubt, of the kind Descartes advocates, ever actually reasonable at all?

To answer the first question, indeed there is at least one alternative to Descartes's route beyond doubt, associated with the other great tradition of modern thought: empiricism (though the pathway takes empiricism to radical extremes generally labelled phenomenalism, further discussed in {7}). I can doubt that there's a real moon there, but I cannot doubt that I see something that appears to be what I normally call a moon. The appearance or phenomenon of the moon is undoubtedly there before me. It is easy to commit a false step here, from the idea that I seem to see a moon to the idea that I actually see a seeming-moon, or what philosophers came to call the sense data, or the qualia (qualities) associated with the moon. Actually, what is going on can only be called "seeing" if there is a real relation going on between the real moon and its observer, myself. But we can validly say that moon-like phenomena or qualia are going on, and that cannot be doubted. In the empiricist tradition, at least in its radical wing represented by David Hume and Bishop George Berkeley, the real world is the phenomenal world: the totality of moon qualia, as they change in an orderly and predictable way. Once we have learnt all we need to know about the moon, there is not something extra—the reality or essence of the moon—that needs to be added to complete the picture. As Berkeley repeatedly pointed out, *esse est percipi*, to be is to be perceived.

Both Descartes and Berkeley lead us beyond doubt, but in different directions. Descartes's direction takes us to the thinking mind, which eventually in his argument triumphs over the treacherous dubitability of the material world; and hence, to rationalism and substance dualism. Berkeley's direction takes us to the world of phenomena, sense data, or qualia as the foundation of all knowledge, and hence via the other great tradition of modern philosophy, empiricism, to phenomenalism. Which is right: Descartes identification of existence with rational thought or Berkeley's identification of existence with perceivability? Or are there other resolutions of these questions? Certainly, we shall find several.

?{2}f: Doubts about Doubt Itself

{1} noted that it does not occur to most people to doubt the evidence of their senses. And a global doubt of all experience, of the kind Descartes started from, is arguably irrational, for two reasons. In the response to ?{1}a it was argued that to doubt, to treat of what we normally trust as delusion, we need an account of something surer. If x is argued to be only appearance, we need to know what is being argued to be real. To begin with an account of the doubtful, in order to get to what is sure and certain, involves a perverse reversal of commonsense logic.

But more profoundly, when we doubt, we are not just making a contrast with what is real; we need to know what we are sure of in order to know what we are doubting, and why. I doubt that the moonlit squirrel is really grey because in better, sunlit conditions I have seen him as red. If asked, why I take the sunlit conditions as showing the true color, I will point out that in sunlit conditions generally I see everything better. I see lots of different colors, and I see many shapes, which in the moonlit conditions I cannot distinguish. I am already working with a sense of how the real world works, and how sight in particular works, and how it objectively needs light in order to work. I might back this up with a rudimentary theory of visual perception. It is this theory of how reality works that leads me to believe some perceptions are unreal, or at least, fail to capture some realities.

It would seem that we need the notion of a real world to identify phenomena in the first place. In the case of the moon, there is no simple moon phenomenon. For the moon changes shape, color, size, and luminosity through time, such that it is impossible to define a single "moon quale."[41] All we can do is define a set of moon-related qualia, and add an account of how these will vary because of the orbit of the moon, cloud cover, my own position, and so forth. We could, from these, predict what the moon quale will be at a given time, and hence would be able to distinguish which of my qualia are sightings of the moon. If one of the moon qualia appeared in an unpredicted time or setting, for example, a full moon right next to the sun, we would probably conclude that it was an illusion, or seek some special explanation. In other words, we look to a scientific account of the real moon to identify the relevant qualia as genuine appearances of the moon. Our understanding of the phenomenal world is structured by our account of the real world. In that case, we cannot identify the appearances without having a notion of the reality of which they are the appearance. A global doubt, which tries to bracket away or remove the real world and leave only the "pure" phenomena, makes no sense.

This is evident also when I decide that some perception is definitely unreal: a phantasm or a hallucination. I may doubt a hallucination because it appears and disappears without an observed cause. If it does so, I will reasonably conclude not that it is a real uncaused event but that the workings of

---

41. "Quale" is the accepted singular of "qualia," meaning a single item of experience or sense-datum. Whether there is such a thing as a quale, as opposed to qualia, is what I am questioning here. It is, I suggest, material objects that come in singular form, not phenomena.

my nerves or mind, or a supernatural angelic or demonic being, must have caused it. Or I may doubt that my friend is really standing there in front of me because I know that he died several years ago. I remember his funeral. There must be some other cause than his bodily presence: perhaps after all people can manifest after death by some mechanism we do not understand; perhaps my longing for my friend is driving my mind to fantasize; perhaps it is caused by the fact that I took LSD an hour ago . . . .

We only ever doubt the evidence of our senses, I would suggest, because of some belief about how things are, and what causes produce what effects. So to exercise a global doubt about everything we experience, there must be some account of reality in which we believe more strongly, that renders everyday experience doubtful. Historically the great systems of global doubt have arisen from (a) the religions that offer an "ultimate reality" beside which the commonsense view is appearance or delusion; or (b) the science that offered an account that rendered secondary qualities subjective, if not a kind of illusion. In the absence of some such global faith in religion or science, global doubt is unreasonable, and hardly likely to help us build a rational world.

?{2}g: Is Dualism Compatible with Faith Traditions?

The reference to religions brings us to a question from a different, faith point of view. Note that the "soul" is often assumed to be a religious idea, if not the belief par excellence for marking out "religious" believers from modern skeptics. It is often assumed that believers (of all kinds) are dualists, while scientists (of all kinds) are materialists. After all, surely it is believers who believe in an immortal soul that, if it guides our actions according to the faith's teachings while we are here on earth, will after death enter judgement, in the hope of going to heaven? Scientists meanwhile—so the story goes—hold that we are machines operating by mechanical laws, and as with all machines, when we cease to work, we will be broken up or left to disintegrate, and exist no more.

This of course is a parody, generalizing wildly in both cases. In fact, the critique of dualism and the immortal soul has emerged as fiercely from religious believers as from scientists. On the one hand there are faith traditions that explicitly deny the existence of the soul, as in the case of Buddhism. Though in Buddhism there is a bundle of causal factors that ripple on after death to converge on another being, this is not understood in the Pythagorean sense as the transmigration of a soul from one body to another. On the other, in the monotheistic faiths, including Christianity, there are strong objections to the idea of an immortal soul surviving death. Many theologians of a Protestant persuasion object to body-soul dualism as a "Greek" idea, preferring instead the "Hebraic" idea of people as unities of body, soul, and spirit.

There is simplification here, of course; Greek philosophers were not all dualists; Pythagoras and Plato were, but Democritus, Heraclitus, and Aristotle were not, or not straightforwardly so. There is little evidence, to be sure, of the idea of the immortal soul in early Hebrew culture, and the Pharisees and Jesus himself pinned their hopes on the resurrection of the body rather than the immortal soul. The immortal soul appears rarely in the Greek Septuagint, and scarcely, if at all, in the Hebrew Bible. The early Christian fathers and mothers often seized upon the Platonic idea of the immortal soul, and Aquinas tweaked his Aristotelian perspective (for which people are body-soul unities) in order to provide for individual continuity between death and resurrection; but as noted, the disembodied soul was unnatural and deficient, needing a risen body to become fully alive again. It was Protestants who explicitly rejected the innate immortality of the soul, and any form of dualism. The rejection though, is vehement and real, and certainly the substance dualism we have been discussing in this chapter could be argued to be profoundly contrary to Christian faith. For this is the faith of the incarnation, affirming the embodiment of God in Christ and in the art, life, and worship of the church, whereas substance dualism gives us two lives, a material life substantially distinct from our spiritual life, encouraging us to think of faith in terms of alienation from and conquest of, rather than involvement in and engagement with, the material world.[42]

?{2}h: Do Other Forms of Dualism Fare Better?

The arguments above apply to Descartes's substance dualism, which posits mind and body as different kinds of substance, that is to say, referring to different subjects, such that, for example, when I say "I think" or "I run" I cannot be referring to the same "I." Rather, the former "I" must be shorthand for "my mind" and the latter shorthand for "my body." But I have already noted that there are gentler kinds of dualism, for which this dichotomy does not arise. In quality dualism (see {6}), there is a single "I" here with two kinds of quality, one nonextended and mental, the other extended in space and physical. In emergent or naturalist dualism (see {9}), there is a single "I" that follows higher-level mental laws and also lower-level physical laws,

---

42. For a thorough philosophical discussion of Catholic and Protestant understandings of life beyond death, see Johnston, *Surviving Death*.

both kinds of law being part of nature. Finally in Aristotelian dualism {8}, mind (or rather, form) and matter are different, but only when they combine can we speak of a unified substance that is in-formed matter.

At this stage I will just summarize the likely way these kinds of dualism might answer our questions. Later Worlds will fill out this summary.

- ?{2}a. None of these alternative dualisms assert a duality of substance. Nevertheless, they are of course more complex than a straightforward monism of matter or mind.

- b and c. Once the substantial duality is denied, it becomes easier to see how one unified thing can have both mental and physical effects. Admittedly there is something a little odd about emergent dualism, where mental and physical laws seem to operate in parallel on a unified subject, leading to what is sometimes called overdetermination.

- d. Though the difference between physical things and their mental representations is acknowledged, these are qualitative and not substantial differences. A qualitative experience can correspond, perhaps, with a physical structure or entity, while words in sentences, qualitatively very different from physical things, may be able to express such a structure or entity.

- e and f. We may be sure of a quality or a causal regularity we perceive, while being unsure as to what physical reality this manifests.

- g. Qualitative and emergent dualisms may save what religions have to save—the idea of a real soul or person—while jettisoning the unhealthy idea that this reality is substantially independent of its physical expression and destiny, belonging to a realm alien from matter.

In all, it seems it may be possible, even necessary, to save the idea that the universe contains both mental and physical aspects, or qualities, or laws, or all three, from the idea of mind and matter as entirely unrelated substances. Worlds {6} and {8} to {10} will explore these possibilities more fully, but in the rest of this volume, {3} to {5} will explore in a quite different direction.

Résumé: An Awkward Transitional Account?

The early modern period witnessed the development of a scientific methodology that proved highly successful in discovering the mathematical relations between observed quantities. Though originally only a methodology, its success made it inevitable that people would generalize the method into a wider epistemology. Thus Descartes developed the method into an epistemology whereby a detached, thinking, and calculating subject looks on at, and tries to mirror, the cosmos by means of rational deductions that produce certainties, on the model of a mathematical deductive system. This picture in turn hardened into a dualistic metaphysics that opposed mind as a thinking substance to matter as extended substance. Science had been successful on the basis of a mechanized universe, which was quite unlike the meaningful, sacramental cosmos of the Middle Ages. But dualism enabled an attenuated version of this religious cosmos to continue on the mind side of the divide, while the matter side, being disenchanted and worthless in itself, became available for technological exploitation and human conquest. However, substance dualism has proven to be an unsatisfactory and highly questionable standpoint, from both philosophical and religious points of view. That said, dualism may be able to present itself in a more reasonable form.

The success of science makes it undesirable, and probably impossible, to respond by "reconquering" the world for religion and so "re-enchanting" it. So the question that now raises itself is whether dualism fails because it is an incomplete transition. Will the tensions in dualism between mind and matter be resolved if we assimilate mind to matter, and simply abolish those factors that Descartes and his age so unsatisfactorily consigned to the immaterial mind? We have seen how for Descartes mind was already incipiently mechanical; would it not be better explained, not as a substance parallel with matter, but as a feature of complicated bits of matter. Should we simply exorcise the Cartesian ghost, and leave the cosmos as a pure, streamlined, monistic machine? {3} will explore this possibility, and the different kinds of issues it raises.

{3}

BITS AND PIECES

Materialism

That man is the product of causes which had no prevision of the end they were achieving; that his origin, his growth, his hopes and fears, his loves and his beliefs, are but the outcome of accidental collocations of atoms; that no fire, no heroism, no intensity of thought and feeling, can preserve an individual life beyond the grave; that all the labours of the ages, all the devotion, all the inspiration, all the noonday brightness of human genius, are destined to extinction in the vast death of the solar system, and the whole temple of man's achievement must inevitably be buried beneath the debris of a universe in ruins—all these things, if not quite beyond dispute, are yet so nearly certain that no philosophy which rejects them can hope to stand. Only within the scaffolding of these truths, only on the firm foundation of unyielding despair, can the soul's habitation henceforth be safely built.[1]

All appearances to the contrary, the only watchmaker in nature is the blind forces of physics, albeit deployed in very special way. A true watchmaker has foresight: he designs his cogs and springs, and plans their interconnections, with a future purpose in his mind's eye. Natural selection, the blind, unconscious, automatic process which Darwin discovered, and which we now know is the explanation for the existence and apparently purposeful form of all life, has no purpose in mind. It has no mind and no mind's eye. It does not plan for the future. It has no vision, no foresight, no sight at all. If it can be said to play

---

1. Russell, *Religion and Science*, 210.

> the role of watchmaker in nature, it is the blind watchmaker.[2]

> How it is that anything so remarkable as state of consciousness comes about as the result of irritating nervous tissue, is just as unaccountable as the appearance of the Djin when Aladdin rubbed his lamp.[3]

THE SIXTH CENTURY BCE onward—the "axial age," which saw the beginnings in India, Greece, and elsewhere of many religious and philosophical traditions—also witnessed the arising in the same places of materialist philosophies that dispense with references to spirit, God, or gods in the explanation of the world. In India the Charvaka tradition espoused materialism; this tradition included Kanada, an early exponent of atomism, versions of which also flourished in some Buddhist and Jain traditions. Better known in the West is the atomism of the fifth century BCE Greek Leucippus, his pupil, Democritus, and Epicurus. The pre-Socratic Greek philosophers were mainly naturalists in the broad sense of explaining the natural world in terms of natural things (water, fire, air, . . .) rather than the gods. However, in the wake of Plato and Aristotle, and later Christianity, such views became eclipsed by a general realism regarding God and the world of ideas or universals.

That realism regarding ideas (but not God) was challenged by William of Ockham, who argued for a nominalist understanding of universals. According to Ockham, the term "dog" does not refer to a real "idea" or "form" of dogness, as both Plato and Aristotle had taught; it merely denotes a collection of things we choose to lump together by way of the *name* "dog" (whence "nominalism"). Ockham was an early constructivist, teaching that only singular things were real, in this case only individual dogs. The class of all dogs was not a reality, but something we humans construct. Ockham's "razor" was designed to eliminate not "entities," but speculative ideas and concepts. Ockham was not an atomist or a materialist, and he was not a great direct influence on early science, but his nominalism shook the foundations of medieval belief in human participation in the real world of ideas, and ultimately in God. God became more remote and inscrutable, while the world became more amenable to human observation and investigation in terms of its constituent parts.

This was certainly the case with Thomas Hobbes, whose nominalist belief that only particular bodies and motions exist led him to challenge

---

2. Dawkins, *Blind Watchmaker*, 5.
3. Huxley, *Elementary Physiology*, 210.

Descartes's dualism in the interests of materialism. The ideas and perceptions that Descartes ascribed to mind could be better explained, he argued, in terms of purely material entities and causation. "Light and color, and heat and sound, and other qualities which are commonly called sensible, are not objects, but phantasms in the sentients," [4] that is, the sense organs. Extension remains intrinsic to matter, but time and space, like the secondary qualities, are illusions produced by our sense organs. Needless to say, society itself is construed on atomistic lines, as consisting of independent bundles of selfishness that need to be constrained into some degree of order by the Leviathan state. (Shades of Dawkins here, though in Dawkins's case the ultimate self-seeking unit is the gene. . . .)

Hobbes's view was exceptional, though not unique in his time, and Hobbes himself drew back from atheism, though unsurprisingly, he was accused of it. Over the course of the following eighteenth century, the nineteenth, and the twentieth, materialism of various kinds has become acceptable and, in many philosophical circles, dominant. Once nominalism is accepted, dualism begins to look like an incoherent compromise between the new science and older, religious views. Materialism begins to look preferable, as it carries the momentum of scientific methodology and discovery forward into an epistemological program for the whole of knowledge, and a metaphysical account of all the reality there is. After Descartes, from the empiricists Locke and Hume through to their twentieth-century successors, many (though by no means all, see {4}) philosophers have embraced nominalism, if not materialism.

{3} will discuss, first, this transformation of scientific method into metaphysical doctrine, examining the impact of nominalism and naturalism on the eight principles. It will then acknowledge that materialism is not a monolith, but comes in stronger and weaker forms. Atheism likewise: its several varieties are discussed in the section that follows, leading into a wider discussion of what (paradoxically?) may be termed the spirituality (or spiritualities) of atheism(s). Finally, as usual, questions are posed regarding the various kinds of materialism.

From Scientific Principles to the Tenets of Materialism

To highlight the change from methodological principle to metaphysical tenet, in the heading for each tenet I offer a name—in four crucial cases an "-ism" name—to show that it is a question of belief that is involved. After

---

4. Descartes, *Elements of Philosophy*, Book IV, ch. 27, paragraph 3. Cited in Burtt, *Metaphysical Foundations*, 131.

each such heading, I repeat from {2} the methodological principle with the same number, on which it is built. In the case of the last two tenets, the tenet is not identical to the principle, but an intensification of it. In these cases, first, the new tenet is stated in italics, and shortly following, the old principle is quoted. To clarify the difference from the older principle, I refer to these tenets as 7* and 8*, with the star signifying that tenet 7* is not the same as principle 7, and likewise, 8* is not 8.

But first, we need to add the new tenets that demanded the change in the others from the dualistic to the materialistic perspective. To avoid changing the numbers, let us call these tenets A and B.

A) Nominalism

Reality consists only of particular things.

This is Ockham's nominalism: the idea just discussed, that particulars, individual things—the "bits and pieces" of the title—are all that exist. As nominalism preceded the modern rise of science, and also influenced the development of the scientific principles into the tenets of materialism, we need to place it at the head of the list of tenets.

Nominalists are not necessarily materialist; Ockham himself believed in God (now reconceived as an individual supreme Being, rather than Aquinas's "Being Itself," which for Ockham could not mean anything). He also believed in immaterial beings such as angels. But it would seem that materialists have to be nominalists. Dualism offered spaces—minds, and the divine Mind—that universals could inhabit. Abolish that space, and ideas have no home to be real in; they can only be collections and human constructions of material particulars. Unless, that is, matter itself is seen as embodying a real world of ideas. Its mathematical structures, for example, could be *identified* with the material structure of the universe. That is the question raised as ?{3}a and pursued in {4}. Meanwhile Descartes's substance dualism is not, of course, the only way to make a home for ideas; we will examine other ways of approaching mind and real ideas later in the book. But our task now is to consider orthodox materialism, which abolishes mind and denies the reality of its ideas and concepts.

B) Naturalism

Everything can be explained by reference to natural quantities; mental qualities or supernatural forces explain nothing.

This is the materialist doctrine *par excellence*, the one that definitively marks the transit from a dualistic to a materialistic perspective. According to it, explanations are sought within nature, rather than by positing occult, supernatural, or otherwise unobservable powers. Philosophers speak of the causal closure of the universe—the idea that nature is not open to causes outside itself—and its nomological completeness, that is, the completeness of the set of laws that govern it. Mind, consciousness, and God, being immaterial, are therefore redundant as far as knowledge is concerned. Dualism loses its mind and becomes monistic materialism, while deism loses the causing God and becomes atheism. Of course, not all scientists, by any means, are materialists and atheists, since God and the soul may be revered for many other reasons than scientific explanation, which never was the main reason for believing in them. But the consensus is now very firmly that God and the soul should not be invoked to explain events in the natural world.

So fundamental is naturalism to materialism that the term is often used in preference to "materialism," as if it were a less harsh way of saying the same thing.[5] However, naturalism and materialism are not equivalent. As we shall see, an idealist metaphysics, or a pantheism such as that of Spinoza, can be naturalistic. There is no obvious contradiction between the view that we need not or should not look beyond the universe for its explanation, or entertain the possibility of supernatural causes, and the view that the "stuff" of which the universe is made is ideal or dual rather than material (see {6}). Personally, I have a lot more sympathy with naturalism than nominalism, and tend to feel that nature should be explained naturalistically; and that it is the possibility of seeing the world as one self-contained whole that invites theistic explanation, not of particular events, but of the whole. Hence, I feel an affinity with naturalistic theism like Spinoza's.

On the other hand, the view that there is nothing in the universe and its causes but matter is in straightforward contradiction with the possibility of transcendent or supernatural causes.[6] So naturalism does not imply

---

5. A third option is "physicalism," which again sounds less harsh and more philosophically sophisticated, perhaps because of the frequent use of "materialism" as a term of moral condemnation, meaning over-interested in money and material possessions. Materialists in our sense are of course not necessarily materialistic in the moral sense. But I retain the terms "materialism" and its opposite "idealism" (which likewise can have a moral meaning) to refer to philosophical stances, or what I call Worlds.

6. The transcendent and the supernatural are not the same, of course. The supernatural refers to the operation of immaterial forces and causes within the universe, while the transcendent refers to realities beyond the universe. The miracles of Jesus, arguably, are transcendent rather than supernatural. In Christian belief, Jesus was not a magician manipulating occult forces, but a divine human being opening the created

materialism, but materialism does imply naturalism. Further, we could say that materialism is what replaces dualism when the principle of naturalism is applied. Materialism is dualism minus the supernatural "ghost." (Matter + mind) – mind = matter, obviously. {3} is definitely about materialism, and this section discusses naturalism as a necessary, defining tenet of materialism. Later Worlds, however, will examine the case for several non-materialistic kinds of naturalism, as well as non-naturalism. ?{3}j will query whether naturalism can provide a complete worldview, paving the way for those alternative options.

The first six tenets that follow are the first six scientific principles under the impact of nominalism and naturalism; they are still stated in the same way, but nominalism and naturalism give them a different "spin" from that which they had in the dualistic perspective. With the final two scientific principles the effect of nominalism and naturalism is more drastic, so that they need to be stated differently, and give rise to the two doctrines most often associated with materialism in the popular imagination: determinism and reductionism.

1) Cosmic Lawfulness

Nature is governed by laws.

This is the widespread ancient belief that remains fundamental to science. However, under naturalism, which rules out a divine or spiritual creator, institutor, or guarantor, the force of the cosmic laws becomes a groundless mystery to be accepted, perhaps, on the pragmatic grounds that it leads to good results. This is one of the many ways in which the grounds for materialism come close to those often advanced for religion: the mystery cannot be proven, but it produces good practice. (See {3}c.)

2) Discoverability

These laws are discoverable by human beings.

Obviously, this other old precept is fundamental to science and to materialism. Opinions would differ, of course, as to whether all the laws are discoverable. Many scientists live in the hope of a "theory of everything," but a theory of "everything" would in fact be a law that unites the laws behind the four forces of nature. This would not, in fact, explain absolutely

---

order to a new, transcendent creativity. If this distinction is valid, naturalism and theism may be compatible; see ?{10}b.

everything. Very often the laws of nature prove to be remarkably simple: Newton's laws of motion, Einstein's two theories of relativity, and those of quantum physics, are all remarkably simple and elegant, and the basic constants (dimensionless numbers) in nature are remarkably few. On the other hand, the search for a theory of everything has got mired down in the complexities of string theory and its rival, loop quantum gravity.[7] Alongside the question of why the universe should be lawful in the absence of a Lawmaker, there is a question of why the universe should obey the laws and constants it does, with such remarkable results—see ?{3}b and c, and {4} and {5}.

3) Formulability[8]

The laws are mathematically formulable.

If the laws of nature cannot be formulated, of course they cannot be discovered, and in the case of physics and astronomy at least, and in the ideal of many of the other sciences, mathematics has been the primary means of formulation. However, in the early days of the rise of science, as noted, the mathematics was most often understood in realist rather than nominalist terms. With nominalism a subtle shift occurs; instead of itself denoting the reality we are observing, the mathematics has to be seen as describing some physical model that is itself the reality. For instance, the formulae of electronics describe actual flows of physical electrons, which are the actual explanation of the relation between voltage, resistance, and current. In classic materialism, the models themselves are often quite literal: electrons really are tiny balls of negative charge, and atoms actually are little solar systems. Only with quantum physics and the like does this literalism begin to unravel into {4}.

4) Empirical Testability

The mathematical laws must be measured and tested by experiment and observation.

Empiricism is even more fundamental to materialism than it was to dualism, since the latter allowed for unobservable events like thoughts in other people's minds. In its extreme twentieth-century form, positivism, all unobservable entities are excluded, and measurements on instruments are regarded as the sole reality. Measurement also gets applied to the human

---

7. Cf. Hossenfelder, "String Theory . . . ."
8. Excuse the neologism, whose meaning should be clear.

sciences, as dualist and vitalist accounts are no longer regarded as valid, and behaviorism prevails.

On the other hand, such accounts, which tend toward the notion that *esse est percipi*, that to exist is logically or actually to be perceived, or (less strongly) potentially perceived, tend away from materialism in the direction of phenomenalism, a form of idealism. True materialism allows the existence of matter even in unobserved and unobservable cases like the neutrino particle, the centers of black holes, and the "dark" matter and energy of which the bulk of the universe is now thought to consist. In such cases, the matter is posited because of effects we can observe (as in the case of galaxies that spin faster than they should, indicating black holes at their heart) or because the mathematical theories that correlate known observations demand their existence.

As in {2}, if mathematical theories are to correlate with models and observations, a kind of correspondence theory of truth is still fundamental to any realistic account, even a positivistic account. In positivism, the meaning of statements is ascribed to the corresponding "facts" that would verify or falsify them. However, the correspondence can no longer be seen as holding between ideas in the mind or concepts in language on the one hand, and things in the world on the other. Quite what is now thought of as corresponding with what is hard to express, and several queries arise: ?{3} d, e, and f.

5) Spatio-Temporal Uniformity

Space and time form the uniform background to the operation of the laws.

For many dualistic thinkers, including Henry More (see {6}) and Isaac Newton, space and time retained a mysterious quality, being the invisible continuum in which all material bodies exist and move, and partaking of the infinity and eternity of God. With materialism, obviously, this divine aspect had to disappear, and space and time, like all else, had to be explained in terms of matter, rather than being its infinite, pre-existent container. The logical pathway was therefore open for Einstein's general theory of relativity, which created a united concept of "space-time," relative to the observer and determined by gravitational forces. Newton had established a uniform space by rendering all continuous motions equivalent; Einstein established a universal space-time by rendering all accelerated motions (under gravity) equivalent.

However, the laws need still to be uniform through space-time. There has been speculation that the laws of nature may be different in far off places or distant times in the universe, and some versions of the multiverse (see {5}) involve a "reshuffling" of the laws and constants of nature.[9] However, either (a) these changes in the laws would be according to a higher law, or (b) they would be random and unpredictable. In case (a), for example, a theory of everything might predict an increase in the gravitational or some other constant through time. But in this case, there would be a uniform law at the higher level, specifying the change in the lower-level law. (All laws, after all, describe the constancy of a change. For example, planets change positions; the law of gravity tells us why and how they regularly do so.) That higher-level law would be validated in the usual way, because of its coherence with other known laws, and because of evidence that its predictions regarding the change in gravity proved true. In case (b), the changes in gravity, for example, would be unpredictable. But in that case, we would not be able to predict what would happen under gravity in the relevant far-off places and times. So the theory that gravity changed unpredictably would be of no scientific use in explanation or prediction. In practice, all the evidence so far suggests that the laws of nature are the same throughout the universe.[10]

6) Quantifiability

Science discovers "primary" quantities and their relations; "secondary" qualities only seem to exist.

The tenet takes a stronger form than the version in {2} because of nominalism, which allows secondary qualities such as "green," being universals, no real existence, and because of naturalism, which allows subjective ideas and experiences no real causal power. In dualism, the secondary qualities are allowed a secondary degree of existence, as phenomena, that is, qualia or "seeming things" that could somehow (albeit in a manner hard to understand) represent real things, and as ideas that could motivate us and so cause (likewise, in a manner hard to understand) real action. In true materialism no such representative or causal efficacy can be allowed. The following section on "Types of Materialism" will examine the possible ways of conceiving of thoughts and qualia within a quantifiable material universe, while ?{3}d will focus on the famous "problem of qualia."

---

9. This speculation, however, seems to me to be invented in order for the multiverse to represent different options regarding these laws and constants.

10. For example, in 2008 research by the Max Planck Institute indicated that the mass ratio between the electron and proton was the same as it is here in galaxies six billion years away, half way across the visible universe.

7*) Determinism

All events are necessarily and sufficiently explained by efficient causes that are preceding physical events.

Here, nominalism and naturalism have effected a drastic change from the weaker Principle 7 in {2}, that "efficient causes are necessary and sufficient to explain events." Nominalism demands that we find causation in individual physical things, which introduces the familiar billiard-ball image of causation as an ongoing interaction between particles ricocheting off of one another. But it is naturalism that demands that all events be sufficiently explained by such causal interaction. If the physical causes are not sufficient to generate the event, the door is opened not only for chance, but also for supernatural causes and/or downward causation by minds.[11] Dualism would then hold true, rather than materialism. As against such arguments, naturalism demands a nature that is causally closed, having causes only within the natural world itself. Most dualists would be happy with the idea that normal events must have some natural causes: that is, natural causes are necessary to natural events. Whether it be an event as trivial as my donning my hat, or as profound and intractable as the origin of life, Aristotle and Descartes would agree that there must be some material cause involved, whatever we say about spirit or divine intervention. (The creation of the universe suggests an exception, of course, if it was *ex nihilo*.) What the naturalist affirms against those others is that the material causes are always sufficient, needing no other cause, and leaving nothing uncaused.

Questions abound (see ?{3}g), such as whether the universe we live in actually is deterministic, and whether that means that the entire future is determined by the present state of the universe, as the present is determined by the past. And if not, is some version of materialism compatible with some form of non-determinism?

8*) Reductionism

All substances reduce to material substances.

Naturalism has made for a big change to the equivalent scientific principle: "*Mechanization: the cosmos and its contents work like a machine.*" For the naturalist abandonment of "supernatural" factors like mind and final causality leaves no place for the notion of nature as a machine, which is inherently something made of interacting parts intentionally put together by an external maker for specific purposes. Though the machine analogy is

---

11. Many argue that quantum indeterminacy does open this door: see {5}.

still often used by materialists, it is misleading: for as Ryle succinctly put it, "avalanches and games of billiards are subject to mechanical laws, but they are not at all like the workings of machines."[12] What is left of the "mechanical" model when naturalism takes away all reference to design and purpose is the notion of being made of bits and pieces: the paradoxical blind mechanism we call reductionism.

Reductionism, as we shall soon see, can mean one of at least three different things, but essentially it means that larger substances should be explained in terms of the parts of which they are made. As with trying to understand a machine, one examines the working parts and observes how they work together to achieve the effect of the whole. In place of the old seeking of the Ultimate as the highest level, the search is for the ultimate explanation at the bottom level of elementary particles, waves, forces, strings, or whatever science conceives the basic elements to be. (As yet, of course, there is no consensus here.) A human being is explained in terms of the brain, limbs, and organs and other parts that make her up, and these organs in turn are explained in terms of the cells that make them up, and the cells in terms of molecules, and the molecules in terms of atoms, and so forth until we reach the elementary particles and the forces between them. Science is assumed to consist in a hierarchy of "levels," descending from the human sciences through biology, biochemistry, to physics, which is seen as the foundation of them all; the foundation that holds most closely to the ideal of being expressed in terms of mathematical formulae. The notion is very familiar, and most of us probably learnt it at school, though in fact a "level" is a varied and disputed notion (see {9}).

The kind of explanation involved here is different from the deterministic efficient causality of 7*, which explains events, and operates "diachronically," as philosophers say, from past to future. Reductionism involves a more static or "synchronic" explanation of a kind of thing (like a tree or a star) in terms of what it is made of. It involves what Aristotle called material causality. In Aristotle's system—see {8}—efficient causality complements final causality, while material causality is balanced by formal causality, or explanation of the parts in terms of the wider whole they help to constitute. In practice, science still often uses formal causality, as when we explain the heart by means of its function in the whole animal to pump blood and so keep the animal alive. (The model at work, once again, is a machine with functioning parts.) But strictly, reductionism insists, the explanation should go the other way: we should explain the animal in terms of its beating heart and other parts. Ultimately the heart is not there because the animal needs it

---

12. Ryle, *Concept of Mind*, 80.

to stay alive; it is rather that animals with hearts tend to survive better than those that lack them, so we, the survivors of an evolutionary process that weeded out the heartless, have hearts. By means of theories like evolution, reductionism is able to sustain itself in the face of the temptations of teleology, and insist that it is not the animal that explains the heart, but the heart (among other things) that explains the animal.

Reductionism is a more complex notion, however, than first appears. Robert Koons distinguishes three kinds of materialism, according to how we understand the reduction of mind to brain, or higher-level events to ultimate material constituents.[13] This may be

1. *Elimination.* Mind is nothing. There is no higher level; everything that "really" happens, happens to the ultimate particles and their relations. Koons notes that eliminative materialism is rare among philosophers. Daniel Dennett and Paul and Patricia Churchland are the best-known examples of those who argue for the elimination of some kinds of "mind" language.

2. *Reduction proper.* Mind is nothing but the brain. Thoughts and minds, and other such higher-level entities, genuinely exist, but statements about them can be translated without loss as statements about the ultimate particles of which they consist. Everything "really" (in a sense that needs defining) takes place at a physical level. This is probably what most people understand by reductionism.

3. *Supervenience.* A concept of uncertain origin, unfamiliar outside philosophical circles. Mind and brain both exist in their own right. But to every mind event there corresponds a brain event. Nothing takes place in the mind without something taking place in the brain: mind events are "epiphenomena," parallel to brain events. Nothing happens on a higher level without something corresponding happening to the ultimate particles and their relations. In "logical" versions of supervenience, this correspondence arises because the brain events cause the mind events. In "brute" supervenience, the supervenience is left unexplained, as just "how it is." Mind and qualia are epiphenomena that just happen when physical things happen in the brain. Logical supervenience, as Koons notes, is hard to distinguish from reductionism proper, while it is debatable whether brute supervenience is a reductionist form of explanation, since the reduction itself is left as

---

13. Koons, *Waning of Materialism*, Loc. 10.

an unexplained mystery.[14] So arguably there may be just two types of reductionism.

?{3}g will ask whether people can be understood on a deterministic basis, while ?{3}h will question whether there are flaws in some or all ideas of reductionism. But the immediate question is what materialism is. We shall find it to be a varied animal, some forms being militantly materialistic, while others lead on naturally to other Worlds.

Kinds of Materialism and Its Relation to Other Views

Scientific method has proven highly successful and transformative in the modern era, in generating an understanding of the natural world that has led to many positive (though some regrettable) technological advances. Modern secular atheism has seized upon the methodological principles for science and turned them into the metaphysical tenets of a total creed. What began as guidelines for pursuing a particular kind of mostly successful investigation into nature have thereby been turned into articles of a reasonable faith to be maintained in one's whole approach to life.

However, materialism is not a monolithic monster. Not all materialists accept all the tenets to the same degree, so there are different kinds of materialism. We have identified ten tenets of materialism, so in theory there are 2^{10} (= 1,024) possible combinations regarding simple yes or no belief in these tenets (that is, excluding the subtle nuances of ways in which they may be believed). This number is lessened by the fact that many beliefs entail or are entailed by others; but still, an exhaustive examination of all the logically possible combinations, and deciding which combinations count as materialistic, would make for a long and rather tedious chapter! In practice it turns out to be the final three, distinctively materialistic tenets that make for the interesting differences between kinds of materialism, and between materialistic and non-materialistic alternatives to be considered in later Worlds. The options are:

- *R or -R*: substance reductionism or not: whether substances (R) reduce to material parts, or (-R) there are irreducible wholes. (The term "reduce" here is intended in any of the three senses just defined: elimination, reduction proper, and supervenience. Thus R includes the view that there are no higher level substances, the view that there are such substances but they are "really" collections of physical substances, and

---

14. Koons, *Waning of Materialism*, Loc. 14.

the view that there are higher level substances, but they supervene on the lower level.)

- *Q or -Q*: quality reductionism or not: whether the qualities of things (Q) reduce to those of their parts. As we shall see, Q means either that only the measurable quantities that physics ascribes to the ultimate parts are real, or (as in panpsychism) that the ultimate particles must also have qualities capable of supporting higher level qualities. -Q would allow higher level realities to have qualities that do not belong to their constituents.

- *D or -D*: determinism or not: whether all events are (D) determined by efficient causes, or (-D) the world is open to other kinds of causality, such as teleology, chance, or even sheer absence of cause.

In theory, the threefold framework of alternatives ought to give us 2^3 (= 8) possible combinations, as follows.[15]

R Q D: Eliminative Materialism

On this understanding, introduced as eliminative materialism above, all substances reduce to material particles having only quantitative properties—extension, shape, mass, position, and momentum—which are all determined by efficient causes. Wider wholes exhibiting qualities, like bodies exhibiting life and minds entertaining qualia and thoughts—do not really exist. The "primitive" language that describes conscious experience and thought is to be eliminated in favor of a more sophisticated description in terms of brain states. An analogy used here is the way, when the theory that combustion was due to the release of phlogiston was replaced by the theory involving oxygen, science did not merely "reduce" phlogiston language to "oxygen" language; it gave up the whole idea that phlogiston existed. Likewise with talk of the ether as the medium though which light propagates, or *elan vital* as the animating force that makes things alive, science does not retain these concepts and explain what they mean in current concepts, it simply abandons the idea that they exist at all, and replaces them with the current concepts. After all, the current concepts generally work together differently from the older concepts; there is nothing in the new framework that could "translate" the old ones. There is nothing in modern chemistry to which "phlogiston" could reduce, no need in modern electromagnetic theory for ether, and modern biochemistry can explain how life works without

---

15. The assumption behind this classification is that the world consists of substances with qualities and powers. Generally, materialism, dualism, and Aristotelianism share this assumption, but there are Worlds that do not, as we shall see.

resorting to life forces. Likewise, it is argued, science should give up antiquated talk about mental events and just talk about physical events in the brain. After all, it proves (as we shall see) probably impossible to translate and so reduce mind states into equivalent brain states; much easier simply to replace mind language with brain language.

So Paul and Patricia Churchland look forward to the day when we have developed an adequate description of physical (including brain) events, enabling us to eliminate folk-psychological statements that refer to the mind and its contents.

> Paul Churchland confidently informs us that it is always false to say that people sitting around a fire "warm themselves next to [it] and gaze at the flickering flames." This is mere unscientific mumbo jumbo. The truth is rather that "they absorb some EM energy in the m range emitted by the highly exothermic oxidation reaction, and observe the turbulences in the thermally incandescent river of molecules forced upwards by the denser atmosphere surrounding." ... And don't expect the Churchlands to feel your pain, for once again, "science" tells us that there isn't any such thing as "pain"; there are only "sundry modes of stimulation in our A-delta fibers and/or C-fibers (peripherally), or in our thalamus and/or reticular formation (centrally)."[16]

But it is the redoubtable New Atheist philosopher Daniel Dennett who presents arguments for eliminating qualia from our conceptual scheme, which we will consider in ?{3}d.

Dennett and the Churchlands apart, however, total eliminative materialism is a rare option in contemporary science and philosophy. And the best it has been able to do, in practice, is to present arguments for rejecting the commonsense view in particular cases, and then to generalize the argument by expressing the hope that as science progresses, and our understandings of the workings of the nerves and brain improves, we will be able to complete the elimination of mind-language in favor of brain-language. Now it is true that our understanding of nerves, brains, information theory, and artificial intelligence is increasing exponentially. But that will only lead to the elimination of mind if there are not conceptual reasons why that elimination is impossible. And we shall see that there are such reasons. Science and technology will undoubtedly enable us to understand and do more and more. But not the inconceivable.

---

16. Feser, *Last Superstition*, Loc. 4261, referring to P. M. Churchland, *Scientific Realism*, 30 and 119.

-R Q D and -R Q -D: two Kinds of "Quality Only" Reductionism

These are two views that suggest that the qualities of things can be reduced to those of the parts, but the things they are qualities of cannot be so reduced. Such ideas can safely be rejected. Both posit the enigma of real higher-level substances like minds, or organisms, existing without the qualities we ascribe to them and by means of which we discern them. In the -R Q -D version, these "quality-free" substances nevertheless make things happen, while in -R Q D, determinism applies. But surely something cannot be a whole that is greater than the sum of its parts unless it has at least some qualities that are likewise greater than the qualities ascribed to its parts. For unless we identify some qualities in a whole additional to those of its parts, what would we be affirming by distinguishing it from the sum of its parts? If we held that the mind was somehow more than its neurons, even though all the qualities of the mind can be attributed to those of its neurons, surely we would be contradicting ourselves?

So -R implies -Q, or equivalently, Q implies R. If this is right, it follows that -R Q D and -R Q -D, can be eliminated. The converse, meanwhile, is not necessarily true: R does not imply Q, or -Q imply -R: so hierarchical materialism and moderate emergence, as described below, are logically possible standpoints. These views affirm (see {9}) that qualities may "emerge" from the parts and their interactions, but these qualities do not need to be ascribed to a new substance such as mind.

R Q -D: Non-Deterministic Materialism

This position differs from R Q D in allowing non-determinism. The universe still consists only of particles in space bearing only primary quantities and relations. But their movements are no longer determined by efficient causes alone. This element of indeterminacy cannot, however, open a space for other kinds of causality, such as final or formal causality. For those forms of causality require the existence of form and pattern over and above the interaction of primary particles, so that either R or Q, or both, have to be negated. Non-deterministic materialism merely denies that everything that happens in or between particles has to happen. Some things happen by chance, or are unpredictable for some other reason than brute chance.

There are two versions of this understanding. On the first, the particles are non-determined, but at a higher level, determinism emerges. The now familiar example is quantum physics, or to be precise, the Copenhagen interpretation of quantum physics. According to this, if we observe a particle's momentum precisely, we can only predict the chances of finding the particle in a particular place, and if we observe its position precisely, the momentum is spread over a range of probabilities. Full determinism, which requires both precise momentum and position, cannot be achieved. And this is not because of the limitations of our measuring apparatus, but rather, a feature of reality itself. One proponent of such a view, Nancy Cartwright, explains that lawfulness may not be a fundamental property of nature, but rather, may emerge in special cases like those described by Newton's laws. Large objects such as pendulums and planets represent what she calls "nomological machines" whereby irregularities cancel out and produce a smooth and predictable operation. More on this in {9}.

The second version is the opposite: at a lower level, determinism applies, but at a higher, macro level—for example, in the case of people and weather systems—we can only make probabilistic predictions. The reason given for this is usually that the amount of calculation required to predict in systems where there are a large number of interacting particles begins to outstrip the time available in the universe. If the only "computer" that can calculate the properties of the particles at some future date is the universe itself, or if even the universe does not have enough time to do so, those properties are effectively unpredictable. In such cases of "complexity" (in a technical sense) we cannot work out the properties, or if we know the properties by observations, we will not be able to work out the laws involved. {4} will consider how the mathematician Kurt Gödel has shown that in mathematics there is no infallible algorithm for generating a true theory; and since the laws of physics are mathematical, this applies to them also. And if we cannot be sure to find all the laws that govern nature, we cannot know whether those laws are deterministic or not. We might then retain a faith in determinism, but it would be a metaphysical, unknowable determinism, which could not be proven true. ?{3}g will consider whether a non-deterministic materialism is feasible.

R -Q D: Hierarchical Materialism

This position differs from eliminative materialism in a different way: determinism is retained, but the ban on qualia or real qualities is lifted. Hierarchical materialism allows a hierarchy of levels of description, in which qualities may apply that are different from those used to describe the basic particles. Nevertheless, the substances to which these emergent qualities apply are ultimately the basic particles of matter. Mental states—thoughts, perceptions, intentions, and so forth—are not nothing, but they are nothing but shorthand, convenient ways of describing what could be described in a much more complicated way, by referring to the matter and events in the brain.

Hierarchical materialism broadly corresponds with what Koons describes as reductive materialism, and also with the logical kind of supervenience. The latter may be identified with reductive materialism because it holds that, though there are many physical events that are not accompanied by mind events (for example, totally unknown events), there are no mind events that are not accompanied by physical events. What kinds of physical event might correlate or vary with mental events? According to Koons, there are three main ways of answering this question. Firstly, "mind-brain identity" holds that minds are nothing but brains, and to every mind event there corresponds a group of brain events. Secondly, behaviorism holds that minds are nothing but behavior, and that descriptions of intentions, thoughts, feelings, and the like are really descriptions of dispositions to different kinds of physical action. Thirdly, functionalism holds that minds are "functions" of the physical properties that realize them; consciousness, for example, is a function of different kinds of representational activity, including self-representational activity.

Hierarchical materialism is undoubtedly the most widespread current form of materialism. It is "hierarchical" because the different qualitative descriptions are held to exist on different "levels," each reducing to, or "emerging" from, the level below: psychology with its mental descriptions reducing to biology, and so on through biochemistry and chemistry to physics, as noted above. In the "weak" form of emergence, consciousness, thought, and the like are seen to be emergent qualities, not identifiable with complex sets of physical qualities, even though they do not attach to irreducible entities like mind or soul. In "moderate" emergence (see below) they effect a non-deterministic causality of their own, while in "strong" emergence, holism, and substance dualism, in addition they belong to higher-level substances in contrast with substances at the lower level.

If consciousness is taken down to the physical level, and the ultimate constituents are said to entertain qualia—being in some sense conscious—panpsychism results: see {6}. Alternatively, some argue that only certain organisms, such as the human ones, possess both mental and physical qualities; this gives us the "property dualism," advocated for example by Michael Jubien.[17] He and many other philosophers would advance such views as crediting the irreducible status of metal properties without denying that humans are physical beings, rather than immaterial minds inserted into bodies, as in substance dualism.

---

17. Jubien, "Dualizing Materialism," in Koons, *Waning of Materialism*, Loc. 524.

It is worth noting, finally, that the philosopher W. V. O. Quine questions whether the distinction between eliminative and reductive materialism amounts to anything significant.

> Is physicalism a repudiation of mental objects after all, or a theory of them? Does it repudiate the mental state of pain or anger in favor of its physical concomitant, or does it identify the mental state with a state of the physical organism (and so a state of the physical organism with the mental state)? ... Some may therefore find comfort in reflecting that the distinction between an eliminative and an explicative physicalism is unreal.[18]

R -Q -D: Moderate Emergence

If the emergent wholes just described not only represent valid descriptions of real qualities, but exercise a real causal activity of their own, while at the same time particles are regarded as the only real substances, then hierarchical materialism gives way to a moderate emergentism. In the case of mind and body, emergentism holds that not only can brain events cause mind events (as for example when light from a flower hitting the retina causes the perception of flower shape and color in the mind); but conversely mental events may cause physical ones (as when my desire and intent to pick the flower causes my limbs to move me in such a way that I pick it.) I call this "moderate" because truly strong emergence abandons reductionism and ascribes mental causes to an irreducible mental agent or substance (see next).

Moderate emergentists often claim to be materialists, arguing that all wholes, including minds, are ultimately made of the basic particles of matter. They hold to what Koons calls the "brute" version of supervenience: the idea that mind states co-vary with physical states such that nothing mental happens without something material happening, but holding that this supervenience is not a causal necessity but a brute, unexplained fact about the way the world is. However, "downward causation" is often hotly resisted by materialists, and with good reason. For moderate emergentism, as for non-deterministic materialism, there exist causal agents that are wholes rather than parts; but in the case of moderate emergentism their causality can no longer be restricted to efficient causality, since minds are said to operate on matter with formal and final causality. Emergentism rejects the idea of minds as additional immaterial bits acting alongside the material bits; nevertheless, if a complex structure of atoms called the brain—or perhaps,

---

18. Quine, *Word and Object*, 265. As I understand it, Quine's "physicalism" is equivalent to what I call "materialism," and he calls "explicative" what Koons calls "reductive."

the whole body—can exercise purpose and accomplish things in the world, then this complex structure is itself an agent and a substance, albeit not necessarily an immaterial mind. This will be discussed further in ?{3}f, g, h, and j, and in {9}.

-R -Q D: Non-Reductionist Determinism

This is a *prima facie* strange position that tries to retain determinism while abandoning substance and quality reductionism. For such a view,

> there are no fundamental particles or qualities that explain all others—no foundation level of the universe—and yet all is explained in principle by a single-level set of laws. At first sight this looks inconceivable, but... fractals provide a model, in that a fractal has no atomic level of subdivision but discloses more complexity the more closely one looks; yet it can be generated by (infinite) reiterations of a single set of laws.... [This raises] the possibility that a world of unfathomable complexity may manifest a deep simplicity. We are left with a view I shall term *transcendent monism*.... "Transcendent" refers to the openness of the world, the way it is explained in terms of activity rather than substance. It is not yet clear what view of mind follows.[19]

I now believe the last sentence betrays the fatal flaw in this position, which is the way that it allows for the existence of minds and other "wholes," and for their possessing and entertaining real qualities, without their being able to exert any non-deterministic causality. The much-criticized epiphenomenalism results: mental states really exist, but without having any real influence over the deterministic sequence of brain events that give rise to them. Minds are then substances with real qualities but no real powers;. But surely it is by their powers that substances are evident.

-R -Q -D: Strong Emergence, Holism, Substance Dualism, and Beyond

This leaves a range of non-materialist options that deny substance and quality reductionism, and determinism. Much of the philosophical literature concerns the particular variant within this range—that is, substance dualism—plus various intermediary states, such as dualizing and dualistic materialisms and non-Cartesian dualisms.[20] However, alternatives to materialistic monism do not have to be limited to views that allow precisely two kinds of substance. {7} will consider idealism, a non-materialistic form of

---

19. Thompson, *Holy Ground*, 207.
20. See Koons, *Waning of Materialism*, chs. 16, 17, and 22 respectively.

monism that has become unfashionable rather than definitively discredited. {4} will introduce triadic "three world" positions that have attracted notice in some philosophical quarters. Pluralistic views such as Aristotelian hylomorphism {8} and Nancy Cartwright's "dappled" nature (see {9}), which allow a variety of substances and kinds of substance, need consideration. There are vast worlds to explore that are in some sense or other non-materialistic, affirming irreducible wholes rather than reductionism, real qualities rather than only quantities, and allowing non-deterministic forms of causality. Some of these may run contrary to the scientific approach; but still, let us explore and see.

Theophobia and the Seven Atheisms

After considering these detailed alternative forms, it is time to widen the focus again to consider the broad impact of materialism on theology. Is materialism necessarily atheistic, and is atheism necessarily materialistic?

The answer to the first question seems obvious. Since God is by definition non-material, eliminative materialism at least is committed to atheism. The naturalistic tenet forbids supernatural causes, causes that lie outside of nature. This does not mean that scientists are committed to atheism, but this is because they are not committed to eliminative or even reductive materialism. The principles of scientific method were seen to allow for deistic or theistic understandings within the dualistic framework of {2}. Indeed, some of the scientific principles, such as (1) and (2), the laws of the universe and their discoverability, seemed to require such an understanding. In that sense, as noted, the God whom materialists reject is the God whom scientific method might seem to require, the dualistic, law-maker God.

Richard Lewontin has made it clear that it is not science itself, but an a priori, "absolute" commitment to materialism, that requires that we do not allow God a foot in the door.

> Our willingness to accept scientific claims that are against common sense is the key to an understanding of the real struggle between science and the supernatural. . . . It is not that the methods and institutions of science somehow compel us to accept a material explanation of the phenomenal world but, on the contrary, that we are forced by our a priori adherence to material causes to create an apparatus of investigation and a set of concepts that produce material explanations, no matter how counterintuitive, no matter how mystifying to the uninitiated.

> Moreover, that materialism is absolute, for we cannot allow a divine foot in the door.[21]

It is strange how theophobic many of the New Atheists are, how determined to keep God at bay, even at the cost of "counter-intuitive" and "mystifying" hypotheses. According to Richard Lewontin here, the justification of such an approach lies in belief in the absolute necessity of the struggle against the divine. Materialistic atheism on this understanding is not so much a skepticism about God—still less a detached evaluation of the divine possibility—as an absolute and unquestionable faith in no-God. As will emerge next, some, but by no means all kinds of atheism, are appropriately described as faith commitments.

For in answer to the second question, not all atheists are materialists. The atheist philosopher John Gray has argued that atheism is a tradition as venerable and as varied as the great religions. He lists seven kinds of atheism, of which the first, New Atheism, is one he is not very fond of: a relatively recent "orthodoxy," rooted in the nineteenth century, based on the success of science in that period and since. The oldest version he lists is secular humanism, with roots in the revival of Greek rationalism in the Renaissance: a "sacred relic" based on the idea of progress in the absence of God, championed by John Stuart Mill, Bertrand Russell, and (very differently) Friedrich Nietzsche. Third comes atheism born of "a strange faith in science," attempting to build worldviews on certain rather dubious interpretations of science, including Neo-Darwinist eugenics, mesmerism, and transhumanism: a "techno-monotheism" preaching salvation by mechanization, in which not only will faith in God be transcended, but also faith in "man" as traditionally conceived. Fourth are the atheisms linked to political ideologies: millenarianism, the Jacobin extreme wing of the French Revolution, Bolshevism, Nazism, and "evangelical liberalism" (by which Gray means proselytizing liberalism). Fifth come the God-haters: de Sade, Dostoyevsky's character Ivan Karamazov, and William Empson, all of whom reject a God whom they appear to hate, rather than disbelieve, through an ethical protest against God's world: thus Ivan "returns the ticket" that God has issued for life in this world. Finally, we arrive at the forms of atheism with which Gray identifies: the progress-free atheism of Santayana, along with the "godless sea" of Conrad; and finally, "the atheism of silence": the mystical atheism of Schopenhauer, and the negative theologies of Spinoza and the Russian Jewish author Shestov. We might add Buddhism to this list, since Buddhists like the others encourage silence regarding God (rather than any vociferous protest) in the interests of our spiritual journey. Such

---

21. Cited in Feser, *Last Superstition*, Loc. 368.

quiet atheism is as far from the rage and dogmatism of some other kinds, as religious pacifism is from religious terrorism.

Gray's "anatomy" of atheism should be required reading for all involved in the "science v. religion" debate. Gray seems to be doing from the atheist side what I am trying to do from the theological side: lift the debate out of simple polarity into a richer variety of intersecting pathways. Regarding the present question, it would seem that there are forms of atheism that are committed to materialism as part of their commitment to science; there are other forms that arise from a wider commitment to a secular, Enlightenment project of political salvation, which necessitates materialism because of a supposed enlistment of science in the wider cause; and there are those (the final two) that arise out of a radical carrying forward of apophatic elements in religion itself (or at least, some religious traditions), which see the rejection of idolatrous understandings of God, and hence some kind of agnostic silence, as necessary to our spiritual progress.[22]

If Gray is right, materialists have to be atheists, but atheists need not be materialists. Atheism is bigger than materialism; it can be spiritual and even perhaps "soulful" (Schopenhauer and Santayana come to mind here). But what does atheist spirituality look like?

Progress, Defiance, and Tragedy

Materialism seems to strike three discordant notes: a steady, marching middle note of progressive self-reliant cheer and hope, a shrill note of angry defiance, and underlying all, a deep lament of inevitable tragic loss.

The middle note is an all-pervasive optimism regarding the inevitability of progress based on the steady advance of science; a "rags to riches" plot, in Booker's terms, in which we lift ourselves out of poverty and degradation by our own scientific bootstraps. It is believed that medicine will steadily eradicate more and more diseases, technology will generate an endless supply of energy and consumer goods, and in the phase now beginning, information technology will give us global communication and markets, while artificial intelligence will enable us to sit back and enjoy ourselves while robots do all the hard graft.

Now progress on the back of science is not simply a false myth. Stephen Pinker has shown[23] how statistically the chances of dying a violent death has steadily declined throughout most of history, even when the terrible wars and genocides of the twentieth century are taken into account. We have, he

---

22. Cf. Johnston, *Saving God.*
23. Pinker, *Better Angels,* and *Enlightenment Now.*

shows, steadily grown more tolerant of one another in our differences, less likely to kill or enslave people of different faiths or nationalities. However, on the one hand, by enabling us to fight wars with more powerful weapons, and to exploit the earth more efficiently, science is now propelling us into ecological crises and conflicts from which we and the earth may not recover. And on the other, scientific materialism cannot take all the credit for the positive developments. Pinker is arguing not for scientific materialism as such, but for liberal Enlightenment values, which include the political system of democracy, which became established in Britain, Holland, the United States, and France before materialist atheism became widespread. The pioneers of democracy were generally either Christian theists or deists. Though Pinker, like many others, links scientific materialism with progressive liberalism, it has been argued that the roots of liberalism are much older, within the Jewish and Christian traditions.[24]

But of course, such arguments can make materialists quite angry, and this brings us to the second note, the shrill defiance often to be found among the New Atheists in particular. Materialism, as noted, is dualism minus God and the soul, and often materialism takes a stance of defiance against the "superstitious nonsense" that preceded it, holding an exaggerated view of the evil oppression of the "age of faith," which in the form of fundamentalist religion, threatens to return. Dualism itself tended to adopt the myth of the slaying of the monster of irrationality by the sword-like clarity of the mind, but in materialism the sense of conflict can seem to be intensified by the absence of a real mind to do the defying and slaying.

And that absence betokens the deeper and darker note of tragedy. Tragedy arises when the forces the hero is battling with are destined to win, either by the inexorable necessity of fate, or because the darkness actually inhabits and directs the tragic hero himself. So it is that behind the notes of progress and struggle in materialism, there lies the knowledge that we have no cosmic allies in our fight, and that in the end we must lose. The second law of thermodynamics states clearly that the universe as a whole is moving towards ever greater entropy and disorder, and first life, then matter, then light itself will peter out into an everlasting darkness. And even in the height of life, an inescapable necessity governs the world, rendering our subjective life unreal. Like tragic heroes, scientists accept the loss of all the cozy, comfortable qualities that give life meaning for the rest of us mortals, contemplating instead the austere beauty of the basic laws and their necessary outworking.

---

24. Cf. Siedentop, *Inventing the Individual*.

So it is that many materialists make a value out of facing up to valuelessness: the tragic stance evidenced in the opening quotes from Bertrand Russell and Richard Dawkins. Meanwhile Christian writers like Blaise Pascal recoil from this vision with fear and horror:

> When I consider the short duration of my life, swallowed up in the eternity before and after, the little space which I fill, and even can see, engulfed in the infinite immensity of spaces of which I am ignorant, and which know me not, I am frightened, and am astonished at being here rather than there; for there is no reason why here rather than there, why now rather than then. Who has put me here? By whose order and direction have this place and time been allotted to me? . . . The eternal silence of these infinite spaces frightens me. . . . How many kingdoms know us not![25]

Post-Enlightenment materialism has more than one form, however, and the three "notes" just discussed function differently in each. In the liberal capitalist form, the note of defiance is directed against the old church and state hierarchies that constrained the freedom of the individual. Here the progress note relates to a sense of political and economic freedom to trade and to develop technological ways of exploiting the earth, so generating utilitarian market value, for which material things are commodities for individual consumption. Meanwhile, the tragic doom note arises from the inverse side of this triumph of individual commodity-value, namely the loss of the "common good," and the emptying of the universe of any ultimate teleology. But it is in dialectical materialism—that other child of the Enlightenment—that the notes of progress, defiance, and tragedy (or at least necessity) sound most stridently, and in a different combination. Here defiance means revolutionary defiance of the oppressors, the upper and middle classes; progress means the inevitable advance of the working classes, and through them (because only when class conflict is overcome in communism can there be true peace) the common good; and the necessity is turned away from tragedy towards securing the inevitability of this march of progress. In communism, tragedy is suspended, though perhaps the denial of tragedy is what has made the story of communism itself so tragic, both in the self-defeating violence of its revolutionary assertion of hope, and in the speed with which in many places communism and its egalitarian hopes have collapsed.

However, what these two versions—which have been in such devastating conflict through the twentieth century—have in common is materialism, the central role of science and technology, and an antipathy to "religion"

---

25. Pascal, *Pensées*, nos. 205–7. Pascal found solace in a fideistic, "blind" kind of faith that, however, shares the atheists' negativity in the way the cosmos is viewed.

(though the liberal version allows religion to survive as an individual consumer choice, provided it does not disrupt society's core myths). Conversely it may be the liberal capitalist version's embrace of final doom that has made it all too indifferent to the tragedies that threaten the earth now as a result of its over-exploitation: it has long ago learnt Nero's habit, of playing the fiddle of consumer delight, while civilization burns.

Questions Regarding {3}

Materialism probably still dominates the English-speaking philosophical scene, yet it may have passed its zenith. Robert Koons presents strong arguments that it is now on the wane, though by no means eclipsed. He lists, roughly in order of birth, just some of the twentieth-century philosophers who have presented criticisms of materialism, including many eminent names:

> Bertrand Russell, Rudolf Carnap, Alonzo Church, Kurt Gould, Nelson Goodman, Paul Grice, Stuart Hampshire, Roderick Chisholm, Benson Mates, Peter Strawson, Hilary Putnam, John Searle, Jerrold Katz, Alvin Plantinga, Charles Parsons, Jaegwon Kim, George Myro, Thomas Nagel, Robert Adams, Hugh Mellor, Saul Kripke, Eli Hirsch, Ernest Sosa, Stephen Schiffer, Bas van Fraassen, John McDowell, Peter Unger, Derek Parfit, Crispin Wright, Laurence BonJour, Michael Jubien, Nancy Cartwright, Bob Hale, Kit Fine, Tyler Burge, Terence Horgan, Colin McGinn, Robert Brandom, Nathan Salmon, Joseph Levine, Timothy Williamson, Mark Johnston, Paul Boghossian, Stephen Yablo, Joseph Almog, Keith DeRose, Tim Crane, John Hawthorne, Richard Heck, David Clalmers.[26]

He also lists many of the philosophical objections.

> Over the last fifty years or so, materialism has been challenged by a daunting list of arguments . . . beginning with the Chisholm-Geach-Putnam attack on Behaviorism and fortified by Kripke's attack on the Identity Theory, followed by a host of others: the multiple realizability argument, the disembodiment argument, the certainty argument, the zombie (or nonconscious automaton) argument, the absent qualia argument, the knowledge argument, the inverted spectrum argument, the argument from the special sciences, the explanatory gap argument, the

---

26. Koons, *Waning of Materialism*, Loc. 10.

anti-individualism argument, the self-consciousness argument, the mental causation argument, and many, many more.[27]

As against this he cites, as noted above, only three main arguments against anti-materialism (by which he means mainly dualism). We cannot hope to present the whole complexity of all the arguments, plus those listed in Koons's book; but these two lists may be of use to the philosophical reader who wishes to follow them up in detail. What follows tries to summarize the main arguments under eleven headings. That in itself (plus the above lists) is not in itself an argument, of course; you must evaluate for yourself.

?{3}a: Is Nominalism True?

We noted how many of the scientists of the early modern era were Platonists taking a realistic view of mathematical and geometrical objects, but that nominalism helped deliver the materialist view for which the only realities were physical objects and their causal relations. Those relations in turn were conceived in nominalist terms as observed correlations rather than real necessities. This move was certainly necessary for materialism, but is it necessary for science? {4} will note how some recent physics seems to be moving away from the nominalist premise, towards a revival of the old realism.

?{3}b: Why Must Nature Obey Laws?

Can science explain the way the world conforms to *any* laws and equations? *Must* nature obey laws?[28] If so, why? What force do laws of nature have? And how do we get from empirical description to prediction? The Scottish philosopher David Hume is generally thought to have challenged the idea of necessity in nature, arguing that when we say that A causes or necessitates B, all we ever actually observe is the constant conjunction, whereby A is always followed by B.[29] Arguably within nominalism, for which the only realities are particulars, causality would have to consist in such a constant

---

27. Koons, *Waning of Materialism*, Loc. 20.

28. ?{8}b and c, in *Embodying Mind*, discuss whether laws offer the best account of causality in nature, but this section restricts itself to the more limited question: if, as materialists argue, nature is law-abiding, why?

29. Whether Hume in fact believed in causality as constant conjunction has been questioned by scholars, notably Galen Strawson in *Secret Connexion*. Henceforward, when I refer to Hume it is to the Hume of broad philosophical tradition. Humeanism is an arguable position with many followers, but I am not competent to judge whether Hume is a Humean.

conjunction; the idea of a real, unbreakable necessity to the following of A by B would require that we impute a reality, not just to A and B, the particulars in question, but to their relationship, that is, to an abstract structure. And that would require structural realism.

The problem here goes further than the nature of the necessity in causal connections between past events, raising the problem of induction, that is, how we can extend causal connections observed in the past to make predictions about future events. Science, of course, needs to be able to turn its laws into predictions in order to make observations that will test whether the predictions are right, and the laws therefore correct. But if all there is to causal connection is conjunction, there seems to be no way of moving from prescriptive mode ("the sun has always risen in the morning, at such and such times") to predictive mode ("the sun will rise at 8.23 tomorrow morning"). According to conventional wisdom, the necessity arises from the laws of nature discovered by Newton (and revised by Einstein), which correlate the rising of the sun with the rotation and orbit of the earth and indeed the movement of all objects under the laws of gravitation. This means that there is more at stake in the sun's rising at the predicted time than the movements of earth and sun right now; the rising at the right time has behind it all movements of all objects as described by Newton's laws.[30] If the sun rose one day at a different time from that expected, we would not conclude that it had disobeyed the law for once, or even that the law was wrong; we would look for other celestial objects that might be causing this difference according to the same laws. But for the laws of nature to have this cumulative, correlating force, they cannot be merely a kind of descriptive record of what has happened in the past. They must have a reality that can accumulate force from all the instances that confirm them. But within nominalism, this is hard to articulate.

{2} noted the historical connection between the dualist God and rise of science. We are now suggesting the scientific notion of causality logically needs grounding. If that is so, then atheism, far from being a logical next step in the unfolding of the scientific worldview, might represent the undermining of one of its foundations. And far from being the opponent of naturalism, "supernatural" foundation might go hand in hand with naturalism. The causal closure of the universe according to naturalism may imply supernaturalism, while the supernatural may, for its definition, require a strong notion of the normal closure of nature. But if this is so, the term

---

30. Hume uses such an argument against miracles: one or two apparent exceptions cannot outweigh all the confirmations of a law.

"supernatural" is a misleading term for belief in a divine foundation of the universal laws; see ?{10}a and b.

?{3}c: Why *These* Laws and Constants?

As well as the sheer obedience to the laws as such, there is a huge question of why nature follows the actual laws that prevail in this universe, as well as the constants that apply to this universe, which seem quite arbitrary. Materialism cannot explain why the world we have is one that contains physical objects obeying certain laws and constants. Even a theory of everything would not explain *why* this particular theory of everything, and not some other theory, explains everything. Nor can it be argued that this "why" question is unanswerable, simply from the fact that science itself cannot answer it. {5} will consider the range of answers that may be put to this question, including the answer that there is no answer: that the laws and constants of nature are just brute facts.

?{3}d: Can Materialism Account for Qualia?

In a well-known passage, philosopher J. J. C. Smart urged us to apply Ockham's Razor to consciousness and see it as, like everything else in the universe, explicable in physical terms.

> Science is increasingly giving us a viewpoint whereby organisms are able to be seen as physicochemical mechanisms: it seems that even the behavior of man himself [sic.] will one day be explicable in mechanistic terms. There does seem to be, so far as science is concerned, nothing in the world but increasingly complex arrangements of physical constituents. All except for one place: in consciousness.... I just cannot believe that this can be so. That everything should be explicable in terms of physics ... except the occurrence of sensations seems to me to be completely unbelievable. Such sensations would be "nomological danglers."[31]

"Nomological danglers" is Feigl's nice term for items that have no explanation in terms of laws of nature. Since Smart wrote (and indeed before) there have been many attempts either to explain consciousness in material terms (as in reductive materialism) or to deny its real existence (as in the eliminative version.) "Consciousness" is of course a very broad term, and essentially

---

31. Smart, "Sensations and Brain Processes," 61.

there are two problems here for materialism. "Consciousness" can refer to our ability to think, imagine, conceive, know, believe, desire, love, fear, and have other such relations to matters that may be, but need not be, themselves physical; here we encounter the "problem of intentionality," discussed in the next section. Or it may refer to "being aware of": in other words seeing, hearing, feeling, and having other sensations in relation to material objects. Here we encounter the "problem of qualia," using the philosophical term of art introduced in {1}. Between them these two problems have largely resisted materialistic explanation, despite many brave attempts.

This is not to deny that many "soft" problems of consciousness have been solved. There is currently a plethora of theories explaining how the brain works, and how the brain may do the things that we expect of a conscious mind. Such successes may lead us to theorize that consciousness arises, for example (following Tononi, discussed in {9}), when the "integrated information" in the brain rises above a certain level. But we cannot know whether or not it arises in all organisms above that level, and none below. And more importantly we cannot explain *why*, at that level of integrated information, or whatever, consciousness arises. This is because information is one category of thing, qualia another.

As Wilfrid Sellars protested to Daniel Dennett—one materialist to another—over a bottle of fine wine, "Qualia are what make life worth living."[32] It is unfortunate then that materialists find qualia problematic. Qualia do so because, as noted, they represent the residue of quality that is left when science has accounted for as much as it can in terms of the primary quantities. Qualia are those properties that we can only denote by qualitative, rather than quantitative, descriptions like "red," "rumbling," "smooth," and "painful." By definition, or by the very procedure of scientific description, these will be precisely the factors that cannot be identified or correlated with scientifically measurable physical quantities, or correlated by science's mathematical laws.

Of course, on one level we may be able partly to explain a quale, at least in terms of some of the causally connected physical events, in the brain and in the outside world, with which it is correlated. We may for instance partly explain the color red in terms of light of wavelength 700–635 nanometers,[33] or pain in terms of the firing of C fibers and/or Aδ fibers in the brain. But even if these explanations tell us (some of)[34] what happens physically when

---

32. Recorded in Dennett, *Consciousness Explained*, 383.

33. Actually it is a bit more complex than a correlation of red with a particular wavelength, but this does not affect the argument.

34. The language here and in the previous sentence is cautious, not only because in practice we are a long way off making complete identifications between mind and brain

we experience red or pain, they do not explain the color red itself, or tell us "what it is like"[35] to experience red or pain. They do not explain why light of wavelength 700–635nm, impacting on the eye and so ultimately exciting the visual cortex the brain, should produce the visual quale we call red, rather than say green or the sound of trumpets; or why the excitation of C fibers should be felt as a throbbing ache, while that of Aδ fibers is felt as a sharp pain. As Huxley famously noted in the opening quote, the arising of consciousness out of the excitation of neurons remains as mysterious as the arising of the djinn upon the rubbing of Aladdin's lamp.

A number of now familiar philosophical fables serve to sharpen our sense of this lacuna, including thought experiments like Mary's room, the inverted spectrum, Nagel's bat, and zombies, and also actual occurrences like coincidental variation. These will now be discussed.

Mary's hypothetical room occurs in the *knowledge argument* of Frank Jackson.[36] Mary has lived all her life in a black and white room, so she has never experienced color. However, she has read many books about the brain and is familiar with the physiology of color perception, so she knows exactly what happens in the brain when someone sees that something is red. According to the materialist hypothesis, these neuron firings provide a complete account of the color red, so there is nothing new for Mary to learn about red on being released from the room and given a bright red apple. But of course, she would learn something she had not known before, namely what experiencing red is like. So the red quale must be something more than the excitation of fibers in the brain.

The *inverted spectrum*, which dates back as far as the English philosopher John Locke, but is still much discussed, raises the conceptual possibility that though color consists in the same physical events in another person and myself (wavelengths of light, such and such firings in the brain, and so forth), for all I know they may experience color differently from me. For example, their spectrum may be inverted, such that when they see light of wavelength 700nm, they see what I would see as violet, and vice versa. As a youth long before hearing of Locke, I wondered about the possibility that others might experience color in more radically different ways, for instance as I experience sounds, or in ways that are nothing like what I experience at all. All of which may seem wildly speculative, but Adam Pautz[37] has argued

---

states, but also because of the problems in principle with making such identifications (see ?{3}f).

35. The phrase introduced by the idealist philosopher Timothy Sprigge, and taken up by Thomas Nagel in his famous essay, "What It Is Like to Be a Bat" (see {6}).

36. "What Mary Didn't Know," in Block et al., *Nature of Consciousness*, 567.

37. Pautz, "A Simple View of Consciousness," in Koons, *Waning of Materialism*, 77.

for the very real possibility of what he calls "coincidental variation," namely, that two people looking at the same object may have very different experiences. Consider a dish of snails, for a person who has only experienced them as slimy garden pests, and another who has happy memories of eating them as banquet delicacies, and can discern the subtle distinctions in flavor between the different species, as others distinguish the various varieties of grape in a wine.[38] What it is like to eat a dish of snails will be very different for each person, though the physical processes involved are the same.

Thomas Nagel drove this point home by asking what it might be like to be a bat[39] (see {6}). We cannot tell, from what a bat is like in terms of physical structure, what it is like to be a bat experiencing the world through echolocation; so he argues that there is no necessary or lawlike ("nomological") connection between physical structure and activity on the one hand, and consciousness on the other. The Australian philosopher David Chalmers makes this very clear in a series of arguments beginning with his now famous "zombie" argument.[40] He argues that if we wish to assert identity of some kind, or some kind of causal relation, between brain or brain function and consciousness, nothing less than a necessary, lawlike connection between them will do. If consciousness just arises contingently in certain cases of brain activity, in the absence of any lawlike connection, then we certainly have not given any materialist explanation of consciousness. However, it is always logically possible for there to exist a brain, or better, an organism with a brain, functioning just as we with our brains do, without there being any consciousness there. In folklore of course we call such organisms—with brains but no minds or experiences or anything it is like to be them—zombies. We may intuitively feel there are no zombies, and we all probably prefer to think there are none because the idea of a zombie "spooks" us. For being animated but not conscious, a zombie blurs the boundary between life and death. But the zombie is not logically impossible.

As hypothesized in the thought experiment, the zombie has all of our brain functions: it can walk, talk, calculate, hold conversations, and work out strategies; it has auditory, visual, and tactile representations of its environment, including us. But it does not see, or feel, or otherwise experience its environment, including us. That is eerie, but alas, not logically impossible. It follows that there is no necessary connection between brain states and states of consciousness, and the latter cannot be reduced to or explained by the former. So we cannot tell from the structure of an organism (brain

---

38. The specific example is mine, not Pautz's.
39. The 1974 essay is reprinted in Nagel, *Mortal Questions*, 165–80.
40. Chalmers, *Conscious Mind*, 94.

included) whether it is conscious. We can conceive of two organisms—even two human beings—that are structurally identical, one of which is conscious, and the other not. No physical structures necessitate the presence of consciousness; therefore they do not cause or explain it.

At least, not on materialist grounds. A dualist might say the functions just cited are functions not of a brain or an organism but of a person, or at any rate something that has sensations, rather than just functional representations, of the world about it. If that is indeed the case, then an organism could not function as if it had consciousness unless it indeed did have a conscious mind, or was a conscious person. That idea would involve a necessary causal connection between conscious experience and physical function; but one that did not seek to eliminate or reduce consciousness as a causal factor. In either case, we fail to identify consciousness with the functioning of matter.

Besides the reduction of mind to matter—via its identification with matter or supervenience on matter—we noted a more drastic alternative, that of the elimination of consciousness; the idea that "really" only matter exists, and qualia and the like are mere appearances without substantial existence. Dennett argues that what we call qualia do not exist, precisely because they are only the appearance of things. Therefore, they only *seem* to exist, they do not "really exist." Referring to phenomenology, the nexus of phenomena, qualia, or appearances that supposedly exists in abstraction from the objective world, he argues:

> There seems to be phenomenology. . . . But it does not follow from this undeniable, universally attested fact that there *really is* phenomenology.[41]

In other words, since qualia are seemings, not sightings—they are how things *appear* to us, not what they *really are*—we only seem to have them, but do not really. There is an important insight here, and a significant error; I shall return shortly to both. Dennett offers several examples, including the acquiring of the taste for beer. He imagines the experienced beer drinker looking back on his first sip, and commenting:

> No one could like that flavor. . . . Beer tastes different to the experienced beer drinker. If beer went on tasting to me the way the first sip tasted, I would never have gone on drinking beer! Or, to put the same point the other way around, if my first sip of beer had tasted to me the way my most recent sip just tasted,

---

41. Dennett, *Consciousness Explained*, 366.

I would never have had to acquire the taste in the first place! I would have loved the first sip as much as the one I just enjoyed.[42]

So has the beer improved over the years, or the beer quale, the beer taste? The same problem applies to qualia generally. Has the squirrel faded, got a bit older and greyer perhaps? Or is it just the squirrel quale that has done so, because the light is poorer today, or because I have just been looking at some bright pictures? So Dennett constructs an argument along these lines:

1. We cannot always distinguish when realities really have changed and when it is our qualia or experience of them that has changed.
2. Therefore, we have no infallible access to our qualia.
3. Therefore, there are no qualia.

The non-sequitur, of course, is the step from 2 to 3. There are many supposed realities to which we have no access (infallible or otherwise), such as the conditions inside a black hole. But that does not mean such things do not exist. There is a missing supposition on the argument, let's call it "0," to the effect that a quale is by definition an experience to which one person, the experiencer, has infallible access. In discussing Descartes, we noted that, while it can be doubted that what I am experiencing is a red squirrel, it is impossible to doubt that I having an experience, and that I believe it to be an experience of a red squirrel. This indubitability argument is often advanced with respect to qualia, but I think what Dennett shows is not that there are no qualia, but that qualia are not infallible or indubitable. In other words, instead of rejecting 3, we can reject 0.

Dennett is using a plausible argument, to the effect that given their uncertain nature we cannot use qualia, as some dualists and idealists have tried to, to establish sure and certain foundations of knowledge. It does seem to be true that I am often surer that I am seeing the same squirrel than that I am seeing the same squirrel qualia; and that in general, our knowledge of qualia relies on a knowledge of objects, not vice versa. Qualia are the appearances of things, not appearing-things in the mind that represent real things "out there." This is the important point that Dennett makes about phenomenology: qualia are not (*pace* the phenomenologists) knowable things in themselves, but precisely as what their alternative name, "phenomena," suggests: the *appearances* of things. But this epistemological point cannot be used to establish the metaphysical non-existence of qualia.

We may put this in terms of the distinction between qualitative and numerical identity. Two things have qualitative identity if they are instances

---

42. Dennett, *Consciousness Explained*, 396.

of the same kind of thing, for instance if they are both red squirrels. They have numerical identity if, in addition, they are instances of the same thing, for example, if they are sightings of the very same red squirrel. What Dennett validly shows is that qualia do not have numerical identity. But that does not prevent them having qualitative identity. As their name implies, they are qualities, not particular things. We cannot identify qualia experienced at different times as instances of the same individual, as we might do, for example, in the case of a squirrel. I can ask if it is just an instance of the same kind of thing, a red squirrel: that would be a case of qualitative identity; or if it is the very same squirrel I saw yesterday: that would be a case of numerical as well as qualitative identity. To know if it is (numerically) the same squirrel, I might identify unique markings, or trace its continuous history from yesterday to today. Though I may know, for example by a particular white patch on the tail, that it is the same squirrel, I really cannot tell if my squirrel qualia are different today from what they were yesterday. They do not have the marks and suchlike that enable us to identify things as the same. But to reidentify it as (qualitatively) a squirrel I just need to be able to identify the characteristics of a squirrel, which may be a little different. Dennett shows we could not identify a recurrence of a quale as the same quale as the one I saw yesterday, but it can certainly be the same *kind* of quale. A quale is not a thing, a particular, but rather a quality, a type.[43]

Now if this is the case, Dennett's argument may be valid in his own terms. For Dennett is, I would assume, a nominalist, believing that only particular things exist. His argument shows that qualia are not identifiable as particulars. But if universals—things like "red" and "triangular" and "good" and qualities in general—exist, then surely qualia exist, as the qualities they are. Now unless you are a *Platonic* realist, qualities are properties that do not float free in their own right: they need to be predicated of a subject. So what do qualia belong to? There are two possible candidates. They could be properties of the mind. In that case, the red squirrel quale is an appearance my mind presents to itself. This would be a natural way of speaking of imaginary qualia where there is no real object for them to belong to. But in the standard, non-imaginary case it might seem natural to ascribe qualia to objects in the world. They are how objects seem to us. That is what they are in naïve realism. But we can improve on naïve realism by allowing for the possibility of mistaken identification: how something seems to me may not be how it really is. The paradigm here is the squirrel that seems grey in the moonlight. But we realize the mistake here precisely because we know

---

43. The singular, "quale" is misleading in this respect, as it suggests a particular thing; perhaps we should speak of "qualia" but not of a "quale"? See ?{3}f.

the squirrel is in fact red. If the squirrel had no real secondary qualities, we could not make a mistake here, or else we would always be wrong, because the real squirrel is thought to be colorless, lacking qualitative characteristics. But I know the squirrel is red because I have seen his "true" color in the optimal conditions of full sunlight, and also know from the tufts on his ears, and so forth, that this is one of the red squirrel species. So when I see him as grey in the moonlight I know that the qualia are wrong, and why.

Two opposite mistakes can be made with qualia. One, as noted in ?{2} d, is to move from the idea that I seem to see something to the idea that I see a seeming something, and so to think of qualia as "internal" realities that I can compare with and measure up against "external" reality. Dennett is right to question this. The other is to argue, as Dennett does regarding phenomenology, that because qualia involve cases of seeming to see, the seeming is itself something that only seems to exist. Appearances—as in "In that light he had a somewhat daunting appearance"—are surely realities in their own right, things we can consider and evaluate. They are not identical with the reality, and sentences like the one just quoted may be inviting a distinction between the appearance and the reality. Qualia, as appearances, are aspects, real things as they appear to someone in some circumstances, though not the totality of the material reality. It is surely a category mistake to ask whether qualia are real appearances or only apparent appearances. It is a mistake, either to think of them as real (in the numerically identifiable sense in which the things they are appearances of are real), or to dismiss them as non-existent.

Consider this contrast. In the first case I am driving along a trunk road. In this case my attention is focused on the reality of the road and the cars around me. It is imperative that I attend to them as material objects, evaluating their primary qualities like size, direction, speed, and momentum, and how they will causally interact with the road in the current weather conditions in relation to my own car. It will not be wise to endeavor to appreciate the finer secondary qualities of the cars and the landscape, admiring just how the red of that Porsche heading towards me blends in with the red of the setting sun. On the other hand, I may pull into a lay-by, set up my easel, and paint the trunk road as it snakes its way into the hills that are lit by the setting sun. Now I will not worry about the primary quantities of the cars, I will consider them as qualia, setting up harmonies and dissonances with other qualia in my visual field. I will notice, perhaps, the way the cars climbing that hill reflect shafts of light from the sun, and as the sun sets and the sky darkens, I will begin to notice faintly the little dots of light descending the hill into the dark valley; I may pick these things out, before I identify them as headlights. If I am (slightly) poetically inclined, I may call them shooting stars, using metaphor: calling things by names they objectively are not, but which call our attention to their appearances, their qualia.[44]

From the example we can see that there is often good reason to disregard the qualia, as when we are doing something like driving, or experimenting and measuring as a scientist does. But there are other situations where we may need to suspend judgement about the objective reality in order to focus on the qualia. There is no good reason to expand the scientific method into a metaphysical generalization.

Smart, in the passage quoted at the start of this section, was presumably considering the way consciousness represents an infinitesimal fraction of the contents of the universe; and in one sense (unless we are strong panpsychists holding that *all* matter is conscious) this is certainly true. At least, it is so if we calculate in terms of mass or volume: in those terms there is unimaginably much more inanimate than conscious matter. But to evaluate consciousness in terms of amount of matter is already to have biased the debate in terms of primary rather than secondary qualities: that is, to adopt from the start a bias against consciousness. If we calculate in terms of complexity and variety of structure: in those terms inanimate matter is relatively simple compared with the rich complexity of the human body and brain.

And considered in yet another way, the universe represents a fraction of the contents of consciousness. For all our measurements of primary qualities, whereby we access the world of physics, involve secondary qualities or qualia. The telescope can only convey the detail of the moon to me if my mind registers color; the pointer on the dial on the measuring instrument in my experiment has to register a conscious measurement. So everything that is known about the universe is registered in sensations or calculated in thoughts. Not to mention that all that makes the universe valuable and beautiful has to do with our perceptions of it and our thoughts, including mathematical thoughts, about it. Add to that, the mind's capacity to imagine infinite worlds of which this physical universe is just one (unless you conceptually inhabit {5}, the multiverse). It becomes clear that, even if physically speaking, conscious minds represent a fraction of the universe, conceptually speaking, the universe represents a fraction of the scope of minds.

44. Painting may of course aim, as in Renaissance Art (I think especially of Van Eyck), to depict the qualia as the appearances of objects as they appear to me, such that they build up a realistic-seeming world as it appears in my perceptive. Differently, as in the Impressionists, and Turner, it may suspend the concern to conjure up a vivid representation of the world, and paint the play of the qualia, the dance of light and color evoked by the world; finally (but not exhaustively), as in the abstract art of Pollock and Nicholson, it may put paint on the canvas with a view to creating new qualia simply so that we can contemplate the interplay of their color and texture.

And that introduces the subject of intentionality: a problem for materialists, and a clue for non-materialists.

?{3}e: Can Materialism Account for Intentionality?

Qualia constitute a very precise problem for materialism, and as noted, these have been discussed in relation to several neat thought experiments. Probably many organisms other than human beings have qualia, since for the most part their sense organs function in similar ways to ours. Echolocation, fishes' sensitivity to magnetism, and suchlike, which have no counterparts in our sense perceptions, are the exception rather than the rule. Intentionality is a much wider and more diffuse matter, concerning the expansiveness of the mind and its ability to relate to and be about anything that exists, as well as things that do not. As far as we know, intentionality occurs only in linguistic animals, which means, for the most part, and perhaps exclusively, human beings.[45]

When philosophers and others speak of "the problem of consciousness," they often mean the problem of qualia. But "consciousness" is an aspect of intentionality, that is, our ability, when undergoing an experience, to be aware of it in different ways, including being aware of this awareness, and being aware of that awareness in turn, potentially ad infinitum. Qualia arise through an aspect of intentionality, namely our ability to attend to what something seems like to us. I can shift from being conscious of the red squirrel itself to being aware of how it appears to me, and what it is like to see that redness. As just noted, I can shift from the attention needed to drive a car to that required for painting the landscape, qualia being attended to for what they are in the latter, but merely a means to an end in the former. So it makes sense to move from the precise problem of qualia to the wider issues of intentionality.

Intentionality arises whenever we entertain ideas *about* something. Anyone who has meditated will be aware of the "monkey mind" that is forever leaping about thinking about one thing after another: one moment, about the nature of dark matter or angels; the next, about what I am going to cook for supper, and whether I have all the ingredients. The intended object may be something that exists physically, like the red squirrel; or only conceptually, like its redness or the fact that it is on the lawn, or a triangle, or

---

45. Some argue that whale sounds and the like indicate a degree of intentionality, and that certain sounds uttered by the higher primates seem to be about, of example, the proximity of food or predators.

the number five;[46] or only in the imagination, like the unicorn. It is through intentionality that the conceptual "world" comes into existence, if indeed it does exist; more on this in {4}. It is also, arguably, through intentionality that final and formal causes begin to operate. Through our wanting, the world comes to possess goals, and things begin to happen not only because they are efficiently caused, but because we want to cause them to happen. And things begin to happen because of their place in a pattern that we understand.

Though Wilfred Sellars believed that qualia are what make life worth living, surely intentionality plays its part also. Imagine the tedium of a world that consisted only of a sequence of qualia, even pleasant qualia, if we lacked the ability to think about these qualia, or to imagine other qualia that might become goals for our actions, so that we might come to enjoy them, or attribute them to others. Some qualia are inherently enjoyable, but others are tastes I might try to acquire, or to overcome. As well as the sheer pleasure (or pain) of qualia there is what we call enjoyment, and dislike, and fear, and other emotions toward qualia, all of which have an intentional aspect of thinking of the qualia as aspects of objects that may do us good or harm.

For as well as having different kinds of object, intentionality consists in different kinds of relation. The five (or so) grammatical moods of sentences provide a good way of classifying these.

- *Indicative*: thinking, meaning, talking about, remembering, depicting . . . that squirrel, or squirrels generally.
- *Interrogative*: enquiring about, arguing about, reasoning, scientifically studying . . . that squirrel, or the red squirrel as a species.
- *Optative*: desiring, wanting, hoping, fearing . . . the squirrel for a pet, or its eating the bird-food.
- *Imperative*: stating what should or must be done . . . about the grey squirrel and its threat to the red, etc. ?{3}k will consider ethics, but clearly feeling something must be done is a case of intentionality.
- *Subjunctive*: imagining what is not but might be . . . a giant squirrel that terrorizes the neighborhood, or a cuddly one that talks to his friend Mr. Rabbit.

It is clear that a lot of intentionality relates to our use of language (in voiced conversations, or silent ones in our minds) to engage with our world. Not all of it does, however: a painting or diagram can be about things in the world, though arguably one has to make some kind of linguistic

---

46. Nominalists would not believe such things "exist" of course.

interpretation of what a painting is about. "Ah yes, it's a red squirrel, isn't it?" One of the arguments for limiting intentionality to the human, linguistic animal is that non-linguistic animals tend not to respond to pictures or mirror images.

In this connection, one of the arguments of the eliminativists may be turned on its head: namely the argument that the self and its qualia represent a fiction in which the brain constructs a supposed unity out of elements that are in reality disparate. This very fiction-making nature, which we undoubtedly possess, is itself a case of intentionality. Something is creating, out of disparate and often discontinuous elements, a seamless and unified narrative. That something is not plausibly a diverse welter of neurons firing. The eliminativists argue, from the diversity of the elements, that the unified mind is an illusion. But the argument points the other way: to the necessity, if this unity is being constructed, of a unifying mind.

That in essence is the problem intentionality presents to materialism. Who or what is making all this story up? Is it plausible that something as diverse yet finite as a brain might construct something as unified yet boundless as the intentionality that is the distinctive activity of the mind? All the areas of intentionality—believing, knowing, studying, reasoning, imagining, inventing, and so forth—require more than mechanical calculation: the demand for a conscious, intention-framing interpreter cannot be avoided.

For example, we all entertain a potential infinity of beliefs, though we are conscious of only a fraction of them at any given time. For example, you and I both believe that 2,333,542 x 414,838 = 968,041,896,196. I believe this on the strength of my calculator. It is the first time I have done that particular calculation, but now that I have done it on an instrument I have always found reliable, I believe it. You could check it on your calculator, and if you do you will find yourself believing it to be true. I could of course check the calculator result using pencil and paper. I don't think I could have worked it out in my head: machines like computers and calculators, and even pencil and paper (which represent arguably the simplest form of computer), are quicker and better than brains in this respect. But the machine alone could not generate the true belief. I might let a monkey watch my keystrokes and observe the outcome on the screen, but I doubt if that would generate in the monkey a belief that 2,333,542 x 414,838 = 968,041,896,196. For my keystrokes and the resulting figures on the screen to be an arithmetical operation generating this result, rather than just a complicated way of producing patterns on a screen, a conscious, intentional being has to interpret the intentionality behind what is going on.

The problem, as I said, is not that the brain lacks power, or that there aren't enough brain states to represent our potential thoughts. There are approximately 100,000,000,000 neurons in the brain, so if each neuron is taken to be either firing or not firing—two possible states—the number of possible global brain states is $2^{100,000,000,000}$ or more than $10^{30,000,000,000}$, 1 followed by 30 billion zeroes. If we all had about ten thoughts per second, then even in the lifetime of the universe we could not have nearly that many thoughts between us. The problem is not the limited capacity of the brain to contain the intentionality of the mind; it is rather that if the brain is a material complex following only physical laws (which is what materialists of all sorts must presuppose), then it is not the right category of thing to do intentional acts like meaning, believing, and knowing propositions, having concepts, and reasoning about and proving truths. For a physical operation producing a physical output cannot give rise to any of those intentional acts without an interpreting mind. If we suppose that a physical process can interpret itself, and so make meaning, by a physical process alone, we create self-defeating paradoxes, and deprive our own arguments (including our argument that intentionality is a physical process) of any meaning.

The functionalist kind of materialist would, of course, try to explain intentionality in terms of function. This is a dubious strategy. What function (evolutionary or otherwise) might be served by devoting so much of our brains to knowing arithmetical truths like 233,3542 x 414,838 = 968,041,896,196, wondering about the right thing to do, and appreciating music, to name but three examples? But even if we did know what functions intentionality serves, it still floats free of genuine explanation, as David Bentley Hart vividly illustrates.

> If I should visit you at your home and discover that, rather than living in a house, you instead shelter under a large roof that simply hovers above the ground, apparently neither supported by nor suspended from anything else, and should ask you how this is possible, I should not feel at all satisfied if you were to answer, "It's to keep the rain out"—not even if you were then helpfully to elaborate upon this by observing that keeping the rain out is evolutionarily advantageous.[47]

Equally vivid as an argument against reducing intentionality to function is a well-known thought experiment by Ned Block.[48] (It is versed as a critique of the functionalist form of materialism, but it would not be hard to tweak it to apply to other kinds.) He notes that the number of neurons in the brain is of the same order as the number of people in China. (The precise number is not vital to the argument.) Suppose we came, as materialists

47. Hart, *Experience of God*, 205.
48. Block, "Troubles with Functionalism," in Block, *Consciousness*, 63.

claim we will, to know the exact way in which the neurons in the brain function and work together. Imagine that we gave the people of China the same kinds of connection and transmission of messages as happens in the brain, so that the way the Chinese people functioned paralleled exactly the way the brain functions. If consciousness is necessarily determined by the function of the brain, we would have to conclude that there was a consciousness pertaining to the people of China, not as individuals but as a collective functioning in this way. The population of China, would have to have thoughts and experiences, as functions of their collective activity. Of course, the Chinese are not special in this regard. Any objects—computer circuits, or bowls of water, correlated and functioning in the same way as neurons in the brain—would have to have consciousness, if consciousness is a lawlike, necessary consequence of brain function. And if consciousness is not necessarily connected, but is just what we have called a "brute supervenience" on brain states but not people-of-China states, then we can no longer assert an identity between brain function and consciousness.

In practice it is not very likely that the people of China could be persuaded collectively to turn their lives over to the stated experiment, or even if they could, that we will ever know the brain in sufficient precision to know exactly what instructions to give them. But it is not in principle impossible for the people of China, or full and empty water bowls, plus suitable instructions, to be what is called a Turing machine, that is, to imitate the functions of a computer. But whether we made the interactions of our Chinese people or our bowls mimic a computer and a brain, it would not generate in our chosen medium any consciousness, any intentional awareness of what it was doing. Our input would generate an output, but these would just be the initial and final states of the medium. To know what these states meant, for the process to carry information, requires a conscious interpreter, an expert in meaning.

The philosopher John Searle presented another Chinese thought experiment to show this: the Chinese Room. This is a room where we can post, through a hatch, questions in Chinese, and get posted back to us intelligent answers in Chinese; but we cannot see what is happening inside the room. Consider these three cases.

1. The questions are entered into a computer, which runs a program designed to come up with the answers and return them to us.
2. The questions are put to a Chinese speaker, who types out the answers for us.

3. The questions are put to someone who doesn't understand Chinese, but is able to check the questions against a phrase book that comes up with matching answers.

Now all three cases are functionally equivalent, giving us correct answers to our questions. For a functionalist, or a strong advocate of Artificial Intelligence, there is nothing to distinguish them.[49] All could be said to understand Chinese. But intuitively there is a deep difference between case 2 and the others, and only the person involved in 2 can be said to understand Chinese, and therefore, to understand that she is engaging in a process of question and answer. The other two are both relying on a mechanical algorithm without any understanding of what they are doing. The example seems to show that only intentionality (possessed by the person doing the asking, and by the hidden person in case 2, but not by the computer or person in the other two cases) gives the physical output *meaning*; the meaning of a physical outcome cannot be settled by physical processes alone.[50] Edward Feser comments:

> There is nothing intrinsic to the nature of anything in the material world that makes it a computer, or that makes it true that it is implementing a program. It is all a matter of interpretation: our interpretation. . . . If computation is observer-relative, then that means that its existence presupposes the existence of observers, and thus the existence of minds; so obviously, it cannot be appealed to in order to explain observers or minds themselves.[51]

Suppose I were to take this typescript that I am writing now, and convert it from being a "Word" file to being a "JPEG" file, a kind of image file. As far as my computer goes, it would be the same file, with a slightly different ending to its name. It would be the same string of binary code. But the picture my computer would produce, if it did produce one,[52] would be gibberish to me. However, it would not be any more meaningless to the computer than it is as a Word document. It is *to me* that the binary string translated into picture format would be gibberish, impossible for me to interpret, by contrast with the Word file, which to me is at least relatively less full of gibberish!

---

49. Philosophers would say they all pass the Turing Test.
50. Searle, "Minds Brains and Programs." Cf also Searle, *Intentionality* and *Rediscovery*.
51. Feser, *Philosophy of Mind*, Loc. 2525.
52. Most computers, of course, are too clever to try to do this.

Could we, in principle, construct a computer more like a brain, such that it could, by its own physical means, interpret its own content, and understand the concepts involved in my Word document, and maybe come up with a refutation proving after all that intentionality has a physical basis? It is true that we now have software that can suggest improvements to grammar, and in the case of pictures, aesthetic improvements. But of course, there is nothing in the computer that has not been put in there by human programmers. And even when computers can rewrite and improve their own programs—which we are beginning to enable them to do—still the programs that result need to be tested by humans to assess whether the changes really are what humans judge to be improvements, or whether the computer is running away up its own blind alley (or worse, beginning to develop an intention of taking over the human species!)

The physical irreducibility of intentionality is not just a temporary limit that our science can overcome; the limit is logical. If we suppose that intention and meaning can be identified with material processes, vicious regresses and strange paradoxes result. Suppose, for example, I were to observe, on my neuron-detector, the brain events associated with understanding the connection between brain events and conscious intentionality. What are my brain events now doing, for *now* I am not just understanding the connection between brain events and mind events, but observing the brain events connected with understanding that connection? And now I am observing the brain events associated with observing the brain states connected with *that* understanding. And so on, in infinite regress. Now infinite regresses do not harm intentionality: one aspect of intentionality, as noted, is self-consciousness, and one aspect of that is consciousness of self-consciousness, and so on. The infinite in this regress is a potential infinite, which we cannot pursue to its end, since after a while we will want to think about something else. But an infinite regress instantiated in the actuality of matter is a more severe problem. It is the kind of regress that lies behind Gödel's proof that no self-consistent system can generate a complete set of truths; that is, there can be no mechanical algorithm for the production of all truth, in arithmetic at least. Gödel's proof is another way of telling us that intentional issues of knowledge cannot be reduced to physical algorithms or "fact factories" in the brain; more on this in {4}.

In the end, if either the eliminative or the functionalist forms of materialism produce a materialist account of intentionality, in the process they necessarily eliminate or functionalize the mind and the rationality on which their own arguments for this depend. For whereas arguments are intentional propositions connected by logic and persuasive power, our brains consist of neurons and synapses connected by physical cause and effect. In materialism, our beliefs are not primarily "true" or "false," but simply something produced by the operation of our brains. In which case, there could be no reasons for believing materialism to be true or false; all we could say is that in some (but not all) brains, such and such nerve processes cause nerve patterns associated with belief in materialism.

If this is so, the aim of the New Atheist should not be to argue and so persuade people's minds not to believe in God. In materialistic terms, the materialists have a brain state that disposes them not to worship or say phrases like "God exists." The aim (if they can have an aim) must be to produce brain states that give other people similar dispositions not to believe in or worship God. To that end, argument regarding truth will be at best a minor part of their effort, since rhetoric and emotive appeals, not to mention threats of torture and physical violence if people do worship God, may prove much more effective in changing such behavior. In which case the dialectical materialists (and shame to say, the Christian inquisitions) in their use of terror, and Friedrich Nietzsche in his reduction of truth to the play of power, have essentially got it right.

?{3}f: Mental Identity and Physical Identity

Behind the issues of qualia and intentionality there lurks the question of physical versus mental identity. Brain-mind identity needs a clear notion of how we identify brain states and mind states so as to be able to correlate them. Functionalism meanwhile requires a clear notion of how brain states could function together to produce the various forms of intentionality. But a mind seems to be a whole thing, a unity, that can reach out limitlessly to engage with anything that exists, and things that have no existence too, and weave relationships of various kinds, including logical relationships, between these things and between itself and these things/nothings. A brain (on the materialist understanding) has to be conceived of as an interconnected complex of parts relating by means of efficient causality only. On the face of it, the idea of any kind of identity between mind and brain, or mind elements and brain elements, seems to constitute a category mistake, like trying to draw comparisons between a squirrel and the idea of courage, or between the color red and the number twelve.

One big problem here is that mental simples, if they are anything physical, are physical complexes, not physical simples; while physical simples are mental complexes, not mental simples. Physically the simplest things in the universe are the entities it is made of, since by definition everything made of them would be more complex. These simple entities may be quarks, or superstrings, or something else, according to your theory. Whichever it is, they are immensely complex in conceptual, mind terms, requiring a mastery of quantum mechanics, chromodynamics (quark theory), and/or string theory. Few human minds possess a full understanding of these mentally complex physical simples.

Conversely, mental simples might include qualia, and also elementary ideas, like that of a circle, that of red, and that of a square. These can then be put together to form slightly more complex ideas like red squares, red circles and square circles. It is immediately apparent to the mind that the first two concepts work well, but the third does not. But what happens in the brain when we entertain these simple ideas would be a much more complex set of neuron firings. The mentally simple is physically complex, so complex that full understanding of the brain will take decades to come, if it comes at all.

The first identity problem we note is that it is hard to identify particular neurons and their synaptic connections. Neurons and synapses do not have labels, and they vary from person to person, and within a given person's life, since they develop and deteriorate through time. So though of course we have general maps identifying parts of the brain associated with the senses, bodily actions, and even emotions, it is impossible to make a detailed map positioning all the neurons of the brain. That means we cannot say, for example, that when people think of squares, the neuron at position 1262 3852 8539 (using some kind of grid reference for the brain) fires, as well as . . . and proceed to list all the firing neurons by their locations.

It is plausible that we can only identify neurons by the ideas they characteristically accompany. This is what we do when we identify the parts of the brain cortex associated with sight, sound, smell, hope, fear, and so forth. But it follows that all we could say in the case of thinking of a square is that when we do so, the neurons associated with thought about squares fire. This is virtually tautological and hardly informative; all we would be affirming in practice is that brain activity and mind activity are associated somehow.

But what then happens when we think about the color red? Would it be the case that the neurons associated with red fired (presumably not the same as those that fire when I see red, or else I would not be able to distinguish experiencing red from thinking about it). And then, when I think about a red square, would the neurons that fired be those associated with thinking about red plus those associated with thinking about a square? Or would that be what happened when I think about red and about a square, simultaneously?

Then when I came to think about a square circle, which neurons would fire? And how would the impossibility of this concept register in terms of neuron-firings? Could we find the answer experimentally? No, for the situation is this: we can only find the answer we are looking for (for example, whether particular neurons are identifiable with thinking about a square) by presupposing the answer (namely, that the neurons that fire when I think of a square are the ones about which I am testing as to whether they fire whenever I think of a square). The situation is analogous to looking for a jabberwock[53] in a forest. Somebody asks me what a jabberwock is, and I respond by saying, "We'll only know when we find one." So it is when we look for the neural correlates of ideas in the forest of the brain.[54]

The situation becomes yet more complex if a materialist tries to hold on to a correspondence theory of truth. Being realists, and with their inheritance from the dualists, most materialists[55] want to say that a belief is true if and only if it corresponds to how things physically are. As noted, the dualist version of correspondence gave us the problem of how a mental squirrel could correspond with the physical one "out there." With reductive materialism the problem of correspondence is doubled: how the brain state arising when I see a squirrel can correspond with the squirrel qualia, and how those qualia in turn might correspond with the actual squirrel. With eliminative materialism, the middle, mental term is eliminated, leaving us with an even huger problem: in what sense can a squirrel-seeing brain-state correspond with the real squirrel?

The root problem here is that, as noted, we individuate both our qualia and physical reality by means of intentionality. When we identify something as a squirrel quale, we are applying our (intentional) ideas of what constitutes a red squirrel. If we did not know about squirrels, we would see rather the quale of a furry red animal. But also, as just argued, we identify a brain state as a squirrel-seeing brain state because, again, we have (intentional) ideas about squirrels. The mind and its various kinds of intentionality has priority in our identification, both of experiences, and of items in the physical world: a fact that leads us towards {4} and {7} especially.

So far I have simplified matters in the interests of clarity. When philosophers speak of brain-mind identity, they have in mind two kinds of identity: type-type identity and token-token identity. The distinction between tokens and types was introduced by the American philosopher C. S. Pierce; it is related to the distinction introduced above between numerical and qualitative identity. To understand the distinction, ask how many words there are in the sentence "A rose is a rose is a rose." We could correctly answer eight or

---

53. A creature featuring in Lewis Carroll's nonsense poem, "Jabberwocky."

54. The question of the relation of intentional versus physical identity and properties, and how ideas combine, is argued with greater subtlety by Michael Jubien in "Dualizing Materialism," in *Waning of Materialism,* esp. 529.

55. There are exceptions, such as the pragmatists and relativists.

three. There are eight *tokens* or instances of words. But some are instances of the same word *type*, of which there are only three: "a," "rose," and "is."

Type-type identity argues that to each type of mind event there corresponds a type of brain event. It is now generally conceded that type-type mind-brain identity is unworkable, partly for the reasons already given: namely, that the types of thing that go on in the mind are radically unlike the types of thing that go on in the brain. Mind and brain "divide up," and also "connect up" in different ways, according to different logics. So mostly when philosophers affirm mind-brain identity, it is of the token-token variety. That is, they assert that to each mind event there corresponds a brain event. Depending on what flavor of materialism one adopts, the "correspondence" involved will be a strong identity, a logical supervenience, or a weaker "brute" supervenience of mind states upon brain states.

Now if all that is being considered here is particular brain and mind "tokens," it seems that no lawlike, repeatable connections could be established. Consider the rose sentence. If we are thinking about types, we can notice repeated patterns: for instance, the word-type "a" is always followed by the word-type "rose." In the same way one might note lawlike connections between types of brain state and types of mind state. But if we consider only tokens, we have, in the case of the sentence, a sequence of words; in the case of the brain, a sequence of brain states; and in the case of mind, a sequence of mind-states. End of story. So all that mind-brain identity is now asserting is that the sequence of our brain states is identical with, or supervenes upon, the sequence of our mind states. If we ask which kinds of brain state correspond with which kinds of mind state, we are asking the type question with all its problems. What is being asserted is now simply that for each individual mind state, we can observe an accompanying brain state. But this observation, being the observation of a particular token, is one-off, not experimentally repeatable. And I suspect that we still face the problem of how we pick out and identify the relevant token brain-state except as the one that corresponds to this particular token mind-state.

In all, then, type-type mind-brain identity (or supervenience) is too strong to work, while token-token mind-brain identity (or supervenience) is too weak to assert anything testable or significant. Mind and brain events have different kinds of identity. Does this mean we have to return to substance dualism? We shall see that there are other options. Meanwhile, one of the ways in which the different identities of mind and brain becomes manifest is in the different kinds of causality involved. Physical causality, for an orthodox materialist, is determinist; intentional causality, if it exists, involves freedom in the choice of goals and how to achieve them. And that brings us to the next query.

?{3}g: Is the World Deterministic?

We considered above the possibility that the world may be materialistically reducible in terms of substances and properties, without being deterministic, suggesting that there may be physical evidence of non-determinism at some levels, and that it may ultimately be impossible to know whether the physical universe runs on deterministic lines. ?{3}b meanwhile discussed the tension between two tenets of materialism, namely nominalism and determinism, in that nominalism cannot articulate the "must" of determinism, explaining why in virtue of its causal laws the world must be as it is. If materialists wish to retain nominalism, then, the best they can offer is the rather paradoxical notion that the fact that the world has to be as it is is inexplicable: that the necessity of what happens is a contingent fact. Or else, more plausibly, they may retain determinism as a methodological principle for science, but abandon any absolute metaphysical determinism. It will then be argued, pragmatically, that scientists prove most successful at discovering theories when they work on the principle that all events are determined by previous events according to deterministic laws.

But determinism is a close ally of naturalism, since if determinism is false, nature ceases to be causally closed, being open to supernatural and other non-physical, non-efficient causes. In the interests of keeping naturalism then, philosophers may wish to dispense with nominalism, as in {4}. The problem with that is that it opens another route beyond naturalism, since ideas, though non-physical, may now be thought of as real. As a more modest alternative, we may wish to retain naturalism but only as, itself, a methodological principle. Naturalism and determinism then become methodological principles for scientists rather than metaphysical tenets for everyone. In that case, while it is held that scientists, to be taken seriously, must operate on naturalistic and deterministic assumptions, others, who are not doing science but, say, making ethical decisions, writing poetry, or worshipping God, are free to be as indeterminist as they like, and maybe have to be indeterminist in order to fulfil their respective non-scientific callings.

One final wriggle available for the determinist who does not wish to take these options is to argue, as some have, that the necessity of laws of nature is "nomological," by which is meant something stronger than Hume's constant conjunction, but weaker than "metaphysical" necessity. It is argued that, though metaphysical necessity requires the reality of laws and the mathematical structures that express them, nomological necessity does not. However, nomological merely means "law-based," and it seems to me a special category is here being invoked just to allow determinists and other believers in natural law to wriggle out of metaphysical realism; no sound explanation is given for why nomological laws have real force in the world without themselves being real.

Finally, the issues of determinism and consciousness interconnect. Mathematical laws can only connect mathematical, quantifiable structures. Qualia and qualities are by definition not quantifiable. So there could be no mathematical law for the production of consciousness and the qualitative, qualia-full world consciousness involves. If the necessity of natural laws derives from their mathematically formulable nature, then there can be no necessary connection between physical states and mind states.

?{3}h: Are Reductionism and Determinism Regressive?

Reductionism explains the properties of things in terms of the properties and relations of smaller things that constitute them, but can this reduction continue forever? As Max Tegmark (whom we will encounter more in {4} and {5}) explains,

> A famous thorny issue in philosophy is the so-called *infinite regress problem*. For example, if we say that the properties of a diamond can be explained by the properties and arrangements of its carbon atoms, that the properties of a carbon atom can be explained by the properties and arrangements of its protons, neutrons and electrons, that the properties of a proton can be explained by the properties and arrangements of its quarks, and so on, then it seems that we're doomed to go on forever trying to explain the properties of the constituent parts.[56]

This regress of explanations opens up the possibility that all we have is what philosophers call "gunk," an endless succession of layers of explanation with no fundamental bedrock. Or else (Tegmark's option) there are no fundamental constituents of the world, only structures of relations without relata.

There is a similar possible regress in determinism, in that it explains events in terms of previous events that necessitated them, and those events in turn are explained in terms of the preceding events that explain them, and so on, ad infinitum. In the absence of some self-explanatory, necessary being that caused events in the first place, how can determinism actually determine and render necessary *any* event? Such arguments have of course been used to "prove" God's existence (see {8}), though there are other contenders for the necessarily existent, regress-stopping bottom layer of the universe. Philosopher of Science Rom Harré argues for ultimate fields of

---

56. Tegmark, *Mathematical Universe*, 266.

force, which have a causal effect without being themselves either material or made up of material constituents. Positing such fields of force as the ultimate level of explanation offers the possibility of a non-reductionist determinism (-R -Q D), as does Tegmark's alternative resolution of the regresses in {4}. However, Harré still leaves unresolved the question of why these particular force-fields are the ones that operate in our universe.

?{3}i: Can Materialism Tell Us What Things Are?

Science hypothesizes many realities of which it could be said we do not know what they are. What *is* a quark, a string, dark matter, dark energy, space-time, a quantum, gravity energy, matter itself . . . ? Such things are defined in terms of each other in a system whereby they coherently interrelate, but no scientist can say what each one is. The world consists of laws and relations connecting we know not what.

Is this reasonable? Bertrand Russell derides the idea:

> There are many possible ways of turning some things hitherto regarded as "real" into mere laws concerning the other things. Obviously there must be a limit to this process, or else all the things in the world will merely be each other's washing.[57]

Philosophers distinguish between intrinsic (or categorial) and dispositional properties. The former are properties things have in themselves, the latter the tendencies they have to change and be changed by other things. Normally science tries to account for dispositional properties by means of intrinsic ones. Lead has a tendency to sink in water because it consists in heavy atoms that bind much more densely than water, which consists in lighter atoms, hydrogen and oxygen. But of course already we are explaining "binding" qualities as dispositions explained in turn in terms of atoms with their intrinsic properties; and those in turn can be regarded as dispositions of yet more fundamental particles. For the structural realists of {4}, dispositions to change and be changed according to laws of nature are in the end all there are.

Russell agrees that dispositions to act according to laws is all that science can tell us about nature, but he regarded this as unsatisfactory, because it led to a superficial view in which everything in nature is, in Russell's striking terms, something else's "washing." Everything is ultimately caused by, or a property of, we know not what. And that means nothing is fundamentally explained, and no properties are fundamentally had by anything.

---

57. Russell, *Analysis of Matter*, 325.

Now it may be the case that science cannot answer the question of what the universe really consists in; what really "has" the properties, and what really causes and undergoes the interactions, which we observe. But we expect more of a worldview than that.

How does the dispositional-versus-intrinsic distinction relate to the familiar primary-versus-secondary distinction? One answer would be that these are different distinctions that cut across each other. But we might like the world to divide more neatly than that. There are two parsimonious ways of folding the distinctions together. One is to say that the only "real" properties and relations are the primary and dispositional ones, and the secondary and intrinsic properties do not really exist, only seem to. This is the austere answer we will encounter in {4}. The alternative answer accepts the same reasonable assimilation of the dispositional and primary as the object of science, and the intrinsic and secondary as that which is too subjective for science to touch; but it affirms the latter as real nonetheless. This is the proposal of {6}, panpsychism. In {4}, matter as a fundamental explanatory substance disappears, leaving only number and relation. In {6}, matter is retained, but expanded to embrace mental or experiential properties. In either case the matter of classical materialism is transcended. In order to give a fully explanatory worldview, both alternatives go beyond what science alone can discover, but in opposite directions.

?{3}j: Can Naturalism Provide a Complete Worldview?

Probably if asked to draw an emblem or icon for science, many people would draw a telescope, that key invention leading to so many discoveries in the early, heroic age of modern science. A telescope diffracts light so that we can see lots of detail we could not otherwise discern: stars, planets, moons, distant galaxies, the surface of our moon. But in the process of enlarging a small area of vision, a telescope shuts out the periphery. It is not a good idea to drive a car using a telescope, because, though the view of the number plate of the car ahead may be superb, vital information, like the fact that you have wandered into the opposite lane, and there is traffic heading straight towards you, may be hidden from view.

Essentially all experimental apparatus is like a telescope, and all science, as it uses such apparatus, is like using a telescope. For such apparatus serves to bring into view, and make discernible and measurable, things we otherwise would not be able to observe and measure. The apparatus turns otherwise non-sensible realities into sensible secondary qualities whereby we can measure primary quantities. But it does so by shutting out, and rendering non-sensible, other aspects of experience. Most experiments enable us to discover things by excluding what is deemed irrelevant to the matter being studied or the theory being tested, and most scientific predictions contain the explicit or implicit rider, "other things being equal." In science as in vision we gain in accuracy by losing out in the complex range of our experience. So the question raises itself: do we get the best view of reality by always looking through telescopes or the equivalent; or for a complete vision, do we need to turn away from our apparatus, and absorb reality in a more diffuse and total way.

Science is often considered as a body of knowledge of the world. That is how a Cartesian dualist and many a materialist would understand it. But it is perhaps better considered as a vast complex of measuring apparatuses plus methodologies for using them to extend our seeing of and operating on the world.[58] The questions that then arise are: how far can science extend our experience; and are there senses in which in the act of doing so, science can also blind us to experience? Are there are limits to what science can help us see, or will science one day, as one story of progress tells us, enable us to understand everything?

In a masterly little booklet, the Nobel prize-winning biologist Peter Medawar asks whether there will always be more for science to discover, or will science one day come to an end? And (our different but related question) are there some things science cannot discover, or will science one day tell us all there is to know? His answer is that there is "no limit upon the power of science to answer questions of the kind that science can answer."[59] He notes the astounding success of science in answering scientific questions, settling issues rationally "beyond reasonable doubt" in a way that philosophy and religion never manage to. But he argues that there are questions that are not of the kind that science can answer: for example, the origin of the universe, and life's purpose and meaning. He concludes,

> I do not believe . . . that the exercise of reason is *sufficient* to explain our condition and where necessary to remedy it, but I do believe that the exercise of reason is at all times unconditionally *necessary* and that we disregard it at our peril.[60]

To sum up, in terms of our analogy, the telescope of science is brilliant at doing what it does, and there is no limit to the ways in which its power to bring reality within our sensible and operational reach may be extended.

---

58. See, for example, Polanyi, *Personal Knowledge*; Barad, *Meeting the Universe Half Way*, and one interpretation of Kuhn's paradigms.

59. Medawar, *Limits of Science*, 88.

60. Medawar, *Limits of Science*, 98.

But there are matters that lie outside the frame of the scientific telescope. To approach them, Medawar insists we must not let go of our exercise of reason, though reason will not settle them. The question remaining, therefore, is whether there are ways of looking at the world that are wide enough in scope to approach, if not settle, the wider issues of origin, meaning, and purpose, while remaining rational.

{5} will visit the question of origins, and the related question of why the laws of the universe are as they are. Later Worlds will look at meaning and purpose. For now, a word about a key, related area where scientific materialism may not be able to help us.

?{3}k: Can Materialism Generate Ethics?

"Sorry, we can't help it. It's the way we're brought up round here."

Such was the half-apology of one member of a gang of youths that had just thrown stones and broken my window in the urban parish where I once served as priest. It illustrates perfectly what determinism can do to ethics. Traditional ethics relies on the idea that our actions result from our free decisions. This requires a teleological causation whereby we, as individuals, entertain purposes and seek to bring them into effect by our actions. As is well known, accounts of ethics vary. For some, what makes an action right are its consequences; in another, it is having the right purposes in doing the action; in another, it is conformity to revealed or rationally derived standards; and in yet another, it is being a good or virtuous person who will be disposed to do the right thing. But in all of these cases, the presupposition is that the person wills and does the action. In materialism, on the other hand—except, possibly, non-determinist materialism—the real causes of the action are efficient causes acting in the brain. Purpose is either non-existent, as in eliminative materialism, or a mere appearance or epiphenomenon. What made the youth throw the stone at the window was not really his desire to break it, or his desire to annoy me by means of breaking it, but rather a causal chain with possible origins in his genetic makeup, his childhood experience, and the complex interactions within his brain.[61]

Now determinism is good news for the dialectical materialist Marxist, since it means that once the conditions in society are changed, and injustices are ironed out, people will change accordingly to fit the new society. There is no need to argue and debate, appealing to people's conscience to

---

61. Of course, the boy quoted showed an ironic understanding of this viewpoint that indicates he may be less determined by his environment, and have more free choice, than his words suggested.

choose the true and the good; rather, it is a case of carefully controlling the information input into people in order to produce better outputs. But for the liberal capitalist version of materialism there is a problem, because liberal capitalism relies so heavily on notions of democratic debate and free choice, but in the post-Enlightenment materialist accounts that so often accompany this liberalism, free choice does not exist.

So there have arisen many attempts to show that morality can indeed be founded on a materialist basis. Now my experience tells me that many materialists are good people, with high ideals. The problem is that on their own account they have no need to be. If determinism is true, our ideals are at best the epiphenomenon attending certain kinds of brain activity, while really our actions are produced elsewhere. What the materialists produce, time and again, with minor variations, is some explanation of the causes of altruism, usually in terms of its evolutionary benefits. But to offer cause as if it were a justification is to commit the "naturalistic fallacy."[62] The youth committed this fallacy when he argued (tongue in cheek, I think) that his bad childhood, which (perhaps) caused or explained his action, thereby justified or excused it. So the fact (if it is a fact) that evolution determines that I will do this generous or self-sacrificial act (say, diving in to save a child) does not constitute its justification as an act; the explanation is not what makes it good. Conversely, the fact that evolution, or childhood upbringing, may have made the boy break a widow does not justify the act; it remains a bad act (because of its consequences, or the boy's intention, or whatever) even if the lad could not help but do it (which I am not convinced about anyway). It may or may not be the case that evolution has made us altruistic; but altruism is *justified*, not because of the evolution (for after all, many seriously bad habits have evolved too), but because of its intention and its benefits. For that kind of justification to make sense, we need a notion of free choices and ends, and it is hard indeed to see how this could be a purely materialistic notion. Of course, it is humane to make allowance for some degree of efficient causality operating in people's make-up and life-experience. But moral (and legal) judgments cannot be based on mitigating circumstances alone.

We are all familiar, I imagine, with cases where the scientific account is valid. Typically, in cases of compulsion, addiction, and sheer hypocrisy, I find myself doing, almost automatically, things I don't want to do, and then find reasons to justify my act, perhaps to myself, perhaps to others. I find myself pouring an eighth glass of whisky, and when I notice this fact, I reason that another glass won't make any difference, and anyway, St. Paul wrote that a little alcohol is good for your health. I have told myself that watching

---

62. A phrase coined, controversially, by Moore in *Principia Ethica*.

such and such a movie would be a complete waste of time, but then, as I find myself reaching for the controller to turn it on, reason that the critics are not always right, and should I not be open minded and see for myself?

However, we all know the difference between compulsion and hypocrisy on the one hand and healthy moral action on the other. The latter is genuinely a case of going through in my mind the pros and cons, and then deciding and acting on what seems the right option. It is true that many of our actions fall somewhere between these two poles, with elements of compulsion and hypocrisy, and elements of genuine moral search and free choice. But if the determinists were right, there would not be this polarity. And it is a polarity that is not only obvious to most of us, but one that we need to be aware of to make good ethical choices.

The determinists make much of an experiment by Benjamin Libet[63] in the early 1980s, in which certain brain events appeared to be associated with the act of choosing. People were asked to make a choice between alternatives, and state when they had decided, while their brain states were recorded. It appeared that the conscious choice came *after* the relevant brain state, suggesting that the "choice" was actually determined by the brain state, which also caused the (later) consciousness of decision. Now there are big questions to ask about how a specific brain state could be identified with the act of choosing unless we have a prior conviction that such identifications are possible: we seem to have to be determinists to get the experiment set up. But the deeper issue is that the experiment also presupposes that a free choice is a matter of having a certain conscious mind-state of choosing. It could well be that often our consciousness of choice comes after our acts of choice; when we realize, looking back, what made us decide to do what we spontaneously did. That in itself does not make the sense of choosing illusory. Here are three examples.

Example One. Walking along a beach, I see someone in the rough waves, flailing and crying out. I see nobody else on the beach. Spontaneously I dive in, and swim out to save the person. Only looking back do I realize what went through my mind: the fact that I can swim reasonably well; the fact, perhaps, that I have read stories and newspaper accounts of heroic rescue attempts, and it has seeped into my soul that rescuing is the right thing to do if you can; the fact that in the absence of any other helper, the outcome will be the drowning of the person or my saving them, or perhaps, my failing to, or perhaps, both of us drowning. There was no time to calculate all the probabilities consciously, but all these considerations

---

63. Libet et al., "Time of Conscious Intention . . ."

created a "gut feeling" that impelled my action, making it my choice, even if the awareness of all the factors came later.

Example Two. My opponent at tennis executes a masterly volley into the top left corner. "Miraculously" I intercept it, taking the speed out of it on my return, enabling the ball to spin past the right of the opponent as he continues to move to my left. I had no time to think, or work out, precisely the action of my legs and body, and the angle and movement of the racket, required to make this superb shot. So was I an automaton, my return predetermined? No. Hours of training of mind and body, and tennis experience, went into the shot. It achieved my purpose without my thinking about it, but it was the product of *me*: not just my nerves, muscles, and neurons, but the complex unity that decided to do all this training and practice. I am entitled to consider that I freely, albeit spontaneously, *chose* just the right strategy and tactic to defeat my opponent, among all the other shots I could have chosen to make.[64]

Example Three is the scientist herself. At the "object" end of her instrument—be it a telescope or electron microscope or particle accelerator or whatever—is a world of what may well exhibit thoroughly deterministic quantities and relations. But at the "subject" end is the scientist, who like the tennis player has chosen to undergo years of training and experience in learning how to suspend her own preconceptions and interpret "objectively" the qualia that dance before her eyes, to discern the quantities behind the qualities, the causes operating through the flux; and then again, the years of training and expertise to devise further instruments and apparatuses to test out her resulting conjectures. We may not find any grounds for ethics in the "object" end, but this is because of the exacting ethical work that takes place in the "subject" end, the scientist as a human being exercising her calling as scientist.[65]

There will be more to be said in later Worlds about the notion of free choices in relation to determinism, and mind in relation to matter, and about virtue ethics, which seems the account of ethics that best fits all three cases. But enough has been said to clarify that scientific materialism with its deterministic focus provides no grounds for ethics, though the work and action of scientists themselves does provide evidence that ethical motives nonetheless exist.

---

64. Needless to say, I have never made such a shot, which are best left to the Federers of this world.

65. Cf. Polanyi, *Personal Knowledge*.

Résumé: Is There a "View from Nowhere"?

Thomas Nagel famously described the materialist standpoint as attempting to view the world "from nowhere."[66] He meant attempting a view of nature from which all subjective bias is excluded, and which will look the same whoever is the onlooker. Whether or not this is a worthwhile aim, and whether or not you think science has achieved it, the fact remains that it is an aim that can only be achieved by excluding many kinds of reality. The scientist may (or may not) succeed in excluding her bias from her experiments, but she cannot exclude herself. Without an observer, the experimental apparatus shows not a view from nowhere, but no view at all.

We have seen that materialism raises a great number of questions. We have asked whether nominalism is right to limit reality to particular realities. We have queried whether materialism can explain why nature is lawful, how natural laws can be justified, and why nature has the laws it has. Then we moved to three big central questions that materialism has not yet answered (though sometimes it has rejected the question): regarding the conscious experience through which all scientific data arrive; concerning the intentional nature of thought and reasoning, including scientific reasoning; and concerning the contrasting criteria of identity for mental and physical events, and the nature of the physical itself. We have specifically asked whether determinism can apply to the real world, and whether reductionism and determinism both lead to an infinite regress. Finally, we have asked whether the closed causality of naturalism can provide a complete view of the world, and sustain an ethic worth believing. All of these questions, directly or indirectly, concern the reality or otherwise of the human subject, over against the material world in general.

The plausibility of materialism derives in large part from its posing as a commonsense, no-nonsense realism, free from the high-flown speculations of metaphysics and religious doctrine. It also gains much from its plausible claim to be the natural mindset of science, with its immense productivity in terms of understanding of the world, and resultant life-transforming technology. However, we have seen how materialism and naturalism expand the principles of scientific method into a metaphysics governing our total understanding of reality. As Orthodox theologian David Bentley Hart writes, "Between the triumphs of the inductive, empirical, and theoretical sciences of the modern age (on the one hand) and the metaphysical premises of naturalist thinking (on the other), any association is entirely a matter

---

66. Cf. his book of that title.

of historical accident."⁶⁷ Hart exaggerates a little, for we have seen that the materialist principles arise when the methodological principles of science are "inflated" by the metaphysical principles of nominalism and naturalism, so that all are lent a metaphysical glow. It remains true that the resulting materialist metaphysics is a compound, shaky edifice demanding a "leap of faith" as bold as anything in theology.

That said, I have argued that, being so compound, materialism is not the dogmatic monolith it can sometimes seem. Its tenets can be unraveled, creating a variety of alternative options, some of them being a qualified form of materialism, others leading to other Worlds. In {4} we shall visit the beautiful world that arises when the tenet of nominalism, and its dependents, are removed.

---

67. Hart, *Experience of God*, 296.

{4}

MUSIC OF THE UNIVERSE
Structural Realism

As the eyes are made for astronomy, so the ears are made for harmony, and these are sister sciences.[1]

Being uncreated and imperishable, [reality] is whole and uniform and unshaken and perfect. It never was nor will be, since it is now, all together, one, continuous.... Nor is it divided, since it all exists alike; nor is it more here and less there, which would prevent it from holding together, but it is all full of being.... It exists without beginning or ceasing.... For strong Necessity holds it within the bonds of a limit, which keeps it on every side.[2]

Besides being complicated, reality, in my experience, is usually odd. It is not neat, not obvious, not what you would expect.... Reality, in fact, is usually something you could not have guessed.... So let us leave behind all these boys' philosophies—these over simple answers.[3]

THE CONVICTION THAT A mathematical harmony underlies the whole universe and the consequent hunger for a theory that can unify and explain everything we know characterize the fourth of our "Worlds." We move from the world that is "nothing but" matter, just described, to a World in which matter is a curious and perhaps redundant concept, and the universe is

---

1. Pythagoras, cited as fragment 253 in Kirk, *Presocratic Philosophers*, 214.
2. Parmenides, Fragments 295–98, in *Presocratic Philosophers*, 248–50.
3. C. S. Lewis, *Mere Christianity*, in *Signature Classics*, 31.

seen mainly in terms of laws and relationships governed by mathematical equations.

Two factors converge here: the belief, deriving from the ancient Greeks, that the subject matter of mathematics is real, indeed more real than what we perceive with our senses; and the more recent development in modern physics and philosophy called "structural realism," which makes "matter" ever more elusive, and suggests that the ultimate objects of physics are quantities and their relations as described by mathematical equations. Put these two factors together, and the view emerges that what is real, and what physics describes, *is* a range of mathematical equations describing abstract relationships. Whereas the atomistic {3} could be said to resemble a pointillist picture made of atomic dots, {4} conjures up a world that cannot really be pictured at all. For {4} is more like a musical symphony, in which there is no reference to physical realities "out there," but rather an unfolding of harmonies and relationships between themes.

So {4} will examine first the ancient realism about mathematics, and consider the implications of the discovery that nature so often abides by rules set out in mathematical equations. Following Gödel and some reflections on rules and games, it will investigate why structural realism is convincing, how it is that mathematics can discover truths without examining the material world, and how the very idea of matter in the world has become questionable. It will then turn to consider the narratives, spiritualities, and possible theologies associated with structural realism, with special reference to the spiritual power of music, being the form of art that is akin to mathematics in being remote from reference to the world. It will then raise questions concerning whether structural realism is compatible with materialism, or constitutes a form of idealism; whether after all it needs experimental science and its reference to the physical, and takes leave of these at its peril; and the even deeper question of what determines whether something—say a physical phenomenon, or mathematical object, or musical symphony—is real or (different question) relates us to reality.

Realism in Early Mathematics

Mathematical notations date back to prehistoric times (much earlier than phonetic languages) and mathematical methods were known to the Sumerians and Babylonians. But it was the Greeks living on the coast and islands of Asia Minor—beginning in the sixth century BCE with Thales of Miletus—who first saw mathematics as a key to understanding the cosmos, and first set the standards for rigorous proofs.

In this tradition, Pythagoras of Samos believed that the world was based on the geometrical harmonies of music, likening (as in the quote above) the study of astronomy (which was then the main science, and relied heavily on geometric theory) to listening to music. Pythagoras observed that harmonious notes correspond with simple geometrical ratios between the length of the strings on which they are played. He believed the same harmonies governed the movement of the heavenly bodies, creating a *musica universalis* or "music of the spheres." This idea persisted until the mechanistic universe prevailed after the Renaissance; it was especially important in Johannes Kepler's understanding of the orbits of the planets. And when modern physicists refer to "string theory," they are referring not to tiny bits of rope, but to harmonies between vibrations oscillating in an unimaginable space that has vastly more dimensions than our own. If string theory proves successful (and at the time of writing, the jury is out) it may turn out that, while Democritus with his hooked-up atoms provides a good model for chemistry, in physics Pythagoras reigns.

In the fifth century BCE Parmenides of Elea (quoted above) added another contribution to the mathematical universe: the hunger for unity, the conviction that reality must be One. He argued that what is not, by definition, does not exist, and therefore there is no empty space, logical or physical, for things to move into from where they are. Change and movement are therefore impossible, and reality must consist of one eternal and unchanging necessary whole—necessary in the sense that it could not be other than it is. Change and time are therefore illusions.

Parmenides's ideal has arguably returned to modern physics. Einstein's general theory of relativity posits a single space-time in which time is but one of four dimensions. Change reduces to a line drawn through a space-time block. Meanwhile physicists are now searching for a theory of everything: equations that will account for all four forces of nature in terms of a single theory. Finally, the search for the One is (paradoxically) a factor leading to the idea of the multiverse of {5}, the whole in which all possibilities are actualized and there is no longer any contingency.

Parmenides's One, like the multiverse, is counter-intuitive. Closer to most of our experience, I imagine, is the world according to Heraclitus of Ephesus (c.535–c.475 BCE), whom Parmenides may have been arguing against (or *vice versa*). Heraclitus was perhaps the closest of these Greek thinkers to Gautama Buddha, who *may* have been a contemporary, and who declared in his fire sermon that all things are aflame with impermanence. Heraclitus likewise viewed all things as impermanent, partaking of the nature of fire. He famously decreed that one can never step into the same river twice, since the watery matter that surrounds you will be wholly different each time.

Arguably the greatest of all Greek philosophers, Plato (428–348 BCE) effectively reconciled Parmenides's eternal One with Heraclitus's flux. He conceded that the material world was ever-changing, as Heraclitus described, but affirmed that above and superior to this material world there exists a world of forms that is, like Parmenides's One, eternal, unchanging, and perfect. The forms include mathematical objects, like triangles and numbers, as well as universals, like goodness and greenness. We (like Plato's successor and critic, Aristotle) tend to regard such abstract things as "abstracted" from material things, but for Plato it was the material things that were pale shadows of the much more concrete and real forms.

Plato was a dualist, believing in ideal and material worlds alongside each other: a view that gave rise to a mystical, contemplative approach, increasingly emphasized in the school that became known as Neoplatonism, which was a heavy influence on the development of Christian theology. We will consider Plato and the Neoplatonists a little more in {7}. Then in {8} we will consider Aristotle's more nuanced understanding of the relation between form and matter. It was his thinking that arguably first enabled us to understand how there can be both change, as Heraclitus affirmed, and things that persist through change, like the Parmenidean One; for he saw how change is always the change of some continuing thing. So change and changelessness, and matter and form, are interdependent.

The Platonic Revival

We have already noted how the conviction that nature was governed by mathematical laws—a conviction largely absent from Aristotle and his medieval followers—underwent a resurgence at the time of the Renaissance and was a major factor in the rise and in the success of modern science. A Neoplatonic understanding of the reality of mathematical and other forms was a big influence on Renaissance astronomers like Johannes Kepler, and figures as what I have called the third principle of scientific method. Notwithstanding the nominalist trend in materialism, this conviction has survived into more recent philosophy and science through thinkers like Gottlob Frege, Simone Weil, Karl Popper, Iris Murdoch, Roger Penrose, Paul Davies, Stephen Hawking, and Max Tegmark, to name only a few.

Hawking beautifully asked, "What is it that breathes fire into the equations and makes a universe for them to describe?"[4] Indeed, to ask a

---

4. Hawking, *Brief History of Time*, 174.

closely related question, why should we believe our equations represent that which comes to fiery life in the existence of worlds? Recently the science writer Graham Farmelo has shown how science has made most advances when mathematicians and scientific experimenters have worked in partnership. The "hard" physical sciences like chemistry, physics, and cosmology rely on the language of mathematics. It is as if "the Universe Speaks in Numbers."[5] To take two examples, matrix theory and multidimensional Hilbert Space gave quantum physics a way of developing the equations that proved experimentally true; and the alternative non-Euclidean geometries of the nineteenth-century Russian mathematicians Bolyai and Lobachevski later enabled Einstein to develop his general theory of relativity, describing space-time in a manner that later proved experimentally valid. Meanwhile the "soft" human sciences like psychology and sociology often ape this use of mathematics by the hard sciences, admittedly with much less success.

What is it about mathematics that makes it such a powerful clue to the nature of reality? Why should physical reality be so predictable, so amenable to obeying the laws expressed in our mathematical equations? And why should we be so sure that mathematical truths are eternal, representing discoveries rather than inventions?

It is obvious that mathematical proofs are, on one level, human constructions, happening in history. And some philosophers of mathematics, notably David Hilbert, have been content to regard mathematics as a kind of constructive game played with rules of our own devising. On his view, mathematical systems reduce to axioms—formulae we just accept as basic—plus rules for manipulating them to construct new formulae. Though we call this construction work "proof," for formalists it is not a case of proving a truth so much as legitimating a move in a game we have decided to play.[6]

There was, presumably, a historical moment when Pythagoras discovered his theorem about triangles, and likewise with every other mathematical theorem. Pythagoras's "discovery" did not come about through his observing how triangles behave, but rather, presumably, through constructing lines on a page and devising a "proof" from basic axioms—the kind of work Hilbert describes. Yet we rightly refer to Pythagoras's theorem as a

---

5. Farmelo, *Universe Speaks in Numbers*.

6. The view that in mathematics we intuit or grasp truths in a Platonic world is called "intuitionism" and is associated especially with the work of mathematician L. E. J. Brouwer. A third view, "logicism," is associated with Bertrand Russell and A. N. Whitehead, who devoted several hundred pages of dense notation in their classic three-volume *Principia Mathematica* to proving from the principles of logic that 1+1=2. But Gödel's work (see next section) problematizes logicism as well as formalism, as both seek to deduce all of mathematics from a set of axioms.

discovery, not an invention. The diameter of a square did not start being $\sqrt{2}$ at the moment the proof was constructed, in the way steam locomotives started to exist in the year (1802) when Trevithick constructed the Coalbrookdale Locomotive. Rather, it had *always* been true, though only after the theorem was constructed did we *know why* it was true. This combination of historical construction and eternal reality is a paradox to which this book will return.

But alongside the "eternal" status of mathematical theorems, which Plato made so much of in his world of forms, there is a seemingly contrary aspect, which also persuades us that we are dealing with something "out there" and real. Why should mathematical reality itself often be unpredictable, offering us the surprises that make us feel we are grappling with a reality outside ourselves. Mathematics repeatedly offers us "something you could not have guessed," which C. S. Lewis, in the opening quote, regarded as the trademark of reality. If you have never studied mathematics except in the routine, utterly surprise-free atmosphere that so often characterizes the teaching of math at school, it may be a surprise to learn that mathematics can be full of surprises.[7] The literature on mathematics contains a host of examples, of which Fermat's last theorem (see next section) is a case in point. It is surprising it was true, as there was no reason to suspect it was; and it is also surprising how long it has taken to prove it.

Now Platonists do not consider that mathematics provides the only inhabitants of the eternal world of forms. Plato himself believed that all abstract qualities—what later philosophers have termed universals—belonged there. Beauty, greenness, humanity, and so forth all had their eternal archetypes, supreme among which was the Form of the Good (which the Neoplatonists identified with God). The justification for this is that "beauty," "green," and "good" are not just names for arbitrary collections of things; they describe something real. But nothing is perfectly beautiful, or perfectly green. Beautiful things have defects in the eyes of at least some beholders. And there are likely to be dapplings of brown or other colors in anything we describe as green. Likewise, no human being is perfectly human; no earthly thing is perfectly good. Moreover, actual beautiful or green things, humans, and good things come and go in time. If words like beautiful, green, human, or good are to have a stable meaning, they must be referring not to these imperfect and evanescent things but to something perfect and eternal that they all manifest or (to use the Platonic phrase) "participate in." And these he called the forms, of beauty, greenness, and so forth.

7. For one illustration, consider the construction of Platonic solids in higher dimensions, in my *Christian Spirituality*, 127–30. There is a host of examples in the book I was mathematically raised on, Sawyer's *Mathematician's Delight*.

In the late nineteenth century, Gottlob Frege added to mathematical theorems and universal qualities a third set of inhabitants of the "eternal" realm: propositions, or what we might call claims to truth. When I say or think (to use Tarski's example) "snow is white," it may be a passing thought, and may have been otherwise expressed, for example by the sentence "*schnee ist weiss*" or "Frozen H2O, when it has fallen onto the ground, reflects all the wavelengths of light." But the *proposition* (or truth-claim) that is expressed is the same in each case, and it is something that has always been the case, and always will be, even in realms where there is no snow. It is true in places where snow never falls, and it was true before the earth had cooled enough for snow to form, that show is white. It is true on planets, and even in universes, where there is no water, because in all these places it remains true that what we here and now call snow is what we here and now call white. Or so it is argued.

Plato believed the eternity and perfection of the world of forms made its contents not only real, but more real than the physical world of matter. It is easy to believe this in the case of mathematical and geometrical objects. Any equilateral triangle you draw with a material pen on material paper will have sides that are not quite straight and equal, and angles that are slightly more or less than 60° and add up to slightly more or less than 180°. But the "real" equilateral triangle, the one that exists on a Euclidean surface, and which we are trying to draw on our paper, does have perfectly straight and equal sizes and angles exactly as just described. The section on contemplation, below, will find reason to doubt the superior reality of other kinds of Platonic form. But that apart, Platonism regarding mathematics, universals, and propositions has become quite widespread among scientists and philosophers.

The philosopher Karl Popper coined the terms, "Third Realm" and "World 3"[8] to describe this world. Gottlob Frege had earlier referred to the Third Realm for such things, and in order to distinguish these realms from my Worlds {1}, {2}, and {3}, that is the term I shall henceforth use. The Third Realm is independent of the First Realm, the material world, and the Second Realm, the world of human experience and consciousness.[9] It is the world accessed through intentionality, just as the Second Realm is the world of sensation and qualia. Even on physical planets without snow, and nobody experiences or thinks of snow or its whiteness—Plato, Frege, and Popper would argue—it remains the case that snow is white. If what ?{1}c argued

---

8. It is important not to confuse Popper's "World 3" with my "World {3}." In this book, {3} denotes the materialistic worldview. For this reason, I prefer to use his term "Third Realm." The Third Realm figures in most of the Worlds {4} to {10}.

9. Popper, *Objective Knowledge*, 43–44.

is true, and if Plato is right, the First and Second Realms depend for their conceptualization on the Third.

We will find reason in this book to look for a closer interpenetration of the three worlds, which means that truths in the Third Realm cannot be wholly independent of Second Realm consciousness to entertain those truths, and First Realm matter for them to be instantiated in. It will prove questionable whether snow would be white if there were no material eyes to receive its light, coupled with minds to perceive and affirm it to be white. But I anticipate; let us see why the reality of the Third Realm has become accepted by many.

Gödel's Impetus towards Realism

In 1931 two papers by mathematician Kurt Gödel proved the two famous incompleteness theorems. Gödel thereby shifted the ground decisively in favor of some kind of realism (or intuitionism, the idea that in mathematics we perceive or intuit truths) in mathematics: some element of surprise and discovery that cannot be reduced to mechanical method.

This theorem concerns the way we prove the truths of arithmetic from basic principles. It appears that we have to make a choice between completeness and consistency. If we want a consistent, self-contained set of axioms, we will never be able to prove all the truths of arithmetic. There will always be statements about the natural numbers that are true, but that are unprovable within the system. If, on the other hand, we want to be able to prove all the truths, our first principles will have to be to some degree incoherent and incomplete.

Though once we have the proof for a theory, we can follow it through step-by-step, there is no step-by-step method (or "algorithm") for discovering the right theories, or their demonstration, either in mathematics or in science. It will always require the inspiration of an Archimedes with his "eureka moment," or the genius of a Newton or Einstein, to discover the right model or theory. It can take a very long time for mathematicians to find proofs for theorems of whose truth they are sure: for example, it took 368 years for mathematicians to prove Fermat's Last Theorem (of 1637) that no three positive integers a, b, and c can satisfy the equation $a^n + b^n = c^n$ for any integer value of n greater than two. This simple theory proved ferociously complex to prove.[10]

As a simpler example, consider this sequence of numbers:

---

10. Cf. Singh, *Fermat's Last Theorem*.

2 ... 3 ... 0 ... 1 ... 0 ... 4 ... 3 ... 0 ... 2 ... 0 ...

You will probably find it impossible to discern any pattern in this sequence. There is no "meta-algorithm" for discovering the algorithm by which it was generated, or indeed, for deciding whether there is such an algorithm, or whether the sequence is entirely random. But this is not because the algorithm is necessarily complex in itself; in our example, quite a simple method is in fact involved. Imagine ten bowls arranged in a circle, with one of the bowls marked as being the first. Take fifteen marbles, drop one in the first bowl, then moving clockwise, drop one in the next bowl, then still going clockwise, miss a bowl and drop one in the next, then miss two bowls and drop one in the next . . . and so on. Our number sequence gives us the number of marbles now in each bowl, counting clockwise from the first bowl.[11]

There is no way you could have worked that out; but the use of a playful imagination might have hit upon it. And once the method is known, whether by creative play or by being told about it, it is easy to verify that it is right and that the method had to give rise to that sequence and no other. Gödel's theorem tells us this is how mathematics works; there is no "meta-method" for discovering mathematical structures and proofs, but once discovered, we can know for sure that the proofs are right and the structures are "really there."

Strictly, the incompleteness theorem applies to arithmetic, and its application to mathematics generally has been disputed. However, all mathematics relies on arithmetic, and the "hard" physical core of science relies on mathematics, so the implications for science are enormous. If you want a complete understanding of the cosmos, you have to rely on more than just proof; you have to embrace a degree of incoherence or paradox. If coherence and consistency are more important to you, then you have to abandon the idea of complete understanding.

This choice obviously also applies to the evaluation of the "Worlds." Maybe we have to choose between Worlds like materialism on the one hand, which appears fairly coherent and consistent, but omits from its view many areas of experience and value; and, on the other, and more idealistic if not theistic views, which appear more complete in this respect, at the expense (arguably) of some degree of coherence and freedom from paradox.

The two questions remain, then, without a universally accepted answer: why is nature so "tame," so predictable, so amenable to mathematical

---

11. Tegmark offers an even simpler example (*Mathematical Universe*, 205). It is very quick to multiply two 300-digit prime numbers, but to factorize the resulting 600-digit number and recover the original two primes would take our best computers longer than the age of the universe.

formulation; and why is mathematics so "wild," so full of surprises and literally unimaginable creativity? Perhaps, if it were not so, it would not be so able to tame the surprising world we live in.

Games and Mathematical Emergence

A clue to the basis of mathematical truth may be found in the theory of games. Though a game may appear to be a very Hilbert-like, formal affair—nothing but rules and moves—a game actually illustrates something of how mathematics works (and also part of what we mean by "emergence," the key concept in {9}).

As a child, I used to delight in devising new board games and trying them out on unfortunate friends and relations. I found out then how hard it is to predict what a game will be like just from the board, the pieces, and the rules. The only way to find out is to play the game. Only then does it become clear whether interesting goals and strategies will emerge, and how long the game will take to win, or whether indeed it will be winnable at all. I remember subjecting people to games that I thought were brilliant in conception, but proved infinitely tedious in the playing!

On one level all we see happening in a board game is a sequence of physical causes. Players in turn take up particular pieces and move them to other places on the board. So is the game really *nothing but* such physical moves? Of course not. In chess, for example, the rules are very simple, and the number of pieces and squares of the board is very small, yet it has been proven that there are more possible games of chess than particles in the universe. Each chess game is effectively unique. And in the course of the game, things like intentions, plans, and strategies come into play, which cannot be ascribed to the pieces; though of course without the physical pieces and the board, there could be no game and no strategies. In that rather trivial sense, the game "supervenes" on the pieces and the board.

The game of chess could be played with pieces and board physically different from the conventional ones—indeed, you can find an extraordinary variety for sale in shops—and on something that does not physically resemble a board. Computer chess programs do not need to know about, or have apparatus that can detect, what is happening on the physical boards and pieces; it is their software program that in some sense "knows" or keeps track of what is going on in the game, and works out the best strategy.

Computers themselves were once made of valves, and then transistors, and these days silicon chips. They could even be made of bowls that were either full or empty of water; or Chinese citizens following instructions. So long as the filling and emptying of the bowls, or the Chinese citizens, followed the same rules as the turning on or off of the valves or chips in the chess program, they would still function—albeit clumsily—as computers, performing the same calculations. They would "Turing complete"—a term named after the famous code-breaker Alan Turing, who showed how any machine that could follow certain rules would be able to perform all the calculations a computer can. Computers then are not reducible to silicon chips (and chess not reducible to pieces and moves), because there are different physical ways of doing what the computer does (or playing chess).

In all these cases we see the emergence of a higher level of reality and relations, a concept {9} will explore further. The game is not reducible to the pieces and the rules, nor is the computer "nothing but" a lot of silicon chips. But we do not need therefore to be dualists and invoke the mind or life force or soul of the game or the computer to explain what these things have in addition to the pieces or the circuits. The game and its rich strategies and possibilities, and the computer and its ability to calculate, are emergent realities that subsist in the pieces or the circuits. And this is a new point: they might subsist in other physical expressions too. Rudolf Hesse's novel, *The Glass Bead Game* suggested that all of our culture might be modelled in a game played with glass beads, so that art, religion, science, and so forth emerge as higher levels of a basically simple game. I remain skeptical about this. But now we are considering the opposite possibility: that a single higher level might be modelled in a number of different lower-level ways, including glass beads on a board, but also silicon circuits, bowls of water, and so forth.

And the ability of the computer to calculate suggests that mathematics might too be about emergent reality that subsists in different physical manifestations. We learn early on that if we take two apples and add another one, we get three apples. The same thing happens with pears and galaxies and . . . anything you can think of. So the mathematical formula $2 + 1 = 3$ describes an emergent truth that holds whatever the physical expression. As we proceed into the truths of higher mathematics, we find that their physical expressions can vary much more profoundly than this.

So we could regard mathematics as a game, or as a group of interrelated games, played by mathematicians in which profound and often unimaginable truths are discovered, some of which help us understand and predict the actual world we live in. Others might help us understand and predict events in possible worlds other than this one.

Once this is understood, the nature of the "matter" you play with or theorize about becomes less important than the rules of the game, or the mathematics you use to play with it or make theories about it. And this is part of the reason why matter has begun to fade from the center of the scientific picture, while structure, pattern, and rule have become all-important.

Matter as Cheshire Cat

Realism regarding mathematics is an old tradition with, if anything, increasing momentum in our own time. Much newer in origin is the way modern physics has erased conventional understandings of matter. We have seen in {2} how science shifted attention from secondary qualities to the primary quantities of number, mass, and extension (or size in space). What was left was a world without qualities, consisting of discrete, countable lumps of matter of various sizes and positions interacting according to basic forces. Several developments in modern science have changed this picture, and forced us to abandon the notion of a material "substance" that possesses the primary quantities. Philosopher of Science N. R. Hanson argued a while ago:

> Matter has been dematerialized, not just as a concept of the philosophically real, but now as an idea of modern physics. . . . The things for which Newton typified matter—e.g., an exactly determinable state, a point shape, absolute solidity—these are now the properties electrons do not, because theoretically they cannot, have.[12]

Bertrand Russell draws an intriguing analogy:

> It has begun to seem that matter, like the Cheshire Cat, is becoming gradually diaphanous until nothing of it is left but the grin, caused, presumably, by amusement at those who still think it is there.[13]

This "dematerialization" is a logical step, following from four kinds of reason. First, the relative indifference of large-scale structures to the nature of their components, as just discussed. Second, what has been called, perhaps prematurely, the waning of materialism as a philosophy, as discussed in the questions regarding {3}. Thirdly, the following through of the momentum of the logic behind the Cartesian doubt and the consequent distrust of secondary qualities and appeals to imagination, leading to an acceptance that reality is unimaginable, either in terms of secondary qualities or in terms of primary quantities.

---

12. Hanson, "Dematerialisation of Matter," 34.
13. Russell, "Mind and Matter," 135.

But fourthly, several developments in science have added impetus to this trajectory. There is a big literature on this for the interested reader to pursue.[14] I will just sketch six factors, associated with developments in twentieth-century physics.

1. General relativity abandons the idea of particles of matter in space exerting attractive and repulsive forces on each other, in favor of a unified space-time manifold in which forces like gravity appear as a geometric warping.
2. The idea of matter and energy as separate gives way to the concept that they are interconvertible, related by the famous equation $e = mc^2$. In nuclear fission and fusion, as well as in the burning of the sun, we witness this conversion taking place.
3. Quantum physics undermines another duality, between particles and waves. Rather than having matter associated with particles, versus energy travelling in waves, all reality has a wavelike and a particulate aspect.
4. This duality manifests when light travels through two slits to form an interference pattern on a screen, as we would expect to happen with patterns of waves. Even if there is only one particle of light (photon) emitted at a time, it "interferes with itself" to produce the same interference pattern, as if it were a wave travelling simultaneously through both slits at once!
5. The notion of particles of matter with definable position and momentum gives way to an uncertainty, whereby the more we know about a particle's position, the less we know about its momentum. We can know where things are, or how fast and in what direction they are going, but not both.
6. And it only gets weirder. In one of the more recent developments in physics, reality consists of "superstrings" in ten, eleven, or twenty-six dimensions (depending on the theory). All but three of these dimensions are coiled up so that we cannot observe them. As noted, strings are nothing like Democritus's atoms of matter, much more like Pythagorean harmonies and ratios between numbers.

The cases involving quantum physics (3–5) are worth a little more discussion. For in quantum physics there is something, called the wave equation, that does evolve deterministically. But it evolves in a "Hilbert Space"

---

14. For a fuller account of the rise and fall of the concept of matter, see the articles by McMullin and Clayton in Davies, *Information*, chs. 2 and 3.

that has many more dimensions than our three. Regarding the wave equation, and its strange "collapse," cosmologist Max Tegmark comments,

> a veritable zoo of interpretations of what's going on has cropped up over the years, including the ensemble, Copenhagen, instrumental, hydrodynamic, consciousness, Bohm, quantum logic, Many-Worlds, stochastic mechanics, many-minds, consistent histories, objective collapse, transactional, modal, existential, relational, Montevideo and cosmological interpretations.[15]

But for our argument we need only focus on three main interpretations.

1. *The Copenhagen Interpretation* pioneered by Hans Bohr and Werner Heisenberg. The wave equation describes only the probability of finding a particle at any point in space; the particle remains "spread out" in a wavelike way—possibly here, more likely there . . . —until observation "collapses" it into an interference pattern on the screen, or a measurement of position, or momentum. You could say it is our minds that turns a range of possibilities into something actual and definite. On this interpretation, the wave function describes the chances of Schrödinger's famous cat being alive or dead, but when we look, the cat becomes definitely alive or definitely dead. A positivist variant of this view refuses to say anything about what is really "out there" before measurement. Following the slogan "Don't speculate just calculate," science should not be speculating about what kind of matter is there, but simply making measurements and correlating and predicting them through mathematical laws.

2. *Many Worlds:* the view developed by Hugh Everett and popularized by Bryce deWitt. The wave equation describes how things actually are, namely a range of actualities in different universes. When Schrödinger's famous cat is observed, on this interpretation, it is not that he suddenly becomes either alive or dead. Rather there is a universe in which he is alive, and another in which he is dead, and we are in one of them. The reality is the multiverse (World {5}) in which many incompatible possibilities are realized at once. We obviously inhabit just one such world, which is why when we look, we just see one version of whatever is going on. If our minds and bodies could reach across all the universes, we would get the full picture that quantum physics describes.

3. *The Implicate Order* of David Bohm. The wave equation describes things as they are, but this exists in just one universe, and consist of

---

15. Tegmark, *Mathematical Universe*, 225–26.

an underlying "implicate order" with non-local "hidden variables." This order is very different from our spatiotemporal world, containing something like Leibniz's universe of holographic monads (see {6}), though the implicate order is ever-changing, lacking the eternity of the monads. We ourselves can only perceive this in terms of our conventional terms of particles located in space-time. So we see a cat, alive or dead, but what is really there is something more mysterious.

Among scientists (c) is not popular because of its metaphysical, some would say occult aspects. Most scientists divide between (a) and (b), with a trend in the direction of (b). But in all the interpretations the idea of precisely locatable matter moving deterministically in our space and time has given way to something more mysterious, if it can or should be described at all. Each interpretation points to a shift in Worlds: the constitutive role of observation in (a) suggests a degree of {7}, idealism; (b) obviously takes us towards {5}, the multiverse; while {c} suggests views discussed in {6}, notably Leibniz's universe-reflecting monads.

What is left after moves 1-6, and the interpretations a—c, is nothing like "matter," but rather is simply quantities, plus equations expressing their relations and patterns of causal interaction. It is here that mathematics comes to our aid, but only if we regard mathematics as itself engaging with reality "out there." It is a natural move to combine structural realism with materialist skepticism: mathematics then supplies the reality with which science engages. Max Tegmark takes the further step of arguing that the reality with which science engages *is* a mathematical object. Or rather, each possible mathematical world, with its axioms, laws, and proofs, constitutes a universe within the multiverse of all possible worlds. Mathematical laws and relations are all that there is, just as the insubstantial grin is all there is to the Cheshire Cat.

This move from {3} to {4}, from a materialist understanding to one based on mathematical reality, is less evident in the "higher" sciences like biology, let alone sociology, than in physics, for two reasons. One is that mathematical approaches have less application in the higher sciences, where qualitative methods of form recognition still have pride of place. The other is that the idea that reality reduces to material atoms is much easier to believe in the higher sciences. It is easy to believe, in sociology, that society reduces to individual "atoms" that are biological units called human beings; and in biology, that these and other organisms reduce to material atoms. It is only at the very lowest, quantifiable level that the atomistic model comes into question. However, this means that atomistic models prove questionable also at the highest level of cosmology, because of the way cosmology is dependent on physics, which alone can describe what may have happened in the early stages of the universe.

In effect, the structural realist universe results from the fact that some physicists and cosmologists have become prepared to sacrifice some of the basic tenets of materialism listed in the preceding chapter, in the interest of others. Before we turn to that, however, it remains to look at the spiritual and theological impact of {4}.

How Can Music Move?

Pythagoras spoke of mathematics and music in the same breath, as co-revealers of reality. Listening to music is possibly the closest some people get to contemplation. But what could be its relation to reality? After all, what music seems to share with mathematics—in contrast with arts like painting, sculpture, poetry and drama, and sciences like physics and biology—is abstractness, the lack of any specific reference to realities outside itself. This raises the question "how can music move?" in two senses. How can the metaphor of music as consisting of the movement of notes, or phrases—so that these, in turn, build into "movements"—have any purchase in a medium that consists of a sheer sequence of sounds? And how can such movement move us (to use another metaphor) emotionally?

Broadly speaking philosophies of art have been of three kinds: formalism, which focuses on the balance and beauty of form in the art object; representationalism, which argues that art serves to represent things in the world in a special way; and expressionism, for which the main goal of art is to express feeling. In the case of music, representation seems to be ruled out (except in the special case of program music, in which the music deliberately imitates the sound of sea on the shore, say, or the howling of wolves). In music, expressionism has probably been the main contender. Philosopher and musicologist Peter Kivy has written much on the basis of a behaviorist account of the emotions.[16] The human body expresses sadness, for example, by adopting a slow gait, a drooping posture, and downcurved lips and eyes. Music that has a slow rhythm and "drooping" and "downturned" phrases will express sadness in the same way.

Another philosopher and aesthetician, Roger Scruton criticizes Kivy here for using unexplained analogies. "Music does not literally move slowly, droop or ponder."[17] Kivy is saying that a certain quality in music expresses sadness because it is somehow like sadness, but the question of what makes

16. E.g., Kivy, *Corded Shell* and *New Essays*.
17. Scruton, *Soul of the World*, 160.

it seem like sadness is left unresolved. Scruton goes on to insist, "hearing the sadness of the music is not hearing an analogy between the music and an emotion; it is hearing the sadness *in* the music." He argues that feelings are embodied in music as they are embodied in people. Scruton therefore focuses on the form of the music, not as something to be cherished in itself, but for its intentionality, the way it offers things like thoughts and feelings that are usually intentional—about objects in the world—in the absence of the objects themselves. "Music is heard as a kind of pure aboutness—an intentional relation from which both terms, subject and object, have been deleted."[18]

What does this mean? The language is not easy, but it suggests to me that what mathematics is to matter, music is to consciousness. Just as mathematics deals with the patterns and relations that hold between items in the material world, in abstraction from those material things and their materiality, so music deals with patterns and relations holding between thoughts and feelings in abstraction from the things that thought and feeling are about. Music offers us thought in the absence of anything thought about, and feelings like love and fear in the absence of any specific thing loved or feared. The form of love or fear does not, in music, focus on a beautiful landscape or a terrifying tiger, but allows love or fear to unfold according to its own dynamic, and its own relation to other thoughts and feelings.

Such a theory could combine expressionism and formalism in suggesting that music is about emotion, but it is about the form of emotion, emotion allowed to generate beautiful structure, in the absence of the things in the world that normally generate emotion. As the great aesthetician R. G. Collingwood argued,[19] art serves not merely to express a feeling (as a grunt, scream, or a laugh might) but to give intellectual articulation to the feelings of the artist and her society. Just as when we play with material objects, mathematical relationships emerge with a structure of their own, so when the artist plays with notes, melding them into melodies and harmonies, and these into musical themes, and these in turn into symphonies and fugues, new structures of relationship emerge with a life of their own.

If this is right, though music consists of material sounds, its meaning cannot be reduced to or explained by anything material. This raises a further question for the reductionism and materialism of {3}. But what about {4}? Do musical works belong in it? Should we assign them to Popper's Third Realm, alongside mathematical objects, eternally true propositions, and universals like the color green? Are Mozart's symphonies, as Einstein

---

18. Scruton, *Soul of the World*, 162.
19. Collingwood, *Principles of Art*.

claimed, eternal, just waiting to be discovered? It is true that a symphony is a universal rather than a particular. It is not impossible, for example, that Mozart's 40th symphony might be stored in a digital format, like a CD, and that this CD might be ejected from a dying earth and find a way to another planet, where millions of years hence, it is discovered by aliens and played, on their own equipment and perhaps eventually by their own orchestras.

But the crucial question is: would the symphony be appreciated? Would it be recognized as art? I think probably not. For if what has just been argued is true, musical works are "abstract" in the opposite way from mathematical objects. They, and works of art generally, are built out of the very things that mathematics abstracts from: concrete human feelings, intentions, and sensations. Conversely mathematics is built out of the very thing music abstracts from: the world of real relations between things "out there." That is why, in exploring whether there is intelligent life elsewhere in the universe, it makes sense to beam out mathematical formulae that an intelligent form of life might recognize to be true, despite its probably very different senses and experience of life. It makes less sense to beam out a Mozart symphony, because to recognize it as art, the alien life would need ears like ours, and probably an emotional life and a culture not too far removed from our own.

It is a beautiful idea, to think of the musical as Pythagoras did, as the other side of the mathematical, such that the mathematical harmonies of the solar system are accompanied by a "music of the spheres." {6} will explore the idea that reality has two aspects, an "outward" physical-cum-mathematical aspect, and an "inward" mental-cum-meaningful aspect. However, whereas we can know, by abstracting away from ourselves, the former, we can only know about and relate to the latter in ourselves and in beings like ourselves. If there is a music of the spheres, perhaps there are angelic beings who will be able to tune into it; but in our case it will fall on deaf ears.

At best, then, the meaning in music adds to and broadens our concept of {4}, rather than raising questions about it. It is a reason for preferring {4} (and other worlds in which music has a place) to {3}.

Contemplating Reality

As noted, Platonism has had a long and deep impact on spirituality, informing a Neoplatonic tradition of contemplation that was a strong influence on Eastern Orthodox theologians and perhaps, through Augustine of Hippo, an even stronger influence in the West. Many mathematicians and physicists speak of the beauty of the equations governing the universe, and the joy of contemplating them. This kind of joy was familiar to theologians of the Orthodox tradition, such as Maximus the Confessor:

> It is the work of the highest goodness not only to have created the divine and incorporeal natures of mental creatures as a reflection of the ineffable Divine glory . . . but also to have imprinted clear traces of its greatness in sensory creatures . . . for these traces can transport directly to God a human mind, which ponders deeply over them, making it soar above all visible things and leading it, as it were, into the realm of higher bliss.[20]

Maximus offers a way of ascent through physical and mathematical to mystical contemplation, familiar in antiquity and medieval times, but largely lost since, though there have been Neoplatonic voices in the wilderness such as Simone Weil and Iris Murdoch. In this light it seems strange that more scientists and mathematicians do not find their biophilia and contemplation of the natural world leading them naturally towards God. {8} will explore the "chain of being" that ascends through creaturely beauty to God.

There is a negative side to Platonism, however, in the way Plato and the Neoplatonists regarded the forms as not only real, but *more real* than their material counterparts. In the famous analogy of the cave,[21] material reality is compared with a play of shadows cast on the wall of a cave by the real forms, which the prisoners cannot turn to see. In Plato's thought context, we can see why he thought this way. The unchanging nature of forms like "triangularity" and "green" (and we might add, the unchanging truth of propositions like "snow is white") enabled them to qualify as partakers in the Parmenidean One. Material things are much more Heraclitan: an ever-changing flux in which is hard to single out what is true.

This aspect of Platonism, however, has not stood the test of time. Aristotle argued (see {8}) that we only find the forms conjoined to matter. Thus "bedness," or the idea of a bed, is not more real than actual beds. Aristotle argued that it is the *union* of form and matter, and neither in isolation, that is real, and has certain potentials that may be realized. Thus, it is when bits of matter (like feathers, fabric, and metal or wood for the frame) are ordered by the idea or pattern of a bed, that we get a real bed with potential to keep us warm and help us sleep. *Pace* the Platonic realists, a mere bed structure, or a plan of a bed, is not a real bed, and cannot keep us warm. *Pace* the materialists, nor can the sheer matter of the bed, the feathers, etc.

---

20. Cited in Kadloubovsky and Palmer, *Philokalia*, 161.
21. Plato, *Republic*, Book VII.

In terms of spirituality, Plato's realism led to a great mistake that has pervaded much of Christian tradition. It suggested that the contemplation of the idea of beauty is nobler that the contemplation of actual beautiful things like landscapes, paintings, people, poems, and symphonies. It is surely these latter that have the power to transform us, not "Beauty itself," whatever that might be when abstracted from the different kinds of beauty in different kinds of thing. It is Van Gogh's *Starry Night* or Bach's *St. Matthew's Passion* or my beloved's face or the murmur of the waterfall in my garden that I love, not something "more real" that each of these poorly replicate. That is why the thought that we will one day encounter the Beauty that was the source of all we loved in our departed does not console us. What we loved was the loved one, the living person, and not something they represented. And we may even experience the mystical ascent as a danger, sucking us away from the material world in which we live and love, toward a pale abstraction. It is widely acknowledged that Christian spirituality has often suffered from a certain disengagement from, or even despising of, ordinary matter.

In that respect, Maximus's ascent would constitute a danger if it involved only abstraction from concrete examples of beauty to "Beauty Itself." But Maximus, unlike Plato, is describing, not a process of abstraction, but an ascent through creatures to a Creator: not to "Beauty Itself," but to a Being who is beautiful in a way that embodies all that I love in my beloved, and in *The Starry Night*, and so forth. It is often recalled that Augustine and Aquinas referred to God as *ipsum esse*, Being Itself. But "Being Itself," though it might inspire a certain intellectual awe, is not lovable unless it is "empersoned." In fact, the full phrase in Aquinas (though not, so far as I know, in Augustine) is *ipsum esse subsistens*, Being Itself subsisting, that is, existing not as a disembodied Platonic quality, but as that to which we can assign qualities. God is not here contemplated as a being, but as Being Itself understood as the activity of one we can relate to and love. In the idea of the incarnation, of course, this personal, lovable dimension is intensified (perhaps even realized and made coherent) as Being Itself becomes "empersoned" in a particular material, knowable, and lovable human being, Jesus Christ.[22]

Does it make sense to believe that all that we have loved on earth is found in this human and divine person? I suggest it makes more sense than believing, with Plato, that there is some abstract form that is the reality behind all the shadows of it that I have loved. Whether one essentially simple divine person who is Being Itself can embody the sheer variety of all the beings I have loved is another question. This perhaps *is* the question

---

22. A lot more thought is needed here, of course. See {10} and also Williams, *Christ*.

of whether God exists: whether Being Itself (*ipsum esse*) is a real subject (*subsistens*), whom I can love and who loves all beings; or whether there are only beings, some of them loved.

Finally, we often speak of a mystical journey of ascent through creatures to God, as if, as time advances, we leave creatures behind and "reach out" (in the *epektasis* of Gregory of Nyssa) towards God. But the approach to God will surely mean transcending this linear time itself, towards something more akin to the space-time of Einstein. The notion of a space-time manifold in which all times are embedded, so that the passage of time is illusory, may offer consolation with the suggestion that past moments of happiness are co-present with present and future times. Occasionally the past comes back to us with a vividness that exceeds the usual re-narration of what we once did, which "never could recapture /The first fine careless rapture."[23] Marcel Proust encountered such a vivid return in the memories evoked by his madeleine cake, which led him to embark on the world's longest novel, his *À la Recherche du Temps Perdu*—Search for Lost Time. Poisons like greed, fear, hatred, and loss, on this view, would represent the false perspective of an ego tunnelling its mole-like way through the space-time manifold, always leaping ahead to anticipate the future, and always trying to retain that which is becoming past. Nirvana then represents, perhaps, what happens when we let go and allow all moments to be eternally present. A Christian believer would see all times as co-present "in the Mind of God," such that the movement from beings to Being Itself, as just described, is not really a letting go of creatures but a letting go of our time-conditioned grasp of them, and a rediscovery of them all in the divine perspective.[24]

{4} and the Tenets of Materialism

The route has come, via abolishing consciousness in favor of matter, to abolishing matter in favor of the Platonic world, whose status needs further discussion—see ?{4}b—but is hardly material. Reality, once thought easy to model in terms of little atoms and their bonds, now presents itself to us in abstract equations and unimaginable spaces. But how exactly does {4} relate to the tenets of materialism? Does it abandon them or take them further?

23. Browning, "Home-Thoughts from Abroad."

24. The non-believer might approach a similar thought via the sheer idea of the space-time manifold, as Brian Cox has described in his TV series on forces of nature. On the other hand, the idea that all times co-exist in an abstract manifold is not quite the same as the idea that they co-exist in a person I can encounter and love. The former idea is called into question in ?{8}d. The latter is harder to grasp and believe, and if true, a greater consolation.

Does it retain their problems or resolve them? We shall see that both answers to both questions are true. Let us take each tenet in turn.

A) Nominalism

It should be obvious by now that the greatest change from {3} to {4} is the abandonment of nominalism in favor of realism, at least with regard to mathematics. This represents a reversal of the move from the Platonic realism that saw the rise of science in {2} to the materialism of {3}. However, overall {4} is far from being a restoration of {2}. In many ways, as we shall see, the release from nominalism enables {4} to carry the scientific thrust of {3} forward beyond dualism, towards a monism of a more refined and less materialistic kind. This development is not one that all philosophers of science would welcome, and it is probably more acceptable to those familiar with physics, where mathematics prevails, than those writing on the basis of the less mathematically orientated sciences such as biology, where the main thrust remains towards physical reductionism and determinism. Let us see how this is so.

B) Naturalism

It would seem that {4} is in general compatible with naturalism: the desire to explain the universe as a unified causal whole without resort to "external" causes, whatever these may be, remains a major motive in {4}. However, we noted that one of the reasons {3} adopted nominalism was to safeguard a thoroughgoing naturalism. Once the reality of mathematical structures and other ideal objects is granted, then we have conceded the cosmological role of non-material, intentional objects that are generated in the process of reasoning, "in the mind." There are then only two ways of holding naturalism and structural realism together: by denying that the mathematically real is non-physical, or by denying its non-physical aspect an explanatory role. In the first case we identify (as Tegmark does) the physical universe with a mathematical structure, so that the latter ceases to be a non-physical factor. In the latter case we hold (as Tegmark also does) that all mathematical objects exist as universes, so that these objects, even if some of them are ideal (and it is hard to see how we can exclude at least some non-physical universes, see ?{5}c and d) no longer represent explanations of *our* physical world; this is the "multiverse" solution, {5}.

The status of {4}, whether ideal or material, will be discussed as ?{4}b, and whether the multiverse can explain this universe (naturalistically or otherwise) as ?{5}e. Meanwhile, if the realism of {4} is allowed to extend beyond the mathematical and the naturalistic, the door is opened to intentional realities that are not mathematically expressed. For example, as noted, it allows for the possible meaningfulness of music. Generally {4} is more amenable than {3} to creativity in the realm of ideas, and less tied to a fixed "matter," but arguably these might be expressed in a broadened definition of nature, allowing {4} to be naturalistic in a non-materialistic way.

1) Lawfulness, 2) Discoverability, and 3) Formulability

These three tenets clearly remain in place in {4}; arguably they are strengthened. The laws of nature are given a precise, mathematical formulation that is clearly discoverable by the human mind. In the process, we note, physics gains a pre-eminence among the sciences because the other sciences cannot so easily be mathematically formulated (if they can be at all), but must rely for credibility on the belief that in principle their laws are reducible to those of physics.

4) Empirical Testability

In philosophy, empiricism opposes rationalism. Empiricists from Locke through the logical positivists have asserted, with varying degrees of dogmatism, that theories can only be true either by definition or by correspondence with what is observed. But {4} definitely takes the rationalist side, regarding mathematical and other Third Realm statements as being true neither by definition, nor because of experience, but because of rational argument and proof. No mathematician, for example, would adopt an empirical approach to deciding on the mathematical proposition that the diameter of a square of side 1cm is $\sqrt{2}$cm, by carefully measuring the diameter of lots of 1cm squares with a ruler, and then calculating the average! She would decide the issue by checking Pythagoras's proof. Some empiricist philosophers have argued that mathematical propositions fall on the other side of their divide, and are true by definition. And it may be the case that, for example, $4 \times 1 = 4$ is simply a definition of what we mean by 4. But nobody has ever shown that all mathematical statements, including for example Pythagoras's theorem, follow from the definitions involved. Hence {4} places such theorems in a realm of eternal, necessary truths that could not be otherwise, truths we arrive at neither by observation nor by definition. {4} allows a lot of mathematical speculation—such as we find in string theory and other such "theories of everything"—that does not cash out with any directness in terms of observable reality.

However—as raised in ?{4}a below—if such theories are to be scientific, they must surely eventually terminate in predictions about what we might observe. Arguably in {4} we do not test propositions one by one, but build a total body of theory that is logically interconnected, which then stands or falls as a whole on the strength of perhaps relatively few critical experiments. Thus it is often thought by the uninitiated that quantum physics has been proven true through experiments like the double slit, and Schrödinger's cat. But Schrödinger's cat never existed; this poor dead-and-alive creature, and the slit experiment, and the like, are *thought* experiments, which argue what must be the case if the theory is true; though in more recent times an actual double slit experiment has been carried out, and needless to say, behaves as the quantum theory predicts, as does all the other evidence.

5) Spatiotemporal Uniformity

Again, this principle is strengthened in {4}. Whereas an empirical law might vary with time and space (though as noted, only if it did so in accord with another law could this be regarded as a case of law-governed behavior), the laws are now mathematical, and mathematics cannot change in accordance with contingent matters of timing and location. {5} will explore the possibility of different laws in different universes, but this possibility exists because those universes might be different mathematical structures. On the other hand, mathematics can suggest other interpretations of space and time than the absolute, uniform container within which Newton's laws play out: including the curved space-time of Einstein, and the more radical relativity of Leibniz and Mach; see {6}.

6) Quantifiability

The originally Pythagorean tenet that quantifiable mathematical relations underlie and explain nature is the essence of the move from {3} to {4}. The tenet is merely taken further, at the partial expense of the empiricist tenet.

As noted, this is the decisive move against dualism, which posits a substantial realm of mind, including secondary qualities, alongside matter, which has only primary properties. {4} allows for a substantial realm of ideas, including mathematical objects; but this is not a parallel world to the material world, but rather, that which underlies that world.

The question raised in the Résumé of {3}—the possibility of a "view from nowhere"—seems to be answered in {4}, in that mathematical truths and other propositions are not dependent on the consciousness of the individual who believes them, but are indeed "views from nowhere," perhaps the only such views there are. The diameter of a square of side 1 unit is $\sqrt{2}$ units long whatever the measuring unit is, and whatever any individual thinks, has thought, or will think. (We would not have known this without a community and a tradition of people making geometric constructions, but that is another story.) In the Multiverse, as we shall see in the next World, this is even more so: most of the universes in it are indeed "viewed" or indeed "thought about" by nobody and nothing.

7*) Determinism

Here, nominalism and naturalism have effected a drastic change—signified by the change to 7*—from the weaker Principle 7 in {2}, that "efficient causes are necessary and sufficient to explain events." Nominalism demands that we find causation in individual physical things. {4} has the potential to resolve the issue (part of ?{3}b) of what makes for natural necessity, how laws of nature can be not just descriptive (as in "the sun has risen at such and such times") but prescriptive ("the sun *must* rise at such and such a time tomorrow"). The laws of nature have a mathematical form, and this form is more than decoration; the mathematics, according to {4}, correlates the real relations between the events we observe. The mathematical Newtonian laws correlate the rotation of the earth and its orbit of the sun such that we can predict exactly when the sun will rise tomorrow, and indefinitely into the future. Could it be that the necessity that applies in the mathematics transfers to the natural laws, making them in turn necessary? To be sure, the events themselves do not become necessary, since the natural laws take the form of conditionals. Typically, they are expressed in statements like: "if ... then ..., other things being equal." For example, if there are no clouds in the way, and no cosmic catastrophes like meteorites striking the earth, and I am still alive and have got up in time, then I will see the sun rise at such and such a time tomorrow. I know this with the same kind of absolute certainty as that by which I know the diameter of a square of size 1cm will be $\sqrt{2}$cm. This too has its *ceteris paribus* caveat, such as "... provided I have drawn and measured it accurately, and I am in Euclidean space ..., etc."

However, this move may be too fast. We know mathematical necessities by means of proof, but natural necessities (if that is what they are) require checking against the evidence. Predictions from natural law, like the sunrise, need to be tested, and it is often the anomalies—the predictions that turn out to be false—that force us to go deeper and discover better laws. And the mathematical law has to be applied to physical reality by means of some kind of physical model that maps the law onto observable events. As a simple example, the model of electricity in a wire as a "flow" of electrons is what enables us to transfer the mathematics correlating pressure, resistance, and flow in a river or a water pipe, to correlate voltage, resistance and current in an electricity-bearing wire. In the absence of the model of current as an electron flow, the mathematics would still make the right predictions, but we would not know why; we would not have a scientific understanding of currents. And in the absence of the model, we might not have thought of applying the mathematics of flow in the first place.

It was for such reasons that Rom Harré, encountered in {3}, argued for a revolution placing the model at the center of scientific enquiry.

> *The Copernican Revolution in the Philosophy of Science* is to see the traditional view that a deductive system of laws is the heart of a theory, and an associated picture of the mechanism and permanent objects are but a heuristic device, turned upside down. It is to see the model as essential and the achievement of a deductive system among the laws as a desirable heuristic device.[25]

Tegmark would take precisely the view that Harré criticizes; for him it would be the mathematics that describes the reality, the model being a crude but dispensable heuristic device to help our imaginations get to the mathematics. But then, as we have seen, Tegmark is a strong realist regarding the status of the mathematics itself. We will return to this debate as ?{4}c below, while {6} will discuss what seems to be a very different, panpsychist approach to natural necessity as an extension of our direct experience of causing things to happen.

Finally, note that at this stage that ?{3}c—"Why these laws?"—remains unresolved in {4}, awaiting possible resolution in {5}.

8*) Reductionism

Naturalism has made for a big change—denoted by the *—to the equivalent scientific principle, *"Mechanization: The Cosmos and Its Contents Work like a Machine."* Reductionism is surpassed in {4}, not by being abandoned, but by being taken further than in {3}. A great deal of the mathematics of the

---

25. Harré, *Principles*, 2.

modern universe cannot be ascribed to particles and their relations, and cannot be imagined as happening in our 3-D space, let alone observed in it. This is because the elements to which science reduces things have been stripped, not only of secondary qualities like color and texture, but of primary ones like mass and location. The questionable bias in materialism in favor of the primary quantities (see ?{3}d) is overcome by the relegation of the primary and the secondary with equal rigor. "Reality" in {4} lies with equations specifying laws, patterns, and relationships, and not with qualities or things of *any* kind, primary or secondary. This in turn resolves ?{3}h, the regress in reductive explanation. Having stated the problem as quoted in ?{3}h, Tegmark goes on to argue:

> The Mathematical Universe Hypothesis offers a radical solution to this problem: at the bottom level, reality is a mathematical structure, so its parts have no intrinsic properties at all! In other words, the Mathematical Universe Hypothesis implies that we live in a relational reality.[26]

Mathematical structures like triangles (unlike physical triangular shapes, which may be colored and have a specific length) and numbers (unlike numbers of say physical oranges, which would be orange and smell a certain way) have no properties of their own, not even "primary" ones. Tegmark argues that "the properties of nature stem not from properties of its ultimate building blocks (which have no properties at all), but from the relations between these building blocks."[27] If he is right, and they do represent the ground level of explanation, they terminate the notorious regress implied in reductionist explanation. Whether such moves take us completely out of materialism into a form of idealism will be raised as ?{4}b.

Summary

{4} abandons the nominalism that led to confusions within {3}, thereby enabling what some would regard as a less confining naturalism, a freedom from reductionism, and a more total, less point-by-point, need for empirical testing. Strict materialists, on the other hand, might regard this move as an abandonment of the naturalistic, reductionist, and empiricist basis of science. Is the move worthwhile in answering the many questions the materialism of {3} raises? Or does it simply raise many more?

I will take the first question first, following through from ?{3}a to j.

---

26. Tegmark, *Mathematical Universe*, 267.
27. Tegmark, *Mathematical Universe*, 267.

a) Is nominalism true? No. Structural realism is by definition realism regarding structures and relations.

b) Why must nature obey laws? Because its structure is mathematically constituted, therefore necessary, as mathematical truths are.

c) Why these particular laws and constants? The answer must await {5}.

d) Accounting for qualia. Qualia do not fill a constitutive role in {4}, but universals like "red" are real, and complex relations between qualia may build up, as in music.

e) Accounting for intentionality. Intentional objects, especially mathematical ones, are at the core of {4}.

f) Mental vs. physical identity. If the universe is identical with a mathematical object, then parts of the universe, like brains or persons, may be identical with intentional structures, though the queries raised about the irreducibility of intention are far from satisfied in {4}.

g) Determinism. This would seem to be upheld by the necessity of the world's mathematical basis, but again, it sits in tension with the intentionality and the ethical aspect of {4}.

h) Regress of reductionism and determinism. The regress is stopped by making (mathematical) relations, rather than entities and their quantities, primary.

i) Completeness. {4} certainly allows a foot in the door, if not for God in the full Judeo-Christian sense, at any rate for a Platonic Good and Beautiful.

j) Ethics. By the same process, ethical decision-making and the pursuit of final causes come to make sense, though this is in tension with mathematical determinism.

There is something Janus-like about {4}. On the one hand, the resort to mathematics, and the idea of the world as a complete mathematical structure or Parmenidean One, could make for a rigid determinism. On the other, the openness to mathematical and by implication other forms of intentionality, and the subversion of the idea of a fundamental bedrock of material objects, could send shivers down the materialist spine. This duality raises further questions.

God, Spirituality, and Ethics in {4}

What story does {4} tell, what spirituality follows from it, and what view—if any—of God? I will defer discussion of these issues till we have considered {5}, which is in many ways an extension or radicalization of {4}, opening up alternative answers to these questions that are implicit in {4}. I hope it will become clear how this approach enhances both clarity and conciseness.

Questions Regarding {4}

In addition to the above ten questions regarding {4} in relation to the materialist tenets, there are the following.

?{4}a: Does Mathematics Still Need Dialogue with Scientific Experiment and Modelling?

The title of Farmelo's book, *The Universe Speaks in Numbers*, suggests a wholesale commitment to {4} in which mathematics might replace the observation of what happens to matter in experiment. But in fact his book shows how the traffic has not all been one way. Physics has progressed best in the periods when mathematicians and scientists worked in partnership. While it is true that new mathematical models have often enabled physics to explore the world in new ways, the converse is also true. Very often models designed to explain experimental data have offered mathematicians new concepts to work on. A wholesale move from {3} to {4} might suggest we could forget experiment and advance physics by rational thought alone. But while this chapter has noted an important sense in which "Third Realm" mathematical objects are "out there" to be discovered, this is clearly not the same as the sense in which physical objects are. The method by which we discover the mathematical objects—rational thought, mathematical notation, and the concepts that go with it, and the construction of proofs— is not the same as the method by which we discover "First Realm" physical reality (or for that matter "Second Realm" contents of consciousness). To discover physical reality, we have not just to think clearly, but to get our hands messy in experiment and observation, as well as (according to Rom Harré) the making of scientific models.

Farmelo does not go into detail about why the partnership between mathematics and physics should work so well. The discussion of Harré and Tegmark suggests that mathematical formulae (for example, the matrix mechanics and the quantum wave equation) serve to correlate relations between different events, while physics interprets the mathematics in terms of models (for example, particle and wave) that suggest generative mechanisms operating in underlying reality. Or the physics may work the other way around: a generative model for what is going on may be intuited, then sharpened up mathematically. The mathematics and the physical model that goes with it have to be tested in experiment and observation to see if the correlations specified in the mathematics do indeed co-vary in the way the formulae suggest. A triad—mathematical formulae, physical model, experimental observation—needs to be in place, but where we begin and end is flexible; there is no rigid, methodologically correct order.[28]

In this sense it may be possible to reconcile Rom Harré, champion of the model, with Max Tegmark, champion of mathematics. After all, a scientific model abstracts away from crude physicality. When we use "flow" as a model for electrons in a wire—to use our simple example—we leave behind the visual and tangible elements of a flowing stream, like weeds and eddies and fish. We focus only on what is "mappable" onto a current in a wire, and this consists precisely of a structure of mathematical relations between pressure gradient, resistance, and current. So, when mapped onto the physical data we are investigating, the model acts as a mathematical structure of relations.

On the other hand, Tegmark's mathematical realism makes his mathematical objects more "real" than bare patterns of relations: something more like Harré's generative mechanisms. In discussing Gödel and game-playing, we noted the way mathematical structures emerge in a surprising, unpredictable way. It is perhaps because of this that mathematical relations can mimic and model the real generative mechanisms behind things. Tegmark's short step is to eliminate the element of analogy in this statement, and to move from "mimic" and "model" to "be." For him the mathematics does not mimic or model reality; it *is* the mechanism generating events. That radical step would clarify an issue which Harré never quite clarified: the status of models and generative mechanisms, and precisely what imparts necessity to their predictions. The conceptual necessity that applies to mathematical proofs would map directly onto the natural necessity linking causes to effects. This might be Tegmark's step of genius.

Or it might not. . . . The partnership between science and mathematics may not prove to be as easy as Tegmark would wish. Our mathematics, for example, includes numbers like $\sqrt{2}$ and π which are enumerated by an infinite, non-repeating sequence of integers. Because of this lack of finite definition, the Greeks called such numbers "irrational." In geometric space, a line

---

28. Cf. Thompson, *Holy Ground*, ch. 5.

between two points A and B contains an infinite number of points. But if we mark a point half way, at C, then there is an infinite number of points between A and C, and between C and B. So the line has the same (infinite) length as each of its two halves, and again, the same length as its four quarters, and so on *ad infinitum*.[29] For this sort of reason, Hilbert rejected the idea that real space can correspond exactly to geometric and mathematical descriptions, declaring that "a really existing infinite set is not possible."[30] But this suggests a divergence between mathematical and physical descriptions. Some speculate that at the ultimate level, just as energy and quantum states come in discrete units, not a variable continuum, so space-time itself may be granular, not continuous. Possibly we could find a mathematical description of this granular space-time. And possibly not. And if not, it might mean that the partnership between physics and mathematics is a marriage of convenience, rather than an indissoluble love bond, and at certain points mathematics and physics may need to go their separate ways, one with its ideal, continuous lines and figures, and the other with its messier, granular objects; each able to shed much light on the other, but amenable to no final "theory of everything." The jury is out on that.

Could we then be left after all with a dualist account, or perhaps a triadic one? Do the different methods appropriate to material, mental, and mathematical realities mean that the realities themselves are substantially different? If the methods have to work *together*, as Farmelo suggests, perhaps not. Perhaps what is involved is a duality or a triad of methods for unravelling a single kind of reality. But such reflections lead us on to the next two questions.

?{4}b: Is {4} Materialist or Idealist?

It would seem that the abandonment of nominalism in {4} forces a threefold choice: to abandon claims to naturalism, to interpret naturalism in a non-materialistic way, or to take a curiously physicalist interpretation of mathematics. If {4} dispenses with all the qualities we associate with matter, and leaves us with numbers and equations only, can this still be called a materialist worldview? Where do equations, universals, and propositions exist? For Plato it was certainly in a non-material world, since matter for him

---

29. This is the basis of several ancient paradoxes, including the race between Achilles and the tortoise. If the tortoise is given a head start, Achilles can never catch up with him. Achilles is forever having to cross the space between them, by which time the tortoise has edged forward a little and opened up more space for Achilles to cross.

30. Cited in Tegmark, *Mathematical Universe*, 69.

was ever-changing, so nothing could be lastingly true of it. Conceptualism, meanwhile, places Third Realm objects firmly in the constructive human mind. However, the angles of a triangle in Euclidean space add up to 180° whether anybody thinks or knows the fact. Popper is therefore probably wise to ascribe these objects to a Third Realm, alongside matter and mind.

We noted how {2}, by reserving a substantial space for mind, rendered mind a kind of universe parallel to matter; a universe equally mechanical, and hence susceptible to elimination or at least reduction to matter in {3}. But now it seems that once it has eliminated the mental ghost, materialism loses touch with the mind-matter contrast, and so naturally develops into the quasi-mental or at least neutral {4}.

On the other hand, if, as just suggested, mathematics cannot dispense with physical investigations, then *pace* Plato, {4} cannot be entirely idealist in the way that, for example, {7} is; it has to retain an element of materialism. But does {4} need to be dualist in the way that {2} is? Does the move from {3} to {4} disguise a regression to the dualism of {2}? Certainly, there are clearer logical pathways to the dualism of {2}, and even to the idealism of {7}, from {4} than from {3}. And as will become apparent, the temptation to walk one of those pathways, in order to avoid {5}, the multiverse, might for some be strong. The fundamental question at stake here is whether in {4} consciousness needs to be given the kind of *constitutive* role that it has in {2} and {7}. Is a substantial consciousness or mind needed, to be the place that "holds," discovers, and entertains the Third Realm objects?

?{4}c: Are Ideas and Mathematical Structures Real?

Part of the answer to this last question is that ideas and mind are "located" very differently in {4} as compared with its predecessors. In dualism the non-quantifiable ideas are located in the mind, in the Cartesian "projector," while the mathematical ideas are located in a mechanized matter, on the Cartesian "screen," as it were, which we are continuously observing. In {3} the ideas (qualia and intentionality) either do not exist, or they are in the brain, or its functions, or in behavior, rather than the mind, and there is no strictly ideal world. In {4}, by contrast, the ideas have neither the Cartesian privacy nor the materialist obscurity. The ideas are "out there," not in brains or dispositions, but in the world itself, constituting its structures. The privacy of the Cartesian theatre and the materialist obsession with the brain are both alike gone; ideas are not in our minds or brains, but in our discourse and in the reality in which we live and move and construct things together. If we emphasize the role of human activity here, we will lean towards constructivism, and see the ideas as human constructs; if we emphasize the reality of the structures, and the way human construction participates in and discovers, rather than invents, structure, then we will tend toward the realism of Plato or Popper. The discussion of games and mathematical emergence should clarify the need to emphasize the Third Realm as that of real structures, or structure as reality, in a manner that prevents constructivism from tipping into nominalism.

But these questions about the reality of Third Realm objects or Platonic forms, *vis a vis* physical and mental reality, raise a deeper question still: how do we decide whether something is "real"; or, what do we mean by calling something real?

?{4}d: What Makes a World Real Anyway?

Does it make sense to rule out consciousness from a constitutive role in world-making? Granted that mathematical truths are independent of conscious thought, if no subject knows the assertions of mathematics to be true, in what sense can they be true? It is one thing, to believe that mathematical truths are not true simply *because* someone has thought them to be true, or *because* they have somehow been "constructed" by the mind. It is another, to believe they could be true entirely without minds to discover them, or thinkers to know them. To be "true," a proposition or formula surely needs to be knowable, by some mind. Is there such thing as an unknowable truth? (Mystics might refer to such ineffables, but they are surely talking about truths knowable only by God, rather than not knowable at all.)

When we affirm that something exists, or some proposition is true, what do we mean? In the case of mathematical truths, we mean (with some qualifications and concessions related to Gödel) that that proposition can be constructed or proven from other accepted mathematical truths or axioms. But what more are we saying when we say something actually or physically exists? Given two objects that are described by exactly the same mathematics, except that one is described as existent and the other as non-existent, what exactly are we affirming of the one, and denying to the other? Consider the dodecahedron: Tegmark would say that, being a mathematical structure, it exists. Another, more empirically minded philosopher might disagree. But is there anything *in the dodecahedron* that can decide between these opposing views? This undecidability is true of most or all mathematical objects. We may debate the existence of the number 4, or the "irrational" number π, or the many levels of infinity described by Cantor, or i (the square root of

-1). But the answer is not provided by mathematics, and philosophers have taken different views.

But the same is true of universes. One philosopher, who believes in the multiverse, might say that such and such a universe exists. A philosopher of another persuasion might say it is a possible world that doesn't actually exist. A theologian might say it exists in the Mind of God, but not in created reality. But the issue between them cannot be determined by examining the universe in question. As Kant put it, existence is not a real predicate, by which he meant "x exists" does not affirm of x any discernible attribute.

But there is perhaps a possibility in the object that such statements affirm. I might be affirming that the alien universe, or mathematical object, in question, is observable. The universe would not be observable by us, to be sure, as we live in a different universe. But I might be affirming that in that universe there would be beings that know what it is like to be there; that the universe enters one or more consciousnesses. (I couldn't know that, of course, but I might meaningfully affirm it.) It is the same with the dodecahedron. If I insisted the dodecahedron was real, I might just be being a mathematical realist, and affirming it is mathematically real. But I might be affirming that there is something it is like to be that dodecahedron, or part of it. As it happens, I find no reason to believe this! But it seems to me that if I were to affirm that the dodecahedron was real, not just in the mathematical sense, but in the sense that this universe is real, I would be affirming that either it could be experienced, or it could experience itself. If this is so, reality is not *just* knowability in experience, but I suggest it is at least that.

For surely part of what we mean when we say that a universe exists is that some being must be able to experience it as existing. A structure—mathematical or otherwise—that people think about or are otherwise aware of, or are even mistaken about, logically must exist. But there would be something contradictory about affirming the existence of a structure that no being, inside or outside of it, ever thinks of or is aware of or mistaken about. This would be what one might call a performative contradiction, for in the act of saying that nobody ever thinks about such and such a structure, you would be thinking about it. To be existent, then, is at least to figure at some time in some consciousness or mind. That is not to say the mind must be thinking about it, or directly aware of it, for it to exist; the mind may just be inferring it from its necessary relation to things it is aware of.

To be real, therefore, something must both be conceptually coherent, and be potentially experienced, or else connected by conceptual or causal necessity to that which is potentially experienced. (We believe that black holes are real, for example, because they make conceptual sense, being a consequence of natural laws that we know about, and though not experienced directly, they have effects we can observe.) It is experienceable effects that select which conceivables (including conceivable universes) are physically or materially real. The real could be identified with "sensible structure," "sensible" meaning experienceable, "structure" meaning the forms and relations typical of {4}.

If true, this has momentous consequences. To be real, something has to be thinkable or conceivable. To say that x exists but that one cannot imagine, deduce, conceive, or describe what x is, is not to say anything at all. In other words, to exist at all, a thing has to exist in the Third Realm, as an object described in mathematical or other universal terms. Some things like mathematical objects and mythical objects, and perhaps musical tunes and symphonies, only exist in that world. But to be physically real—in other words, to qualify as an object in the First Realm, the material world—it has in addition to be potentially real, or to have potential consequences, in the Second Realm, the world of experience and consciousness. Conscious experience is what answers Hawking's famous question. Might we even define the material world, the First Realm, as that part of the Third Realm that has the potential to make things happen in the Second Realm?

Such are the thoughts that open up the logical pathways to Worlds that honor a constitutive role for Mind, or minds, or both. But before we consider the Worlds that do justice to Mind, we need to consider the World that is most successful at eliminating a constitutive role for Mind and/or minds: the World that needs nowhere to view it from; the World that consists of many worlds ({5}).

?{4}e: Is Goodness God?

Finally, if the Third Realm consists of real constructs, is there good reason for limiting those real constructs to mathematical ones, after the manner of Tegmark? The real is often mathematical, and mathematics has disclosed many realities, but not all the sciences are amenable to mathematics, and to limit reality to the mathematizable may well be arbitrary. Certainly, as we have seen, while there is something paradigmatic about mathematical realities, there are many more conceptual constructs or "forms" that might qualify as real. Do unicorns and other imaginary concepts, and music and symphonies, have their own kinds of reality?

For Plato, the supreme reality was the form of the Good, which grounds all other realities, as we shall see in {10}. Moreover, a Good that grounds both the material world and consciousness, including experiences of the Good, is not necessarily far from what monotheistic faiths have called

God. Goodness might qualify as real in our sense of being both supremely coherent, and connected to experience. And this real Goodness that motivates our wills and transforms our experience might reasonably be called God. But there are many ways of conceiving such a God, as we shall see in the worlds from {5} onward.[31]

---

31. The Résumé after {5} will cover both {4} and {5}.

{5}

EVERYTHING THAT CAN HAPPEN MUST

The Multiverse

Everything that can happen does happen.[1]

Inasmuch as for God all things are possible, it may be said that this is what God is: one for whom all things are possible.... God is that all things are possible, and that all things are possible is the existence of God.[2]

Our physical world not only is described by mathematics, but . . . it is mathematical (a mathematical structure), making us self-aware parts of a giant mathematical object.[3]

THE "WORLDS" CONSIDERED IN this book involve different ways of conceiving the relation of mind to matter, or as we now might put it, the relations between Popper's First, Second, and Third Realms. All these ways have implications in turn for how we conceive of the relation between God and the world of mind and/or matter. The multiverse is not obviously a way of understanding the relation between mind and matter, or the three Realms. So why should it have a chapter to itself in this book?

The multiverse arises out of several kinds of development. Philosophers have found modality—possibility and necessity—mysterious. It is relatively easy to know what we mean when we say something actually

---

1. Subtitle of Cox, *Quantum Universe*.
2. Kierkegaard, *Sickness unto Death*, 173.
3. Tegmark, *Mathematical Universe*, 271.

happened, but what do we mean when we say something must have happened, or might not have happened but did? And what kinds of fact make such statements true or false? One way around this is to speak of possible worlds. Something that must happen is something that happens in all possible worlds; something that might not have happened but did is an event that happens in this world but not all possible ones. This makes clear the kind of "fact" that makes modal statements true or false.

However, arguably putting things this way only passes the buck from facts about possibility in this world to facts holding true in "possible" worlds, whose status remains questionable. David Lewis argued for "modal realism,"[4] the idea that all possible worlds are really actualized, though not in our particular neighborhood. Many philosophers have found this idea extravagant, and the idea of an actual possible world looks on the face of it contradictory, or else the term "actual" appears redundant.

It is possible, of course, to relegate the conceivable or possible to the conceptual world that is Popper's "Third Realm," leaving this universe as the sole physically real "First Realm" universe, and/or the sole universe that we are conscious of ("Second Realm"). But if you have trouble with the idea of the mind creating worlds (albeit only conceptually) it is tempting to give the other possible worlds physical existence too, as well as mental existence in the sense that we can imagine and conceive of them (though not experience them). Then we can affirm (paraphrasing Brian Cox, above) that every possible universe actually exists. In that sense the multiverse is, after all, a way of relating our three worlds of matter, consciousness, and concept, giving them all as it were equal reality status. It is therefore not necessarily a materialistic concept. Other universes might be made up of angels and disembodied spirits, if these are indeed conceivable. But the multiverse is most commonly advanced as a way of holding on to materialism and minimizing the role of mind, while at the same time doing justice to the claims of mathematics.

And there is a closely connected reason for advocating the multiverse. In the search to understand why the world is as it remarkably is, it avoids the need to resort to the designing Mind of God. The multiverse does not have to be godless. There might conceivably be some worlds that a god has created, and others where chance and necessity have been given free range. Deciding we are in one sort of universe (whichever way we decide) would not preclude there being the other sort.

On the other hand, while this god who creates some but not all possible worlds might be an interesting being, he, she, or it would not be the

---

4. Lewis, *Plurality of Worlds*.

God of mainstream theism (and indeed mainstream atheism), who is either the only conceivable way of explaining all the worlds, or a total misconception which cannot explain any of them. If the latter holds, and God is a misconception, the godless multiverse may seem the more viable alternative. But if God *is* conceivable, God seems to require much less effort of imagination and conceptual invention than the multiverse, and the demands of simplicity and parsimony point to belief in God. In practice, without atheist presuppositions, the immense claims and effort of imagination that the multiverse requires of us are hardly worth making.

The multiverse dispenses with the transcendent God, because, the realization of every possibility, it is *actus purus*, actuality without unrealized potential, and hence, on at last one definition, is God (see {8} and options (A) and (D) below). To avoid this pantheistic identity, a classical theist who believed in the possibility of the multiverse might try to distinguish the mind of God, which entertains all possibilities, and the multiverse, which is all possibilities as realized by God. God might then be said to "make the multiverse." But in the multiverse the difference between possibility and actuality—and hence between being entertained in the mind of God and being realized through the action of God—becomes blurred. In the multiverse, every possibility is actualized. For many, the abolition of the notion of non-actual possibilities is one of the main attractions of the multiverse. In it, there just is nothing conceivable even in the mind of God that does not exist. In a sense, the multiverse makes a pantheist of God; God's world emanates by necessity from his thought. Such is the radical overhaul of how the multiverse bids us understand reality, and our world, in relation to the conceivable and possible.

Now, being a mathematical realist, as in {4}, does not force a belief in {5}, the multiverse. We can coherently be mathematical realists, as Plato and many others were, without believing in the multiverse; and we can coherently believe in the multiverse, as many scientists do, without being mathematical realists. On the other hand, {4} helps us on our way to {5}, for two reasons.

Firstly, being a mathematical realist means that you ascribe reality to the conceivable, and the multiverse is a way of ascribing reality to what others would see as merely possible or conceivable worlds, existing in human minds and perhaps the divine Mind. In {4}, the world we see and touch ceases to monopolize our thoughts. It may be that what best satisfies the hunger for Parmenides's necessary One is the multiverse; though as we shall see, multiverses themselves come in several kinds, with several ways of justifying them; and none of them is strictly "necessary."

Secondly, as already noted, the actual equations used in quantum mechanics and string theory lend themselves to the idea of the multiverse. The multiverse is in one way the simplest explanation of the "collapse" of the wave equation, though in another way, of course, the multiverse seems complex beyond belief.

Actually, this complexity may be partly resolved if the number of universes posited is infinite. As John Leslie points out, the simple numbers are 0, 1, and infinity.[5] It would require considerable argument to prove, for example, that there are exactly 153 universes. But to argue for an unlimited number of universes would require no special pleading, any more than to argue for just one, or no universes. (The latter would make sense on some definitions of "universe": for example, we might well argue that there is no universe in the sense of a causally unified totality of entities, just lots of unrelated events or things; see option (C) below.)

However, the main reason to support the multiverse has little to do with {4} and mathematics. It has to do with our response to what has been called the "anthropic" structure of the universe, alluded to in the introduction. Among the five main possible responses, the multiverse most clearly does without God. If by "naturalism" we mean explaining things without reference to things and forces beyond the universe, nothing could be more "unnatural" than the multiverse. But if we mean explaining things specifically without reference to minds or Mind (which is what naturalism is often used to mean in practice, even though the broader meaning is arguably a more "natural" interpretation) then the multiverse indeed offers a naturalistic approach.

So let us look more closely at the anthropic question[6] and see how the multiverse sits with the four other contenders for an explanation of why the universe we know is so finely tuned for life and consciousness.

The Anthropic Question[7]

Only relatively recently have scientists come to realize the "anthropic" dimension of the cosmos, that is, the degree to which laws and constants that could have been otherwise seem to be tuned just right for the evolution of conscious beings like ourselves. The many factors that are "just right" for us to exist include the three-dimensionality of space (at least on our "macro"

---

5. Leslie, *Infinite Minds*, 25.

6. It is really more a question—a focus for discussion—than a principle or an answer.

7. The first two paragraphs in this section are adapted from my *Buddhist Christianity*, 222–23.

level); the balance between the basic forces (gravity, electromagnetism, the "strong" force that binds the nucleus of each atom, and the mysterious "weak" force); and the distribution of matter in the early universe. All in all, the chance of getting just one of these factors (the balance of forces) right for life to form has been calculated as 1 in 10-followed-by-sixty-zeroes. This represents the chance that a blindfolded archer would hit a one-inch bull's eye on a target set up at the opposite end of the known universe, twenty billion light years away![8]

And this is just the beginning. Once the universe has been tuned so very carefully to be capable of producing life, and not just, say, clouds of vapor or rocks of iron, there has to be a sun that burns for just the right length of time and intensity, with a planet of just the right size and distance from it, capable of receiving and retaining water and other crucial elements, with a moon created in just the right conditions, a big planet the size of Jupiter to scoop away dangerous meteorites, and so on and so forth.[9] Even then the chances of life evolving seem infinitesimally small; for in laboratories where just the right materials are present in carefully optimized conditions, at the time of writing, no scientist has ever seen anything like life emerging. Life requires something very strange to happen on a very strange planet with a very strange sun and a very strange moon in a universe that is strangely "right." But strangely, life exists.

The existence of this extraordinary and unexplained "fine tuning" in the universe has given rise to an anthropic cosmological principle, which comes in two forms. In its strong form it states that something must have done the fine tuning and caused the universe to have just the conditions that make for life and eventually us. In its weak form it simply states the tautology that any universe that beings like us can observe must have the conditions that would make it possible for beings like us to evolve. In Popper's terms, since the Second Realm, consciousness, patently exists in us, the material First Realm and the laws of the Third Realm must be such that the Second Realm arises.

There are, I suggest, five main ways of responding to the anthropic principle. The first two keep to all of the tenets of materialism, while the others involve an abandonment of some or all of them. (D) explicitly affirms the strong form of the principle, while the others accept only the weak form.

---

8. Davies, *God and the New Physics*, 178. For a longer summary of these factors and the disastrous effects of not getting them just right, see my *Holy Ground*, 215–19, and for a full account, Barrow and Tipler, *Anthropic Cosmological Principle*.

9. Morris, *Life's Solution*.

A) A Necessary Universe

We can accept all of the materialist tenets and still avoid the multiverse if this universe itself is necessary and self-explanatory. That is to say, everything that can be exists in this universe, and has to exist and be the way it is. Such a cosmos would resemble the One of Parmenides, in being a self-contained and self-explanatory, necessary whole. Such properties are traditionally ascribed to God. So on this understanding we can, with the Dutch Jew Baruch Spinoza, speak of *Deus sive Natura*: "God or (if you prefer) Nature." For Spinoza, "there is in the world only one substance, and this substance is God. Spinoza regarded all things as modes or attributes of God, who exists necessarily, and imparts necessity to all God's modes or attributes."[10] The universe is necessary because everything in it is a mode (attribute) of the one and only necessarily existent Being.

The necessary universe has obvious attractions for scientists (and drawbacks for orthodox theists such as the those who excommunicated Spinoza from the synagogue). It means absolutely everything is explained, and the ultimate theory of everything is achieved, without resort to any mysterious factors "outside" the universe, whether other universes or a God who is in some sense "other" than the universe. For the *Deus* in question is for Spinoza a pantheist God, not external but *identical to* nature. Most scientists would probably prefer to use the term *Natura* to *Deus*, to refer to a universe that has to exist and be the way it is for reasons of its own. (More on Spinoza in {6}.)

However, nothing *in* the universe necessarily exists. All things in the universe are contingent, that is to say, they are brought into being, changed, and eventually destroyed by forces outside of themselves. A necessary being would be unchangeable, like the Parmenidean One. Of course, {4} argues for truths and mathematical objects that are unchanging; but that is because they exist in the manner of concepts, not (*pace* Tegmark) as material objects, nor do they cause anything to exist or to change within the universe, in a manner that might impart their necessity to it.[11]

Could it be that though it is made of contingent things, the universe itself is necessary? In Buddhism the universe comes into being by a "co-arising" in which things cause one another to be in a circular fashion. {10} will explore this idea. But this is put forward as an argument for *sunyata*, emptiness, defined as contingency or lack of self-explanatory existence,

---

10. Scruton, *Spinoza*, Loc. 179.
11. Davies, *Mind of God*, 163.

precisely the opposite of necessary existence. And it is hard to see how it could be argued otherwise.

What *could* make the universe necessary and inevitable? Is ours a *logically* necessary universe? Are the laws and conditions of the universe as they are because any alternative would be a logical contradiction? Or is it a *mathematically* necessary universe? Are the laws of nature like the geometric law, for example, that demands that (in the Euclidean plane) the angles of a triangle have to total 180°, or that parallel lines never meet? I have argued that in some senses they are; but this is not a sense that would make for a necessary universe. Those very examples give the game away, because self-consistent, non-Euclidean geometries have been devised in which the angles add up to some other total, and in which all straight lines meet somewhere. We are not sure at this stage which geometry is the geometry of our space and time. But mathematics is always devising alternative possible worlds, and then working out what is necessary within them. In mathematics, as noted, necessity applies only given certain chosen basic rules (called axioms); it is always possible to choose different ones. If Gödel is right, the idea of global, all-embracing necessity based on consistent axioms is doomed in any case, even before we try to apply it to this universe.[12]

Finally, would a necessary universe answer our anthropic query? Hardly so. Even if the world has to be the way it is through logical or mathematical necessity, the fact that this world gives rise to life and consciousness is left unexplained. It remains freakish that the universe that has to be for logical reasons should be such as to give rise to us.

That is why the search for the Parmenidean One takes us beyond this universe to the multiverse.

B) A Necessary Multiverse

We can accept the materialist tenets, and apply them not to this universe alone but to a range of universes, or multiverse. On such a view, everything that can be actually is. All possibilities are realized. If everything that is possible exists, then nothing that is possible can fail to exist: everything that can exist must necessarily exist.[13] This contingent universe we inhabit is only one among an infinity of universes; it has to exist simply because it is possible.

---

12. Davies, *Mind of God,* 166–67, with reference to the arguments of Stannard and Barrow.

13. The idea of the multiverse as necessary is queried in ?{5}f.

To consider some examples, if unicorns may exist, they must exist in some universe. On the face of it, unicorns could arise in an evolutionary process on a planet relatively like earth. Other possibilities, like bats with a wingspan of 100 meters, or birds the size of bumble bees, or land-living dinosaurs as heavy as blue whales, or spiders the size of elephants, are ruled out given the physical, including gravitational, constraints of our planet and the properties of living structures. But a unicorn could conceivably evolve, say, by sexual selection from the horse—horned horses proving more attractive to mates, or more able to fight off sexual rivals, or both—or by natural selection from the rhino as a more agile, speedy, horse-like version. But if this is indeed conceivable, in the necessary multiverse there *must* be unicorns.

Of course, there is also the possibility of a contingent multiverse, in which only some possible universes are realized, others not. But while a contingent universe is worthy of consideration (as option C), a contingent multiverse is not, for two reasons. One is that there would be no way of knowing which possible worlds actually existed. In our own universe we can observe, and in the necessary universe we can work out by conceptual and mathematical methods, which worlds are possible, knowing that according to the theory these are actual. But regarding a contingent multiverse there can be no observation, and no assurance that what is possible is actual. Both empirical and conceptual methods fail. And secondly, a contingent multiverse does not explain anything, in the way that a necessary multiverse might. Because the choice of universes is left contingent, everything in each universe is ultimately contingent.

Among the possibly infinite range of universes, only an infinitesimal proportion of them are right for the evolution of life and consciousness. But this one which we are conscious of living in would by definition have to be one of those! So the "just rightness" of this universe for the evolution of life is explained by a kind of "cosmological natural selection"[14] by consciousness. Our consciousness would have to be in one of the universes that are right for its evolution. Those unfit for consciousness are by definition doomed to exist unknown. (On another account, option E, they are "doomed" not to exist at all.)

The multiverse has come into favor with many (but by no means all) physicists and cosmologists fairly recently, but it is an ancient idea. Hindu and Buddhist thought envisage "beginningless" time cycles in great *kalpas* of up to 1.344 trillion years, in which universes are created, reach their zenith, decline, and are destroyed. However, all the universes are more or less

---

14. Cf. Smolin, *Life of the Cosmos*.

the same, and do not appear to explore radically different possibilities. Such exploration is needed for the multiverse to fulfil its main role, which is to arrive eventually, by random reshuffling, at the right conditions for life.

Sometimes it is argued that an everlasting universe is inevitably a multiverse. Give the universe long enough, it is said, and every possibility will turn up. However, this is dubious. It is easy to imagine an everlasting universe that offers very limited possibilities indeed: for example, a universe that consisted of a single blob that flashed random sequences of red, yellow, green, and blue. It is true that any sequence of colors you might describe, even one a million flashes long, would someday turn up. For the same reason, an everlasting monkey typing on an everlasting typewriter would one day type the complete works of Shakespeare. But there are many possibilities that would never, ever be achieved, either in the colored blob universe or in the monkey and typewriter universe. The blob universe would be unlikely, I suspect, ever to give rise to life or consciousness (and for that reason it might never really achieve even the colors, as there would be no perceivers). The monkey (unless it evolved considerably, which of course it has plenty of time to do!) would never achieve the consciousness and appreciation of the works of Shakespeare which we have, so again it is doubtful in what sense the works of Shakespeare would be accomplished by the everlasting monkey, if he and the typewriter were the only things in his universe. Our universe has considerably more variety in it than the four colors or the letters on the typewriter, but it too is constrained by its contents and laws, and even if it lasted forever, would be unlikely to accomplish *every* conceivable possibility.

So is there any reason to believe in a multiverse; or is the multiverse just a desperate measure to keep faithful to materialist tenets? Max Tegmark has listed four levels of multiverse, reached by different routes, each "larger" than the level before and with a broader rationale for crediting it with existence. These levels include most of the kinds of multiverse that have been argued for.[15]

Level I: Distant Regions of space that are currently but not forever unobservable. These would have the same effective laws of physics as us, but may have different histories. In time these universes might be drawn into our "event horizon" so as to become observable. The existence of such areas of space is uncontroversial, but it is questionable whether they make up with our and other universe a "multiverse" in any clear sense, and whether such a multiverse would possess the "necessity" our universe on its own lacks.

---

15. Tegmark, *Mathematical Universe*, Table 6.1, 166.

Level II: Inflationary Bubbles. These are also distant regions of space, but they remain forever unobservable because space between here and there keeps inflating. (Inflation, a sudden expansion of space-time, is widely accepted to have taken place in our early universe.) These regions obey the same fundamental laws of physics, but their effective laws—the constants of nature and balance between forces—may differ. This last possibility relies on there being mechanisms involved that could reshuffle the constants and so forth. Tegmark himself favors inflation as a possible means of reshuffling, but there are other candidates; for example, the intriguing cosmic cycles described by Roger Penrose.[16] The reshuffling enables a range of different laws and constants to be "explored," which might eventually result in those that are right for life. Of course, we ourselves would have to be in one that is right for life.

Level III: Different Parts of Quantum Hilbert Space. This is the space in which the quantum wave equation unfolds. On the "many worlds" interpretation the universe "splits" into different universes when an observation is made. The result is an unimaginable infinitude of universes. Many scientists believe in such a multiverse, in preference to taking the view that consciousness itself selects which universe is to exist. (The latter option gives us the "participatory" possibility discussed below.) Tegmark claims to have proven that the diversity of the Level III multiverse is the same as that of Level I and possibly (though he cannot prove this) Level II.

Level IV: All Mathematical Structures. This is a much vaster multiverse arising from Tegmark's own mathematical universe hypothesis (MUH). According to this, every mathematical structure corresponds to a real universe. He defines a mathematical structure very broadly, as "a set of abstract entities with relations between them. Take the integers, for instance, or geometric objects such as the dodecahedron."[17] He takes a Platonic view of such structures, but takes the unPlatonic step of identifying the physical structure of our own universe with a mathematical structure. (In other words, he regards the forms, at least the mathematical ones, as physical, rather than, as they were for Plato, inhabitants of an eternal world over and above the material one.) The multiverse, for Tegmark, is simply the totality of possible mathematical structures, each of which corresponds with a real universe.

If what science discovers is a mathematical object, then events follow causes by a total necessity. Earth's orbit and rotation, which determine that the sun will rise tomorrow, are geometrical objects within a much vaster

---

16. Penrose, *Cycles of Time.*
17. Tegmark, *Mathematical Universe,* 259.

mathematical object that is our universe. So its rising is as necessary as the diameter of a square of side 1cm being √2cm.

Tegmark believes his MUH follows from an ERH or external reality hypothesis—"that there exists an external reality independent of us humans."[18] It is not quite clear what sense of "independent" is meant here. Most scientists would not wish to make everything dependent for its existence on the existence of the human species. On the other hand, many have argued that physical existence partly means the possibility of being perceived—or conceptual or causal connection to things that could be perceived—by some perceiver, whether human or not. Note that this does not make things "dependent" on human or any other consciousness; our consciousness of a thing is not part of what causes it to exist, but part of what we mean by its existence. When we observe or perceive things or events, generally speaking we perceive them to be independent of us. Scientists do not generally regard what they perceive as dependent on their observation (except in one interpretation of the quantum collapse), but most scientists would not wish to forgo the demand that their theories be put to the test of experiment and observation, and that nothing be affirmed to exist unless there is direct or indirect empirical evidence for it. The language of Tegmark's ERH is misleading in this respect, and makes the MUH seem more reasonable than perhaps it is.

Though Tegmark's argument from the ERH to the MUH is not altogether clear, it does seem that once we have let go of the principle of perceivability, in the broad sense in which I have stated it, then the obvious criterion for real existence left is conceivability. In that sense the ERH, interpreted broadly to mean the existence of non-perceivables, leads naturally to the MUH, the existence of all mathematical conceivables (and perhaps further, to conceivables in general.) This "leading naturally" is not a strict logical entailment, since people might suggest other criteria for existence. But the main contenders in the field are now clear. There are two simple alternative understandings of reality. Either we believe that, along with conceivability, the perceivability of a thing or its effects is part of what we mean by affirming its real existence, or we believe that conceivability is the only thing we mean by affirming its real existence. In the latter case, we have the multiverse in Tegmark's strong Level IV sense, if not something even stronger. There are possible positions in between, but these are the clearest and simplest options.

The Level IV multiverse is, nonetheless, highly controversial, and we shall examine some questions and criticisms at the end of this chapter. But it

---

18. Tegmark, *Mathematical Universe*, 270–71.

has the strong logical merit of being, unlike all the lower levels of multiverse, the only version that covers all the mathematical possibilities. It looks like being the only really "necessary" multiverse, indeed, the only multiverse that satisfies all of the materialist principles (3)—(6). It is necessary, since it exhausts all the mathematical possibilities; it is naturalistic, simply because there can be nothing mathematically conceivable outside of it, so "external" factors are ruled out; it is, by definition, mathematical, since it includes only mathematical possibilities, not fictions like unicorns (unless unicorns exist as part of some universe's mathematical structure, which for all we know, they may); and it does not require consciousness as part of the explanatory structure. In that sense, Tegmark's Level IV mathematical multiverse is the one that satisfies the logical pressures that led toward {4}. In {4} we come to believe mathematical objects are real; in {5} we come to believe that they are all that is real, and that we live inside one of them. If you want a Mathematical Universe that explains everything, this is it.

However, these arguments about necessity may be fundamentally wrong; see ?{5}f.

C) A Contingent Universe: "Just-So" and "Landscape" Versions

Many find the bewildering multiplicity of the multiverses, and the vastness of Level IV in particular, too high a price to pay for this explanatory power. And that may lead people to reject determinism and reductionism, and deny that the world needs explanation, or forms a naturalistic whole. It can be argued that an empirical approach, and a belief in laws of nature, can be applied pragmatically to particular cases, without building the laws into universal principles. It is possible to take the view (and arguably most practicing scientists do take the view) that, while some things in the universe are explained by other things, and scientists should always be trying to explain events in terms of general laws, there is no explanation for the universe as a whole. There are two main ways of justifying such a view.

The first is just to accept that not everything is necessary, not everything is explicable. Not everything that is has to be, and not everything that might be actually is. This represents the commonsense view that the actual is only part of the possible (because only some possibilities are realized) and the necessary is a part of the actual (because only some things have to be the way they are, others could be different). The world is said to be contingent, meaning it is the way it is without having any reason for being so. We can call this the *just-so universe*.

Some scientists accept the just-so universe. Though the whole thrust of scientists' work is to try their best to explain things, there comes a point—these scientists say—where questions cannot be answered by the methods of science, and the most scientific thing to do at this point is to avoid the temptation to resort to metaphysical explanations like God, which are beyond scientific testing. It is better to accept with humility that science cannot know the ultimate answer to why things are as they are, or why they are at all. (Of course, this does not mean that we cannot know this ultimate answer by other means than science. This is what these scientists say *as scientists*; they may or may not say other things as the people they are. See ?{3}j.)

The alternative approach is to hold on to the idea that everything has an explanation, but maintain that the universe is not a thing and therefore not in need of explanation. This may sound paradoxical, but consider a simple example, like a landscape. In the scene in front of me, it makes sense to ask about the cow grazing in the field, or the mountain, "what caused it?" But this is because the cow and the mountain are specific things, with a specific history we can ascribe to causes. We can explain the cow in terms of the biology that gave it birth, and perhaps the economics that made the farmer decide to put it in the field. We can explain the mountain in terms of the geology of its hard rock and the pattern of rivers that have eroded it, and so on. But what about the landscape as a whole? Does it make sense to ask, "What caused it?" No, because it is not a thing. It is a collection of things: mountains, rivers, grass, cows, villages perhaps. Each of these requires its own explanation.[19]

Now what is a universe more like: a cow or mountain, or a landscape? The answer is not straightforward, but I suggest it is not stupid to regard the universe as more like the landscape. We could call this idea the *landscape universe*, according to which the universe is a collection of many different kinds of thing, each with its own explanation, but it makes no sense to ask for an explanation of the universe as a whole. Cartwright's "dappled" nature, according to which laws can be discovered in nature but nature is not universally subject to law, indicates a "landscape" universe; though the landscape universe is also compatible with the idea that all nature is subject to laws, but not laws that build into a tidy hierarchy so as to form a cosmic whole.

Buddhist co-arising, a concept introduced while discussing the necessary universe, accepts this understanding, deeming it a futile distraction

---

19. In {8}, with help from Aristotle, we will be able to apply more sophisticated terms than "thing," such as "substance."

to ask about the fundamental reason why things are as they are. This is not because there is no causality in the universe. Far from it: the law of *karma*—the law whereby good and bad deeds produce good and bad effects respectively—is often presented as the reason why things are as they are. However, bad karma for example is said to be "beginningless," and therefore unexplained: there just is bad karma and suffering in the world, and always has been. Buddhists speak of things as causing one another to be, in an interdependence that has no first cause. We will consider this in {10}, while {9} will consider ideas of self-organization, whereby an interdependent web of causes may arise, as in an organism or an ecology, which perpetuates itself without there being some original cause of it all. The web may come into being by chance, but once it exists it has to be the way it is.

However, it remains possible to give the opposite answer: that the universe is a causally interconnected thing with a history and development; or as Aristotle would call it, a substance, rather than just an aggregate. Even the landscape in front of us may seem to possess a unity that suggests a single cause behind the many causes. (More on this in the discussion of beauty in {8}.) And the paradox is this: *the more we see the universe naturalistically, as a closed causal whole admitting of no outside intervention, the more pressure there is to understand it as an entity, and therefore, to need to explain it somehow.* Paradoxically, the more we accept the principle of naturalistic explanation as the best guide to exploring our universe, the more we need logically to take one of the following two options, which take us toward views that are either more theistic or more dualistic, or both.

D) A Universe Grounded in Necessary Being

In the quote at the head of this World, Kierkegaard suggests enigmatically that God *is* the fact that everything is possible. If we define the multiverse as the totality of possibilities, then we can equate God with the multiverse. In the multiverse, everything possible is actual, or as Cox put it in his opening quote, everything that can happen does happen. But following Aristotle, Aquinas defined God in terms of precisely this identity: God is "pure act," that in which every potential is realized, and nothing remains merely possible. God, thus defined, is the multiverse: at least the multiverse conceived of as a unified whole, as a Parmenidean One. All possibilities exist in God, or (amounting to the same thing, since God is not generally thought to be material or to have a body) in the Mind of God.

This enables us to move from the idea that this universe is part of an existing multiverse, to the idea that the multiverse that is God grounds and causes the existence of this universe. The divine multiverse does not "exist" in the sense that this world exists. Rather, this world exists as the subset of thoughts in the Mind of God that God chooses to have substantial reality. Figuratively speaking (not implying an actual time sequence, but a logical precedence) first there is the multiverse, and then, with creation, there is the coming to be of time, place, and all creaturely realities within what we call our universe.

Such a move would involve a bold step away from naturalism, mathematical quantifiability, reductionism, and determinism, since we are invoking something that cannot be described in mathematical terms (though we are describing it in logical terms) and we are locating our explanation "beyond" this universe. But it could be argued that the idea of the multiverse does that already, since the multiverse by definition far exceeds this universe.

Precisely what makes for "creaturely reality" remains to be defined. On the most familiar understanding, all possibilities exist in the Mind of God, and God chooses this universe on the analogy of a person entertaining lots of possibilities and then making up his mind to take one course of action in particular. (God may of course have chosen others as well. For example, an angelic universe interacting rarely with ours, consisting of disembodied minds—having a {7} type structure—or perhaps minds embodied in a different, fire-like medium, would be in harmony with the teachings of the monotheistic faiths.) This analogy may sound all too human, but {7} and {8} will examine whether the mysterious relation between mind and body, or more precisely consciousness and action, might have something profound to say about that between God and the world.

For people of faith, of course, God cannot simply be identified with the multiverse. In itself, the multiverse does not offer us any sense of meaning or purpose; we shall soon see that it can be the reverse! If the universe with its vast spaces terrified Pascal (see quote in {3}: Progress, Defiance, and Tragedy), how much more would the infinity of the multiverse? However, the notion of this universe as chosen, from among the multiverse of possibilities, to be, might bring us closer to a traditional sense of God. But that notion of divine choice involves a step away from the awesome purity of {5} towards views discussed later in this book. It is a step we will find other reasons to take.

E) A Participatory Universe

A possibility remains: that we find the reason for selection among the multiverse of possibilities not outside this universe but within it. Instead of regarding this universe as selected by the divine mind, we see it as selected by our own minds. Such a view would hold on to one aspect of naturalism: keeping the universe closed, with all causal factors operating inside it, not from beyond. It would do so, however, by invoking a teleological causality, a causality that operates backwards in time, being a kind of purpose towards which things move. Scientific investigations, at least according to {2} and {3}, have preferred to consider only efficient causality, meaning past events that cause things to happen in the present. Option E would invoke something beyond matter and mathematics, because it would invoke consciousness as a causal factor. For that reason, it would reject determinism, reductionism, and the stricter forms of naturalism. This is the suggestion cautiously preferred by Paul Davies, following physicist John Wheeler: that the universe is as it is because only so can minds arise to contemplate it. We could call this idea the *participatory universe*.[20]

The participatory universe is necessitated teleologically, in virtue of the end or goal of its process (which may not be the temporal end-point; see {9}d). Another variety of teleologically necessitated universe is John Leslie's understanding in {10}, according to which goodness justifies the universe and teleologically causes it to exist.[21]

At the heart of the participatory universe is a logical necessity: if we know of the universe as something that includes us, then that universe has to be such that we can arise within it as its knowers. There would be a contradiction in saying, "I know that the universe I am in exists, but it contains no knowers." This would not be a direct contradiction between two assertions, but a "performative" contradiction[22] between what is asserted and what the act of asserting it implies.

We can arrive at the participatory universe by two routes, as it were. One is by wielding a massive Ockham's razor to trim the multiverse down to just this one known universe. Instead of allowing all possible universes to exist, whether knowable or not, we rule out all universes that cannot be known, and ascribe existence just to this one universe that can be experienced and known. Of course, there is no problem in other universes existing in the conceptual way that mathematical objects do. If a concept is coherent

---

20. Davies, *Mind of God*, 224–26.
21. Leslie, *Infinite Minds*.
22. Philosophers Jaakko Hintikka and Jürgen Habermas, among others, have used this notion.

and clear, we can surely grant it existence in the (limited, Third Realm?) sense in which concepts exist. Tegmark's mathematical universe hypothesis is true by definition if by "universe" we mean "mathematically conceivable interrelated totality." But I have argued that part of what we mean by "physically real" is the possibility of being known. If that is true, only universes with knowers that know them can be physically real. Ours may not be the only known universe, but we know that it is one.

We have seen that one motive for the multiverse, at least at Level III, is to avoid the suggestion that, at the quantum splitting, consciousness selects which alternative is to exist. The Level III multiverse arises when we insist on keeping both universes after the splitting. The alternative is to accept that consciousness has a real role in determining reality. The physicist John Wheeler conceives the cosmos as a closed loop that includes physical reality at one end and mind at the other. Mind emerges from matter and yet also determines matter and the way the universe is.

But we can, alternatively, arrive at the participatory universe from the divinely grounded universe, by applying Ockham's razor to render the divinity more participatory. Instead of the dubious notion of a necessary being designing the whole universe from "outside" with the intent of forming conscious minds within it, we take the bold step of equating the causing Mind with the minds in the universe that select the universe by their observations. Instead of resorting to a divinity whose necessity is itself unexplained, we ground the universe in the necessity of knowers. The universe has to be here, and as it is, because otherwise it would be unknowable and hence, according to our understanding, it would not justify the assertion of its physical existence.

This would be a move Buddhists might welcome. One school of Buddhism, the "Mind Alone" school, posits Mind as the fundamental reality. "Mind" here does not mean the individual ego or self, which does not ultimately exist, but something much more universal. Likewise, the Mind that grounds the universe is not my individual mind, since I on my own could hardly conceive of the universe. It is the totality of conscious beings interacting through science and art and religion, and so coming to know the universe in its totality, in a process that is not yet complete and may include other forms of intelligence than the human. And we add something that the Mind Alone school might not agree on, though it is suggested in the Buddhist notions of emptiness and interdependent co-arising: that this Mind is itself part of and grounded in the universe that it grounds. To many of us with a Western philosophical training, co-arising and the strange loop of causation by consciousness may look absurdly circular by comparison with causation by a necessary Being; but see {10}.

It remains our task, among these alternatives, to evaluate the multiverse. I shall begin with some comments about the spirituality it might evoke—offering a positive comment—before turning to the usual series of specific questions, which counterbalances this with a rather negative final question.

No Regrets; Imagine Boldly

Postmodern spiritually coheres well with the multiverse, but it is more plausible to suggest that the multiverse is a typical postmodern idea than to imagine postmodernism has arisen because of belief in the multiverse! This kind of chicken-and-egg problem, of course, applies to all the links we make between scientific ideas, spiritualities, and cultural trends. Having noted the problem, I move on to suggest some links between {5} and what may loosely be called postmodern spirituality.

The reality of possible worlds could be regarded as freeing us from regret at wrong and harmful decisions, since there is always a universe in which I have made the right decision. Reincarnation is perhaps the simplest means of allowing there to be a multiverse of "me"s trying out different decisions and different ways of living in the succession of lives. (However, in virtue of *anatta*, the teaching of "no self," that would be a very simplistic understanding of reincarnation in the Buddhist context.) This could be seen as a benefit (taking from decision-making the nail-biting anxiety that the future for myself and others depends on what I do next) or as a drawback (taking away the sense that my decision has such eternal consequences, which some regard as essential to ethics): see next section.

In any event, the multiverse could be seen as giving us license to imagine boldly. Mythologies, fairy stories, and science fiction could be seen not as escapes into fantasy worlds, but simply description of other worlds in the multiverse. Such worlds would be "real" of course, only if they are possible; but good fairy story and science fiction writers generally take great care to make their worlds coherent and possible according to the circumstances and natural laws of the worlds they conjure up. Consider the efforts of Tolkien, Le Guin, and Pullman—to mention only three of the greats—to make their different worlds self-consistent and physically credible.

In a sense, the new worlds are not just becoming more imaginable, but are already appearing. If {3} gave us secular humanism, perhaps {5} represents the "post-human": the opening of the imagination of ways of living to incorporate, not only diverse "queer" sexualities, but diverse ways of (arguably) enhancing the human by means of technology, including prosthetic limbs and artificial intelligence, which may in many ways surpass what natural human beings can achieve.[23] If the hero of {3} is Frankenstein, the intelligent and inquisitive scientist who becomes arrogant and narrowly determined as he pushes forward the bounds of human possibility; then the hero of {5} is his monster, in whom a transhuman technology "pushes back" into the human world, replicating that world too well for comfort.

Normally we think of our novelists and other creative artists as inventing rather than creating worlds, but the concept of the multiverse can effect a shift toward seeing them as world-making rather than world-inventing. Two features of mathematics convince us that it relates us to reality. One of them, noted in {4}, is the surprise aspect, the way mathematical theory comes up with things we would not have been likely to invent. In the same way, novelists can be surprised by their characters and their interactions, as they take on a life of their own. The other is that however strange and alien the worlds mathematics can describe, those worlds often turn out to change the way we understand our own. Likewise, by imagining another world boldly, great writers often enable us to see this world more creatively, as a possible world that is not inevitable, but can be changed. In this way, for example, Le Guin's naturally transgender world in *The Left Hand of Darkness* relativized the way our own societies construct gender.

So for Proust, worlds are as many as there are artists to make them:

> Thanks to art, instead of seeing one world only, our own, we see that world multiply itself and we have at our disposal as many worlds as there are original artists, worlds more different one from the other than those which revolve in infinite space, worlds which, centuries after the extinction of the fire from which their light first emanated, whether it is called Rembrandt or Vermeer, send us still each one its special radiance.[24]

Now if we are prepared to take the step of thinking of the multiverse as existing in the Mind of God, then the creativity of the artist or writer can be thought of as a sharing in the world-creativity of God. There might even be ways of following Paul Klee's advice to the novice artist to

> follow the ways of natural creation, the becoming, the functioning of forms. . . . Then perhaps, starting from nature, you will achieve creations of your own, and one day you may even become like Nature yourself, and start creating.[25]

23. Cf. Graham, *Representations*.

24. Accessed at https://www.goodreads.com/author/quotes/233619.Marcel_Proust on 04.03.2020.

25. Cited by Haftmann, *Paul Klee*, 115. Cf also Klee, *Pedagogical Sketchbook*.

Klee goes on to speak, in almost pre-Socratic terms, of his search for "a remote point of original creation, where there is one invariable formula for man, animal, plant, earth, water, fire, air and all the directive forces."[26] If there is anything in this idea of working with and from the origin of creation, it might give some directional thrust to the artist's creation of worlds, and save her from the tedium of random wanderings in the multiverse as described in ?{5}g.

Questions Regarding {5}

?{5}a: Is the Multiverse Too Complex?

The multiverse seems brazenly to defy Ockham's Razor, the principle, mentioned in {3}, named after the fourteenth-century English theologian who urged that "entities should not be multiplied beyond necessity." Ockham urged that we should not introduce concepts into our theories unless we really have to, but aim for the simplest explanations that are compatible with all the evidence. Nothing multiplies unobservable entities quite like the multiverse with its boundless array of whole universes unknown. By contrast, theism merely adds to the universe one quintessentially simple reality: God, whom it is said to be possible to know.

At this point Dawkins objects that, to be a conscious Mind, a Creator would have to be extremely complex, so that explanation by a divine Mind only adds more complexity (though arguably, still less complexity than the multiverse).[27] Classical theism, however, regards God as primordially simple: so simple there is not even a distinction in God between nature and existence. Conscious beings *in the universe* seem to have to be complex, having good sense organs and an intricate nervous system and brain. But in the classic understanding God is not a living organism within the universe, but the consciousness associated with the self-explanatory simplicity of uncreated being. That is not an easy idea to understand, and it may not make sense, but *if* the idea of God does make sense, God is by definition primordially simple. (More on this, especially in {8}.)

---

26. Cited by Haftmann, *Paul Klee*, 118.
27. Dawkins, *God Delusion*, 114.

?{5}b: Is There Any Evidence for Other Universes?

The multiverse is necessarily a collection of separate universes, not interacting, since if they interact, they are interconnected parts of one universe. But without interaction, there can be no exchange of information, hence no knowledge of other universes, and hence no evidence of a multiverse. Martin Gardner writes,

> There is not the slightest shred of reliable evidence that there is any other universe than the one we are in. No multiverse theory has so far provided a prediction that can be tested. As far as we can tell, multiverses are not even as plentiful as two blackberries.[28]

It may therefore be argued that the multiverse sacrifices tenet (4)—the need for evidence and testability—on the altar of keeping the laws of the universe simple. But it may be asked whether it achieves that goal; and even if it does, whether this is a sacrifice that anyone committed to scientific method should make.

?{5}c: How Do We Define the Multiverse?

?{3}b asked why we should expect the universe to obey mathematical laws. The question remains unanswered. Indeed, though Tegmark has become very generous in his definition of the multiverse at Level IV, he still presupposes that the universes are mathematical structures. Is this too limiting? Or too generous? George Ellis has asked, as we might put it, what qualifies a possible universe to be part of the multiverse? And how are these qualifications decided? "What range of possibilities will be contemplated? Where does this structure come from?"[29]

On the one hand, is it too generous, to allow *all* mathematical structures? A mathematical program needs to "halt" to be decidable. But only a minority of mathematical programs halt, so as to give a determinate answer. Tegmark concedes this. He limits his mathematical universe hypothesis to apply only to *decidable* mathematics. However, it has not been shown that the mathematics that describes our universe is decidable. As noted in {4}, Gödel has shown that in any mathematical system whose axioms are consistent, there will be truths that are undecidable. Moreover, infinite sequences of digits are required to describe basic geometrical quantities like π and

---

28. Gardner, *Are Universes Thicker?*
29. Ellis, "Multiverses," in Watts, *Creation*, 65.

even the sequence of points on a line. Tegmark himself prefers to do without the infinitely large and the infinitely small (including the infinity of points on a line) in his universes.[30] So is our own universe to be excluded from the mathematical multiverse? Or if our universe, despite appearances, excludes such infinities, why should there not be universes that do include them?

On the other hand, if we do not limit our truths to those that can be mathematically decided, how widely should we cast our net in fishing for multiverses? If mathematical structures cannot be listed or counted, is there any way we can tell if a unicorn, say, or a giant troll, or the goddess Aphrodite, or—Dawkins's favorite example—the tooth fairy, corresponds to some configuration in some mathematical structure, and hence, some universe in the Level IV multiverse? (Indeed, can we even tell whether there are such things corresponding to our laws of nature in the Level I multiverse?) More profoundly, could there be, in the multiverse, immaterial universes, and universes created by God? Indeed, could not all the kinds of "Worlds" described in this book, so long as they are self-consistent, be accommodated in a generous multiverse? And should there not be worlds that include magic, so long as it is consistent magic?[31] But if everything that is possible is actualized, how do we know it is impossible that there is a world that is exactly like ours till now, but will plunge into a hell of everlasting torment in five minutes time? And if that is possible, how can we be sure we are not in that universe? The multiverse is unnerving (to say the least!) because we can never be sure which of its universes we are in.

?{5}d: How Do We Count and Define the Universes within a Multiverse?

If the multiverse is to be a coherent whole that we can think about and define—rather than an arbitrary rag-bag—there has to be some way not only of limiting, and defining, but enumerating and calculating the universes in it. So Ellis asks, what determines the distribution of universes in a multiverse? "What is the meta-cause that delimits the set of realizations out of the set of possibilities?"[32] In ordinary language, what determines which of the possible universes are realized? As noted, Tegmark's Level IV multiverse has the merit of containing all mathematical structures, or at least, the decidable ones.

---

30. Tegmark, *Mathematical Universe*, 316.
31. Ellis, "Multiverses," 68–69.
32. Ellis, "Multiverses," 66.

?{5}e: What Do We Mean by Possibility and Necessity?

We noted how {4} raised the profound question of what we mean by calling something "real" or saying it "exists." {5} raises this question too, but by asserting that everything that can exist does exist and must exist, it also raises the question of what philosophers call modality; that is, what we mean when we say something can or must exist or occur. {5} and the various alternative explanations of the anthropic principle force us to ask, "what are possibility and necessity?'

In logic these are called the "modal operators," and it is easy to define them in terms of each other.

- *Necessary* = *not possible not*. To say something has to happen is to say that it is impossible for it not to happen.
- *Possible* = *not necessarily not*. To say something may happen is to say that it is not necessarily not going to happen.

But this leaves us with a circularity, which can only be resolved if we can find an independent way of defining either possibility or necessity.

In the twentieth century, an alternative was proposed: modal logic, according to which "necessary" was said to mean "true in all possible worlds." But again, this only deferred the question to the definition of "possible." It was tempting to drop the word "possible" and regard "necessary" as meaning "true in all worlds we can conceive of." "Possible" then meant "true in some of the worlds we can conceive of" and "impossible" meant "true in none of them."

This represents the logical, philosophical route to the multiverse described at the outset of {5}, which parallels the scientific and mathematical routes. It allows us to replace the mystery of the modal operators with the straightforwardness of ordinary description of actual facts. When we use these modal operators, we are really just describing what actually goes on in different universes. But to some, that may seem more mysterious than the modal operators themselves!

If that is so, the alternatives seem to be two. We can follow Hume and abandon modality, causality (in the sense of natural necessity, see ?{3}b) and other universes alike, and reconstruct science so that it only describes what actually goes on in this universe, rather than what might be or cannot be. Science would then be purely descriptive, noting the regular patterns whereby events we observe follow other events.

However, such a view encounters the problem of induction. Science has proven useful because, as well as observing, it makes predictions. As well as saying things like, "y has always followed x," it typically says "y will always follow x" and it bases this on laws, often mathematical laws, that inform us, "y must necessarily follow x." A mere description of what has happened in the past could never justify such prediction about the future, unless mediated by mathematical laws and models that say what must happen. Many scientists, though not all, therefore view the idea of natural necessity as indispensable to science.

That thought encourages us to take the alternative option, which follows our commonsense understanding, whereby future and past are connected via the present. For the commonsense view invokes (whether its supporters realize it or not) an older, Aristotelian understanding, which expands on the commonsense account of causality, necessity, possibility, and time; see?{8}d.

?{5}f: Does the Multiverse Make Scientific Explanation Redundant?

We noted that the mathematical universe resolved the regress of explanations, and this positive point carries over to Tegmark's mathematical multiverse. On the other hand, it may be argued that in another way the multiverse undermines explanation. We noted that the step to the Level III multiverse was taken partly in order to answer ?{3}b, why the universe has the particular laws, starting conditions, and constants that it has. But the response seems somewhat like the proverbial sledgehammer that only smashes the nut to pieces. If the multiverse cycles through random universes until it comes up with the one with the right conditions for life, then the origin of life is fundamentally not understood at all; it remains a product of an infinite series of random circumstances.

Hence the multiverse has been widely criticized for undermining the need for explanation. For if all possibilities are realized somewhere, we no longer need to explain why only some of them are realized in this universe. The multiverse rules out the idea of worlds that are possible but not actual. All potency is act; no potential is unrealized. (There are of course some multiverses that are less than the totality of possible worlds, but they are exceedingly hard to define, and somewhat messy, which is why I have restricted discussion to the pure multiverse as the totality of possible worlds.) Often this is taken to mean that the multiverse is necessary existence, which means in Aristotelian terms that it is God. However, as just noted, possibility and necessity are mutually defined. If we cannot conceive of possibility without actuality, we cannot formulate the idea of non-possibility, that is, impossibility. It follows that we cannot conceive of there being "no possibility not," and hence we cannot conceive of the multiverse being "necessary," defined above as impossibility not.

All we can then say is that the multiverse means that everything is actual. It follows that nothing is necessitated, or rendered necessary, by anything else, and so in the universe there is no causal explanation. For everything that happens, there is some world in which it has not happened; so nothing *has* to happen. Nothing then is made to happen, therefore nothing is caused to happen; hence nothing is explicable. The multiverse is something like the Parmenidean One, but without its necessity; it is a One that just is. It turns out after all to be just the biggest possible "just so" universe..

?{5}g: Is the Multiverse Metaphysically Suffocating?

Just as the multiverse could be regarded as undermining scientific explanation, so it could undermine moral responsibility. If whatever I do, I do the opposite in some other universe, ethical choice is lost. Just as nothing needs explaining in terms of causes, so nothing needs justifying, because whenever I make a choice in this universe, I choose the other options in other worlds. In this way the multiverse drains away our sense of time and of freedom to act. Normally we think of the future as a realm of possibility, which our free actions in the present, working alongside other causes, condense into the fixed necessity of the past, which nobody can change. In the multiverse, and any kind of deterministic universe, the future is in reality necessitated like the past. The multiverse, and indeed any idea of a static, deterministic space-time, could give rise to a resigned metaphysical sloth.

The plot appropriate to the multiverse is surely the murder mystery, except that in the multiverse there is no need to solve the mystery, because there is a story in which every character, and every possible combination of characters, did the evil deed. Of course, a good murder mystery will make many, or all, of the characters likely candidates, so that we see the possibility that x did it, only for that option to be snatched from us as y becomes a likelier possibility. But in the multiverse mystery, this tantalizing aspect is taken away, because we know for sure that x did it in one universe, and y did it in another, and so forth. Not to mention the universes in which the deed was not done, or done in a different way, or to someone else.

In the end the multiverse can come to resemble Jorge Luis Borges's *Library of Babel*, whose interminable shelves in their hexagonal rooms contain books made up of all possible combinations of the letters of the alphabet. Every book ever written, and every book that will be written, is to be found on its shelves:

All—the detailed history of the future, the autobiographies of the archangels, the faithful catalogue of the Library, thousands and thousands of false catalogues, . . . the gnostic commentary of Basilides, the commentary on that gospel, the commentary on the commentary, . . . the true story of your death, . . . [t]he treatise Bede could have written (but did not) on the mythology of the Saxon people.[33]

The joy people experience on learning of this library, which must contain the answer to both their personal problems and the mysteries of the universe, gives way to despair, as they realize that finding the relevant book would take longer than their lifetime, indeed, unimaginably longer than the lifetime of the universe, though not quite infinitely long.[34] The library offers unimaginably small hope to any seeker, inducing despair, but not quite zero hope. The same is arguably true when we think seriously about the multiverse.

A spirituality that harnesses scientific, artistic, and religious forms of contemplation is perhaps the greatest legacy of {4}. And the idea that all times and all possibilities are co-present in the Mind of God is an inspiring one, which invites me to widen my own grasp of the mathematical structure of our own world and possible others. But the idea behind {5}—that all possibilities are actualized in an unimaginable infinity of universes—is, I suggest, suffocating to the human spirit in the search for explanation and for the good life. ?{3}k above questioned whether science can answer questions like those of meaning and purpose. Such questions are only intensified by the multiverse: it is meaninglessness multiplied infinitely.

Résumé of {4} and {5}: More Questions Than Answers?

The questions raised by worlds {4} and {5} are fewer than those raised by {2} and {3} but deeper. {4} raises ?{4}a as to whether mathematics plays the major role in enabling us to understand the universe, or whether scientific experiment is still crucial. {5} takes this question further, asking ?{5}e, whether the multiverse may make explanation redundant. In this respect the multiverse seems to represent a kind of terminus: radically following

---

33. Borges, "The Library of Babel," in *Collected Fictions*.

34. Borges assumes a modest alphabet of twenty-five characters. Each book contains at most 410 pages, each of forty lines of eighty characters each, which is 1,312,000 characters per book. If someone were to peruse each book for an hour it would take by my calculations 251,312,000 (approximately 1 followed by 1,834,000 zeroes) hours to search the whole library.

through the (purported) logic of scientific explanation leads in the end to the abandonment of such explanation. On the other hand, ?{4}b questioned the status of {4}, whether it is essentially "material" or "ideal," and indeed whether these polarizing terms still apply. Meanwhile the multiverse raises related questions: ?{5}c, whether there is a limit to the reality of imagined worlds, and ?{5}d, what kinds of languages, mathematical or otherwise, should be allowed to "construct" the worlds. And finally, ?{4}c asks, if mathematical ideas at least are thought to be real (indeed, to constitute reality), what makes a universe and its contents real rather than simply imaginary? The multiverse raises related questions: ?{5}f about possibility and actuality in our universes, future, present, and past, and intentionality, experience, and actuality. Finally ?{5}g asked whether the multiverse is in the end metaphysically suffocating.

All these questions converge on issues that must be confronted more directly in the sequel, *Embodying Mind*, on the place—constitutive or otherwise—of experience, consciousness, and mind in our Worlds.

CONCLUSION TO *OUTGROWING MATERIALISM*

> Humpty the Clever thought mind came from matter
>   Till he came to the multiverse, where he did shatter.
> Dualists, materialists, structuralists too
>   Tried hard to fix him with metaphysical glue.
> Ask panpsychists, idealists, and Aristotle,
>   Whether there's stronger stuff in their bottle.

I HOPE YOU WILL forgive this doggerel, which is my attempt to summarize *Outgrowing Materialism* and lay the ground for the second volume. This volume has unraveled a basic tension in the principles of dualism and—even more—the tenets of materialism, between the emphasis on experience rather than dogma or reason on the one hand, and reliance on mathematical formulae, reductionism, and determinism on the other. The latter can lead to elimination of experience which is the very basis of the former, leaving us with a pure mathematical multiverse for which matter is reduced to a "something I know not what."

In this sense {5} completes the modern trajectory that runs through the doubts of dualism, the eliminations of materialism, and the triumph of the mathematical world. It offers a world where mind and its perceptions and choices are redundant or delusory; where logical and mathematical necessity run the real show. But the viable alternatives—the participatory universe that gives consciousness a decisive role in world-making; the theologically necessitated universe, which exists because chosen from the multiverse that is the Mind of God; and the just-so and landscape universes—have not been out-argued by the multiverse. Each of them offers a simpler alternative; and each will find a place in the World I advocate, {10}.

Admittedly some materialists might find the price of such simplicity too high to pay, in terms of their central tenets. But in the end, tenets they are, and it is tenets—articles of faith, whether atheist or theological—that will probably decide the issue for each of us. In any event, we shall see, these three alternatives developed into full blown Worlds in the second volume, where they are finally reconciled in {10}.

The second volume will begin with a brave attempt to combine reductionism and determinism within a naturalistic account that includes experience at the root of matter. Though we shall find fault with this attempt, it will open the way to other ways of honoring experience and so embracing mind embodied in matter.

BIBLIOGRAPHY FOR OUTGROWING MATERIALISM

Baggott, J. *Quantum Space: Loop Quantum Theory and the Search for the Structure of Space, Time and the Universe.* Oxford: Oxford University Press, 2018.
Barad, K. *Meeting the Universe Half-Way: Quantum Physics and the Entanglement of Matter and Meaning.* Durham, NC: Duke University Press, 2007.
Barrow, J. D., and F. J. Tipler. *The Anthropic Cosmological Principle.* Oxford: Oxford University Press, 1988.
Beckett, C. *Dark Eden.* London: Atlantic Books, 2012. Kindle edition.
Black, M. *Models and Metaphors.* New York: Cornell University Press, 1962.
Block, N. *Consciousness, Function, and Representation: Collected Papers, 1.* Cambridge, MA: Bradford Books, 2007.
Block, N., O. Flanagan, and G. Guzeldere, eds. *The Nature of Consciousness: Philosophical Debates.* Cambridge: MIT Press, 1997.
Booker, C. *The Seven Basic Plots: Why We Tell Stories.* London: Continuum, 2004.
Borges, J. L. *Collected Fictions.* Translated by A. Hurley. Harmondsworth, UK: Penguin, 1998.
———. *Labyrinths.* Harmondsworth, UK: Penguin, 1970.
Browning, R. "Home-Thoughts from Abroad." In *The Poems of Browning*, edited by D. Karlin, 283–85. London: Routledge, 2014.
Brüntrup, G., B. P. Göcke, and L. Jaskolla, eds. *Panentheism and Panpsychism: Philosophy of Religion Meets Philosophy of Mind.* Leiden: Brill, 2020.
Burtt, E. A. *The Metaphysical Foundations of Modern Physical Science.* Mineola, NY: Dover: 2003. Kindle edition.
Cartwright, N., and K. Ward. *Rethinking Order: After the Laws of Nature.* London: Bloomsbury, 2016.
Chalmers, D. *The Character of Consciousness.* Oxford: Oxford University Press, 2010.
———. *The Conscious Mind: In Search of a Fundamental Theory.* Oxford: Oxford University Press, 1996.
———. *Reality+: Virtual Worlds and the Problems of Philosophy.* London: Penguin, 2022. Kindle edition.
Churchland, P. M. *Scientific Realism and the Plasticity of Mind.* Cambridge: Cambridge University Press, 1979.
Collingwood, R. G. *The Principles of Art.* Oxford: Oxford University Press, 1938.

Cox, B. *The Quantum Universe: Everything That Can Happen Does Happen*. London: Allen Lane, 2011.
Cupitt, D. *Taking Leave of God*. London: SCM, 1980.
Davies, P. *God and the New Physics*. Harmondsworth, UK: Penguin, 1984.
———. *The Mind of God*. Harmondsworth, UK: Penguin, 1993.
Dawkins, R. *The Blind Watchmaker*. Harmondsworth, UK: Penguin, 1986.
———. *The God Delusion*. London: Penguin, 2006.
———. *Outgrowing God: A Beginner's Guide to Atheism*. London: Penguin Bantam House, 2019.
Dennett, D. *Consciousness Explained*. Harmondsworth, UK: Penguin, 1991.
Descartes, R. *Descartes: Philosophical Writings*. Edited by E. Anscombe and P. T. Geach. Rev. ed. London: Nelson, 1970.
Dijksterhuis, E. Van. *The Mechanisation of the World Picture*. Oxford: Oxford University Press, 1961.
Eliot, T. S. *Collected Poems 1909–1962*. London: Faber, 1963.
———. "The Metaphysical Poets." In *Selected Essays*, 3rd ed., 281–91. London: Faber & Faber, 1951.
Ellis, G. F. "Multiverses and Ultimate Causation." In *Creation, Law and Probability*, edited by F. Watts, 59–80. Aldershot, UK: Ashgate, 2008.
Farmelo, G. *The Universe Speaks in Numbers: How Modern Maths Reveals Nature's Deepest Secrets*. London: Faber, 2019.
Feser, E. *The Last Superstition: A Refutation of the New Atheism*. South Bend, IN, 2008. Kindle edition.
———. *Philosophy of Mind: A Beginner's Guide*. Oxford: Oneworld, 2011. Kindle edition.
Freeman, A., ed. *Consciousness and Its Place in Nature*. Thorverton, UK: Imprint Academic, 2006.
Fukuyama, F. *The End of History and the Last Man*. London: Penguin, 2012.
Gabor, D. *Inventing the Future*. New York: Knopf, 1963.
Gardner, M. *The Ambidextrous Universe: Left, Right, and the Fall of Parity*. Harmondsworth, UK: Penguin, 1964.
———. *Are Universes Thicker Than Blackberries?* New York: Norton, 2003.
Goodman, N. *Ways of Worldmaking*. Indianapolis, IN: Hackett, 1978.
Graham, E. *Representations of the Post/human: Monsters, Aliens and Others in Popular Culture*. Manchester: Manchester University Press, 2002.
Haftmann, W. *The Mind and Work of Paul Klee*. London: Faber, 1954.
Hanson, N. R. "The Dematerialisation of Matter." *Philosophy of Science* 73.1 (1962) 27–38.
Harré, R. *The Principles of Scientific Thinking*. London: Macmillan, 1970.
Hart, D. B. *The Experience of God: Being, Consciousness, Bliss*. New Haven, CT: Yale University Press, 2013. Kindle edition.
Hawking, S. *A Brief History of Time*. New York: Bantam, 1988.
Holland, T. *Dominion: The Making of the Western Mind*. London: Little, Brown Book Group, 2019.
Hossenfelder, S. www.quantamagazine.org/string-theory-meets-loop-quantum-gravity-20160112/.
Huxley, T. *Lessons in Elementary Physiology*. London: Macmillan, 1866.

Jaki, S. L. *Science and Creation: From Eternal Cycles to an Oscillating Universe.* Rev. ed. Edinburgh: Scottish Academic Press, 1986.
Johnston, M. *The Manifest*, forthcoming. Chapter 5 downloaded from www.nyu.edu/gsas/dept/philo/courses/consciousness97/papers/johnston/chap5.html, March 2022.
———. *Saving God: Religion after Idolatry.* Oxford: Oxford University Press, 2009.
———. *Surviving Death.* Princeton: Princeton University Press, 2010.
Kadloubovsky, E., and G. E. H. Palmer, eds. *Early Fathers from the Philokalia.* London: Faber, 1954.
Kastrup, B. *Why Materialism Is Baloney: How True Sceptics Know There Is No Death and Fathom Answers to Life, the Universe, and Everything.* Winchester, UK: Hunt, 2013.
Kierkegaard, S. *Fear and Trembling and the Sickness unto Death.* Translated by W. Lowrie. Princeton, NJ: Princeton University Press, 1968.
Kirk, G. S., J. E. Raven, and M. Schofield. *The Presocratic Philosophers: A Critical History with a Selection of Texts.* 2nd. ed. Cambridge: Cambridge University Press, 1983.
Kivy, P. *The Corded Shell: Reflections on Musical Expression.* Princeton, NJ: Princeton University Press, 1981.
———. *New Essays on Musical Understanding.* Oxford: Oxford University Press, 2002.
Klee, P. *Pedagogical Sketchbook.* Translated by S. Moholy-Nagy. London: Faber, 1953.
Koons, R., ed. *The Waning of Materialism.* Oxford: Oxford University Press, 2010.
Koyré, A. *From the Closed World to the Infinite Universe.* Baltimore: John Hopkins University Press, 1957. E-book edition.
Kuhn, T. *The Structure of Scientific Revolutions.* Chicago: Chicago University Press, 1962.
Lennox, J. C. *God's Undertaker: Has Science Buried God?* London: Lion Hudson, 2007.
Leslie, J. *Infinite Minds: A Philosophical Cosmology.* Oxford: Oxford University Press, 2003.
Lewis, C. S. *The Complete C. S. Lewis Signature Classics.* London: HarperCollins, 2002.
Lewis, D. *On the Plurality of Worlds.* Oxford: Blackwell, 1986.
Libet, B., C. A. Gleason, E. W. Wright, D. K. Pearl. "Time of Conscious Intention to Act in Relation to Onset of Cerebral Activity (Readiness-potential): The Unconscious Initiation of a Freely Voluntary Act." *Brain* 106 (1983) 623–42. Doi:10.1093/brain/106.3.623 pmid:6640273.
Locke, J. *An Essay Concerning Human Understanding.* Edited by A. D. Woozley. London: Collins, 1964.
Manzotti, R. "Mind-Object Identity: A Solution to the Hard Problem." In *Frontiers in Psychology*, February 5, 2019. https://doi.org/10.3389/fpsyg.2019.00063. Accessed July 2020.
Medawar, P. *The Limits of Science.* Oxford: Oxford University Press, 1986.
Miles, J. *God: A Biography.* London: Simon and Schuster, 1996.
Moore, G. E. *Principia Ethica.* Cambridge: Cambridge University Press, 1903.
Morris, S. C. *Life's Solution: Inevitable Humans in a Lonely Universe.* Cambridge: Cambridge University Press, 2003.
Nagel, T. *Mortal Questions.* Cambridge: Cambridge University Press, 1979.
———. *The View from Nowhere.* Rev. ed. Oxford: Oxford University Press, 1989.
Noble, D. *Dance to the Tune of Life.* Cambridge: Cambridge University Press, 2017.
Pascal, B. *Pensées.* New York: Dutton, 1958.

Pears, D., ed. *Bertrand Russell and the British Tradition in Philosophy*. London: Collins, 1967.
Penrose, R. *Cycles of Time: What Came before the Big Bang?* London: Vintage, 2011.
Pinker, S. *The Better Angels of Our Nature: A History of Violence and Humanity*. London: Penguin, 2012.
———. *Enlightenment Now: The Case for Reason, Science, Humanism, and Progress*. London: Penguin, 2019.
Polanyi, M. *Personal Knowledge*. London: Routledge and Kegan Paul, 1958.
Popper, K. *Objective Knowledge*. Oxford: Oxford University Press, 1972.
Pullman, P. *The Amber Spyglass*. London: Scholastic Children's Books, 2000.
Quine, W. V. O. *Word and Object*. Cambridge. M.I.T. Press, 1960.
Rorty, R. *Philosophy and the Mirror of Nature*. Oxford: Blackwell, 1980.
Russell, B. *The Analysis of Matter*. London: Kegan Paul, 1927.
———. "Mind and Matter." In *Portraits from Memory and other Essays*, ch. 8. London: Routledge e-book, 2020. https://doi.org/10.4324/9781003090359.
———. *Religion and Science*. Oxford: Oxford University Press, 1968.
Ryle, G. *The Concept of Mind*. Harmondsworth, UK: Penguin, 1970.
Sawyer, W. W. *Mathematician's Delight*. Mineola, NY: Dover, 2008.
Schrödinger, E. *Nature and the Greeks*. Cambridge: Cambridge University Press, 1954.
Scruton, R. *The Great Philosophers: Spinoza*. London: Orion, 2011. E-book.
———. *The Soul of the World*. Princeton, NJ: Princeton University Press, 2014. Kindle edition.
Seager, W. ed. *The Routledge Handbook of Panpsychism*. London: Routledge, 2020.
Searle, J. R. *Intentionality: An Essay in the Philosophy of Mind*. Cambridge: Cambridge University Press, 1983.
———. "Minds, Brains and Programs." *Behavioral and Brain Sciences* 3 (1980) 417–57. doi: 10.1017/S0140525X00005756.
———. *The Rediscovery of the Mind*. Cambridge, MA: MIT Press, 1992.
Siedentop, L. A. *Inventing the Individual: The Origins of Western Liberalism*. London: Penguin, 2015.
Singh, S. *Fermat's Last Theorem: The Story of a Riddle That Confounded the World's Greatest Minds for 358 Years*. London: HarperCollins, 2002.
Smart, J. J. C. "Sensations and Brain Processes." *Philosophical Review* 68.2 (1959) 141–56.
Smolin, L. *The Life of the Cosmos*. Oxford: Oxford University Press, 1999.
Spinoza, B. *Ethics*. Translated by A. Boyle. Rev. ed. London: Dent, 1959.
Strawson, G. "Panpsychism? Reply to Commentators with a Celebration of Descartes." *Journal of Consciousness Studies* 13.10–11 (2006) 184–280.
———. *The Secret Connexion: Causation, Realism, and David Hume*. Rev. ed. Oxford: Oxford University Press, 2014.
Taylor, C. *A Secular Age*, Cambridge: Harvard University Press, 2007.
Tegmark, M. *Our Mathematical Universe: My Quest for the Ultimate Nature of Reality*. London: Penguin, 2014.
Thompson, R. *Buddhist Christianity: A Passionate Openness*. Winchester, UK: Hunt, 2010.
———. *Holy Ground: The Spirituality of Matter*. London: SPCK, 1990.
———. *The Interfaith Imperative: Religion, Dialogue and Reality*. Eugene, OR: Cascade, 2017.

———. *Spirituality in Season: Growing through the Christian Year*. Norwich, UK: Canterbury, 2008.

———. *Studyguide: Christian Spirituality*. London: SCM, 2008.

———. *Studyguide: The Sacraments*. London: SCM, 2006.

———. *Wounded Wisdom: A Buddhist and Christian Response to Evil, Hurt and Harm*. Winchester, UK: Hunt, 2011.

Van Dijksterhuis, E. *The Mechanisation of the World Picture*. Oxford: Oxford University Press, 1961.

Watts, F., ed. *Creation, Law and Probability*. Aldershot, UK: Ashgate, 2008.

Watts, F., and C. Knight. *God and the Scientist: Exploring the Work of John Polkinghorne*. Farnham, UK: Ashgate, 2012.

Williams, R. *Christ the Heart of Creation*. London: Bloomsbury, 2018.

Wittgenstein, L. *Philosophical Investigations*. Translated by G. E. M. Anscombe. Oxford: Blackwell, 1963.

———. *Tractatus Logico-Philosophicus*. Translated by D. F. Pears and B. F. McGuinness. London: Routledge and Kegan Paul, 1961.

INDEX

anthropic principle, 14, 171–85, 190
Aquinas, Thomas, 10, 38
    God, 151, 181
    soul, 61, 70
Aristotle, Aristotelian, IX, 10, 93, 181,
    191, 195
    causality, 82–83
    and dualism, 54, 57, 61, 62, 70–71,
        74
    early modern rejection, 37–40,
        43–49
    realism 24–26, 135, 150,
art, 26, 27–28, 33, 109, 147–49, 187–8
    see also music, poetry
atheism, 170
    and dualism 18–20, 50, 59, 77, 85,
        100
    kinds, 94–95
    New Atheists, 3–5, 7–8, 9, 19, 27,
        39, 87, 94, 96, 117
    own, 13–14
    spirituality, 95–98, 105
atomism, 74
    logical, 65

Barrow, John D., *see* anthropic
    principle
behaviorism, 80, 90, 98
Berkeley, George, 16, 55, 56, 67
Blake, William, 8–9, 55
Block, Ned, 103, 113–14
body-mind interaction, 51–52, 62–63,
    91
Bohm, David, 145–46
Booker, Christopher, 11

    see also plots
Borges, Jorge L., 192–93
brain in vat, 19
Buddhism, 32, 40, 74
    co-arising, 173, 175–76, 180–81
    illusion, 25, 28
    Mind Alone, *Yogacara*, 184–85
    non-theism, 94
    no-self, 69
    own, 13–16
Burtt, Edwin A., 40, 43–49, 55–56, 58

Cartwright, Nancy, 89, 93, 98
cat
    Cheshire, 143, 146
    Schrodinger's, 145–46, 155
cause, causality, causation, 68–69, 84,
    111, 116–17, 127, 173, 181 , 183,
    189
    God as, 57–59
    see also body-mind interaction,
        determinism, necessity
Chalmers, David, 29–30, 104
Chinese
    Block's argument, 113–14
    room, 114–15, 141–42
Christianity, 2, 7, 10, 26–27, 74, 135
    and dualism, 36–37, 69–70, 151–52
    miracles, 77
    own, 13–16
    and science, 17–18, 42, 58, 96–97,
        117
Churchland, Paul and Patricia, 84, 87
computer, 89
    and brain, 112, 113–16

simulation, 29
software v. hardware 141–42
contemplation, 135, 147, 193
  of nature, 41, 56, 97, 147–52
Copenhagen interpretation, 88, 145
Copernicus, 37, 38, 39–40, 43, 50
correspondence theory, 23–25, 29, 63–66, 80, 119–20, 154
Cox, Brian, 16, 152, 168, 169, 181
Cupitt, Don, 35, 55, 56

Davies, Paul, 14, 172, 173–74, 183
Dawkins, Richard, 3, 7, 27, 49, 59, 73–74, 75, 187
deism, 8–9, 17–19, 49–50, 55, 57–59, 77, 93, 96
dematerialisation, 143
Dennett, Daniel, 3, 5, 51, 84, 87, 102, 105–8
Descartes, René, 17, 19, 25, 82
  doubt, 28–31, 64, 67, 106
  dualism, 35–39, 55–57, 62–63, 74–75
  God, 42, 50, 53, 57–59
  relation of doubt and dualism, 50–55, 72
determinism, 72, 82, 83, 85, 86, 88–89, 90–93, 120–23, 130, 144, 159, 179, 182, 183, 192, 195
  and ethics, 126–29
dissociation of sensibility, 18, 55, 59

Eliot, T. S., 18, 55
Ellis, George F. R., 188–89
emergence, 88, 90–92, 141–43, 164
empirical, 9, 39, 44, 79–80, 99, 130, 154–55, 158, 175, 178, 179
empiricism, 30, 67, 75, 79, 154, 155, 158
entropy, 96
epiphenomena, epiphenomenalism, 84–85, 92, 126–27
ethics, 8, 111, 159, 185
  and materialism, 126–29
evolution, 2, 84, 127, 171, 175

faith, 3–4, 7, 17–18, 37, 58–59, 69–70, 195

atheist, materialist, 85, 89, 94–95, 95–98, 131
  naïve, 26–28
  own, 13, 15
Farmelo, Graham, 136, 160, 162
Fermat's last theorem, 137, 139
Feser, Edward, 87, 94, 115
Frege, Gottlob, 135, 138–39
functionalism, 90, 113, 115, 116

Galileo, 17, 30, 37, 38, 39, 43, 46, 47, 49, 50, 58
games, 136, 141–43, 161
Gardner, Martin, 46, 188
Gnosticism, 26, 36–37
God, *see* deism, mind, necessary being, pantheism, theism, transcendence
Gödel, Kurt, 89, 139–41, 161, 164, 174, 188
Gray, John, 94–95

hallucination, 54, 68–69
Hanson, Norwood R., 143
harmony, 35, 43, 58, 108, 132–34, 144, 147–49
  see also music
Harré, Rom, 122–23, 157, 160–61
Hart, David B., 113, 130–31
Hawking, Stephen, 135–36
Hobbes, Thomas, 38, 74–75
Hume, David, 55, 67, 75, 190
  causality, 99–100, 121
  God, 50
Humpty, 195

idealism (philosophical), 6, 10, 15, 25–26, 51, 60, 77, 80, 92, 106, 133, 140, 146, 158, 162–63, 195
identity, mind-brain, mental v. physical, 23–24, 29, 61, 66, 90, 106–7, 114, 117–20, 130, 159
illusion, 25, 28–30, 50–55, 64, 66, 68–69, 75, 112, 132
intentionality, 102, 110–17, 119, 138, 159, 163, 194
  and music, 148–49
intrinsic v. dispositional properties, 2, 75, 115, 123–24, 158

inverted spectrum, 103

jabberwock, 119
Johnston, Mark, 24, 61, 65, 70, 95
Jubien, Michael, 90, 119

Kierkegaard, Søren, 168, 181
Kivy, Peter, 147
Klee, Paul, 28, 186–87
Koons, Robert, 59, 84–85, 90, 91, 92, 98–99
Kuhn, Thomas, 39–40, 43, 125

law
   divine, 18, 41–43, 50, 93
   mathematical, 174
   natural, 41–43, 56, 58, 71, 78–79, 80–81, 96, 99–101, 121–22, 155, 156–57, 180–81
Lewis, C. S., 30, 132, 137
Lewis, David, modal realism, 169
Lewontin, Richard, 93–94
Leslie, John, 171, 183
Libet, Benjamin, 128
Locke, John, 30, 46, 75, 103, 154

Manicheanism, 36–37
Mary's room, 103
materialism
   eliminative, 84, 86–87, 89, 91, 93, 101, 116, 119, 126
   hierarchical, 88, 89–91
   kinds, 75, 84, 85–91
   reductive, 90–91, 93, 101, 119
   tenets, 75–85, 121, 131, 152–58, 172–73, 174, 176, 195
   see also reductionism
mathematical universe, 134, 158, 177–79, 184, 188, 191
Maximus the Confessor, 150–51
mechanization (of world picture), 39, 49–50, 55, 72, 82, 157, 163
Medawar, Peter, 125–26
mind
   divine, Mind of God, 49, 152, 165–66, 169–71, 181–82, 183–85, 186–87, 193–94, 195
mirror, 37, 65, 72

model, 44, 53, 60, 72, 79, 80, 83, 92, 139, 142, 146, 152, 157, 160–62, 191
modernism, modernity, 9, 19, 38, 58–59
monkeys with typewriters, 112, 176
moods (grammatical), modality, 111, 168, 190–92
moon, 66–68, 109, 124, 172
multiverse, 9, 10, 19, 81, 134, 145–47, 153, 165, 168–71, 173–79, 181–87, 187–94, 195
music, 133, 147–49, 154, 159, 166
   of the universe, 134, 149
   see also harmony

Nagel, 98, 103, 104, 130
naturalism, 4, 10, 75, 78, 81, 82–83, 121–22, 124–26, 130–31, 155–56, 157, 158, 162, 171, 182, 183
   and materialism, 19, 76–78
necessary being, 122–23, 181–82, 184
necessity, 19
   cosmic, 132, 169, 173–74, 183–84
   divine, *see* necessary being
   multiverse, 174–79, 195
   natural, 99–101, 121–22, 156–57, 159, 161, 165
   and possibility, *see* moods, modality
   tragic, 96–98
neurons, neural correlate of consciousness, 23, 88, 103, 113–16, 117–20, 129
nominalism, 38–39, 74–76, 77–78, 79, 81, 82, 99, 100, 107, 111, 121, 130, 131, 135, 153, 156, 158, 159, 162, 164

Ockham, William of
   razor, 39, 60, 101, 183, 184, 187

panpsychism, 6, 10, 38, 60, 63, 86, 90, 109, 124, 157, 195
pantheism 10, 57, 77, 170, 173,
   see also Spinoza
Parmenides, 25, 132, 134–35, 150, 159, 170, 173–74, 181, 192
Pascal, Blaise, 27, 97, 182
Penrose, Roger, 135, 177

perception
  childhood, naïve, 22–25, 28, 30
  and existence, 67, 80, 109, 110, 133, 139, 146, 176, 178–79
  and physical sense-organs, 61, 62–66, 75, 91, 103
  veracity, 54, 50, 58, 68, 71, 195
phenomenology, 65, 105–6, 108
physicalism, *see* materialism
  why "materialism" preferred term, 77, 91
Plato, Platonism, IX, 24, 159, 166
  dualism, 36–37, 38–39, 47, 54–55, 60, 70, 135, 149–52
  realism, 9, 25, 43–44, 74, 99, 107, 153, 162–64, 177
  revival, 135–39
plots, seven basic, 11
  mystery, 132
  rags to riches, 95
  struggle, good v. evil, 36–37
  tragedy, 96–97
poetry, 55–56, 147
Polanyi, Michael, 40, 125, 129
Popper, Karl, 19, 60, 135, 138–39, 148, 163, 164, 168, 169, 172
postmodernism, -ity, 5–6, 18, 32, 185
prediction, 44, 45–46, 81, 89, 99–101, 125, 155, 156–57, 161, 188, 190–91
Presocratic philosophy, 41, 132–35
progress, 6, 17, 95–98,
  scientific, 1, 3, 28, 31, 56, 87, 94, 125, 160
Proust, Marcel, 152, 186
Pullman, Philip, 50, 185
Pythagoras, Pythagoreanism, 41, 69–70, 132, 134–35, 136, 144, 147, 149, 154, 155

quantum physics, mechanics, 79, 118, 123, 136, 144, 155, 161–62, 171
  determinism, 82, 88–89, 177–78
  interpretations, 144–46, 184
qualia, quale, 129,
  elimination of, 86–87, 101–10, 122
  and intentionality, 110–12
  reality of, 21, 23, 66–69, 81, 84, 89–90, 117–20, 138, 159, 163

quality, 4, 26, 71, 86, 88, 92, 102, 107, 151
  dualism, 70
  primary v. secondary, 30, 46–48, 50–51, 54, 69, 75, 81, 108–9, 124–25, 143, 155, 158
quantity, quantification, 4, 9, 46–48, 53, 71, 76, 81, 86, 87, 91, 102, 108, 124, 129, 133, 143, 146, 158, 159, 188–89
  see also quality: primary v. secondary
Quine, Willard van O., 91

Realms, three, 19, 138–39, 148–49, 154, 160–61, 163–64, 166, 168–69, 172, 184
reduction, reductionism, 5, 10, 19, 23, 82–85, 105, 148, 153, 157–58, 163, 179, 182, 183, 195–96
  kinds, 85–93
  and naturalism, 38–39
  regress 122–23, 159
regress, 116, 122–23, 130, 158, 159, 191
relativism, 5–6, 15, 32, 40, 119
relativity, 79, 80, 134, 136, 144, 155
representation, 21, 23–24, 65–66, 71, 81, 90, 104–5
  art, 28, 109, 147
Romanticism, 10, 51, 55–56
Rorty, Richard, 65
Russell, Bertrand, 21, 23, 136
  atheism 73, 94, 97
  non-materialism, 98, 123, 143
Ryle, Gilbert, 83
  dualism, 36, 38, 54–55, 56–57, 62–63

Schrödinger, Erwin, 145, 155
Scruton, Roger, 147–48, 173
Searle, John R., 98, 114–15
Smart, John J. C., 101, 109
space
  extension, 54, 62, 64, 70
  geometric, 161–63, 171
  Hilbert –, 134, 136, 144–45, 158, 177

-time, 45–46, 49, 53–54, 80–81, 134, 143–44, 145–46, 152, 155, 166–67, 192
Spinoza, Baruch, 16, 27, 77, 94, 173
spirituality
  own, 13, 15
  and the Worlds, 8, 11, 12, 56, 75, 95–98, 149–52, 185, 193
squirrel, red, 22–23, 28, 30–32, 53, 64–65, 68, 106–8, 110–12, 117, 119
Strawson, Galen, 38, 99
string theory, 79, 118, 134, 154, 171
structural realism, 6, 100, 133, 146, 153, 159
supernatural, 69, 76–78, 82, 93–94, 100–101, 122
supervenience, 61, 84–85, 85–86, 90, 91, 105, 114, 120, 141

Tegmark, Max, 135, 140, 145
  levels of multiverse, 176–79
  mathematical universe, 146, 153, 157–58, 159, 161–62, 166, 168, 173, 177–79, 184, 188–89, 199
  regress problem, 122–23
testability, 44, 45, 52, 79–80, 120, 154–55, 188
theater, Cartesian, 51, 56

theism, 14, 49, 53–54, 77–78, 93, 140.170, 181, 187
theophobia, 93–94
thermodynamics, second law, 46, 96
Thomas Aquinas, *see* Aquinas
Thompson, Ross, 66, 92, 161
time, *see* space-time
tragedy, *see* plots
Turing, Alan, 114–15, 142

universals, 38, 74, 76, 81, 107, 135, 137–38, 148–49, 159, 162–63
  see also Realms
universe, *see especially*
  contingent, 178–81
  grounded in necessary being, 181–82
  landscape, 180–81
  necessary, 173–74
  participatory, 183–85
  see also Tegmark, mathematical universe

Whitehead, Alfred N., 37–38, 136
Wittgenstein, Ludwig, 65
Worlds, defined, 12–13

zombie, 99, 104–5

www.ingramcontent.com/pod-product-compliance
Lightning Source LLC
Chambersburg PA
CBHW052214240426
43670CB00037B/606